Economic and Legal Issues in Intellectual Property

T0355587

Economic and Legal Issues in Intellectual Property

Edited by

Michael McAleer and Les Oxley

© 2007 by Blackwell Publishing Ltd

First published as a special issue of the 'Journal of Economic Surveys' (volume 20, issue 4)

BLACKWELL PUBLISHING
350 Main Street, Malden, MA 02148-5020, USA
9600 Garsington Road, Oxford OX4 2DQ, UK
550 Swanston Street, Carlton, Victoria 3053, Australia

The right of Michael McAleer and Les Oxley to be identified as the Authors of the Editorial Material in this Work has been asserted in accordance with the UK Copyright, Designs, and Patents Act 1988.

All rights reserved. No part of this publication may be reproduced, stored in a retrieval system, or transmitted, in any form or by any means, electronic, mechanical, photocopying, recording or otherwise, except as permitted by the UK Copyright, Designs, and Patents Act 1988, without the prior permission of the publisher.

First published 2007 by Blackwell Publishing Ltd

Library of Congress Cataloging-in-Publication Data

Economic and legal issues in intellectual property / edited by Michael McAleer and Les Oxley. p. cm.
Includes bibliographical references and index
ISBN-13: 978-1-4051-6074-2 (alk. paper)
ISBN-10: 1-4051-6074-8 (alk. paper)
1. Intellectual property. 2. Intellectual property–Economic aspects. I. McAleer, Michael. II. Oxley, Les

K1401.E246 2006
346.04'8–dc22

2006036030

A catalogue record for this title is available from the British Library.

Set in 10.5pt Times
by Techbooks, New Delhi, India

The publisher's policy is to use permanent paper from mills that operate a sustainable forestry policy, and which has been manufactured from pulp processed using acid-free and elementary chlorine-free practices. Furthermore, the publisher ensures that the text paper and cover board used have met acceptable environmental accreditation standards.

For further information on
Blackwell Publishing, visit our website:
www.blackwellpublishing.com

CONTENTS

1

INTELLECTUAL PROPERTY AND ECONOMIC INCENTIVES

Michael McAleer and Les Oxley

1. Introduction

In popular writings, many see 'knowledge' as *the* key driver of economic and social well-being. As Foss (2002) argues, '*[w]hatever we think of this journalistic concept* [of the Knowledge Economy], *it arguably does capture real tendencies and complementary changes.*' Knowledge is embodied and disembodied, codified and non-codified. The extent to which it can be codified affects the ability to register the knowledge and potentially protect it from infringement. Protection increases the returns to the creator, but at a potential (and often actual) cost to the consumer. The knowledge economy should grow, so the argument goes, so that the economy grows, and with it the welfare, health and well-being of all. Knowledge is assumed to be good for everyone (how can more knowledge be bad?) and we should strive to create ways to increase its quantity and quality, (perhaps) focusing specifically on science-based education.

In economic theorizing and policymaking, the relationships between the knowledge economy, knowledge society and intellectual property are often not clearly articulated. Should new knowledge be protected to ensure that the correct incentives are provided for the 'inventors' rather than the consumers (if so, for how long?), or should governments 'acquire' the intellectual property and distribute the gains widely? Issues here relate to AIDS drugs and pharmaceutical companies. History tells us that each time a new piece of knowledge (especially technological knowledge) is revealed, there are winners and losers (see Mokyr, 2003). This new knowledge brings with it issues of ownership and control (property rights) versus the 'intellectual commons'. These issues are not new, but are central to 'political economy'. At the centre of these issues sits the idea of economic incentives and the need to protect, often by legal means, the rights of producers and consumers.

The nine papers by Carlaw *et al.* (2006), Hausman and Leonard (2006), Hoti and McAleer (2006), Hoti *et al.* (2006), Liebowitz and Watt (2006), Marinova and

Raven (2006), Ramello (2006), Towse (2006) and Verspagen (2006), which have been brought together in this special issue represent a unique combination that focuses on intellectual property issues. We are most fortunate to have been able to assemble such an excellent group of contributors and trust that the readers will also find the contributions to be stimulating.

2. Overview

The first survey paper by J. Hausman (Massachusetts Institute of Technology) and G. Leonard (NERA Economic Consulting) considers what happens to economic incentives to innovate when the legal landscape is changed. This is a key theme of this special issue on the *Economic and Legal Issues in Intellectual Property*. In particular, they analyze the incentives to infringe registered intellectual property rights following a landmark legal case in the USA in 1999. As they state, 'while jury awards in excess of $100 million were relatively rare before 1990, they are now quite common. . . . where these damages have been calculated via a lost profits approach'. The infringement results in two forms of cost to the holder of the patent: first, the profits they might have earned (that the infringer took), namely, the 'but-for' world, and second, 'price erosion' where the infringer creates more competition, and hence lower prices and profits for the patent holder. These two sources of lost profits are compounded by lost 'convoyed sales' and lost 'learning by doing', which would have reduced marginal costs (and hence profits) for the patent holder.

As the authors highlight, in 1999 the legal framework under which patent damages are calculated changed after a decision by the US Court of Appeals for the Federal Circuit (CAFC) in the *Grain Processing* case. The issue revolved around the sale of non-infringing substitute products and how the court calculated damages. What the authors do, for the first time, is to consider the economic consequences of granting a 'free option' – the consequence of the *Grain Processing* case. In particular, they analyze how the incentives of companies to risk litigation by using patented technology without a licence have changed. The patent now only provided the holder with the right to sue, whereas the court decides whether the patent is valid and has been infringed. The change in legislation effectively reduces the deterrent effect of litigation and encourages infringement, bringing back to the fore the 'old' problem of whether the returns to R&D and incentives to innovate are decreased.

Hausman and Leonard consider the effect of the *Grain Processing* case, which effectively led to the granting of a 'free (real) option' for potential patent infringers. They calculate that the *Grain Processing* case will increase significantly the incentive to infringe, will increase the propensity to litigate by the patent owners and reduce the incentive to innovate. They conclude by saying, '[t]he economic basis for the Grain Processing decision is at odds with most models of profit maximization of firms acting in an economically rational manner.' This shows the importance of understanding the nexus between legal and economic aspects of intellectual property protection and is central to the theme of this special issue.

The second survey paper by S. J. Liebowitz (University of Texas at Dallas) and R. Watt (University of Canterbury) continue the theme raised by Hausman and Leonard, namely, by considering the effects on copyright law and infringement in the music industry that have resulted from the technological changes stemming from digital industries and the Internet. This is a special case of the more general one that each time a new piece of knowledge (especially technological knowledge) is revealed, there are winners and losers. Using the topical example of the music industry, the authors consider how copyright law, which not only defines the right of ownership but also provides some protection of this right, has effectively been challenged by digital technologies. Again incentives (this time to 'create') are affected and legal boundaries are challenged. As the 'technology' changes (analogue to digital), then there is increasing pressure to change the legal 'checks-and-balances' and the ability to enforce across national boundaries and jurisdictions. Copyright, which was developed in an era of the written word, changes in enforceability when the copiers are effectively anonymous and hence are impossible to trace.

The topical example that the authors analyze is the impact of file sharing on the music industry. Economists have noticed the problems of the music industry and, as in many cases, have developed two alternative solutions. On the one hand, some have argued that with sufficient alterations copyright can meet the challenge, while others have argued that copyright should be abandoned altogether since remuneration can be adequately guaranteed by other means. The authors find significant evidence that economic harm is being done by the music 'pirates', in spite of the fact that new artists are emerging and existing artists continue to produce new recordings. The incentive to create still seems to exist even without adequate copyright law. However, as they argue, it is hard to generate the appropriate counter-factual in this case – what would be the equivalent of the 'but-for' world raised in Hausman and Leonard's paper on patent violation? Liebowitz and Watt conclude that they believe 'all the economic alternatives to copyright law are likely to be second-best solutions to the problem of efficient creation and distribution of "information products", where the market failure based on copying renders the first best solution unworkable'.

Economists do not yet have a simple solution. However, it is clear that the solution also lies with careful legal support – not one that creates the negative incentives as in the *Grain Processing* case!

In the third survey paper, G. Ramello (Università del Piemonte Orientale*)* considers the economics of trademark. The idea of a trademark is to facilitate purchase decisions by 'indicating the provenance of the goods, so that consumers can identify specific quality attributes deriving from their own, or others', past experience.' The theory proposes that this creates an incentive for trademark holders to invest in quality to create a reputation, enhance profitability and in the process, maximize market efficiency. However, with legal power bestowed on the trademark holder, other incentives are created – those of rent-seeking behaviour that come with market power. Trademark does more than correct the market failure created by the separation between the points of production and sale, as it also has an effect on market efficiency more generally.

This area of intellectual property protection has attracted far less coverage than the 'economics of patenting'. However, the Ramello paper provides both a broad, extensive survey and outlines a research agenda of (as yet) unanswered questions.

The fourth survey by R. Towse (Erasmus University Rotterdam) continues the theme of copyright, this time the effects of copyright in relation to artists which, to quote Towse, refers to 'creators and performers in all the various art forms'. Towse demonstrates that cultural economics offers another view to the standard economics of copyright. The themes of incentives to create and consume, to innovate and to pirate are again explored in this paper, the extra dimension here being the issue of the public goods benefits the 'arts and culture' might offer and the potential for government cultural policymaking to increase public access to the arts.

Towse argues that most of the standard economic literature on copyright ignores a number of aspects for cultural production and for artists. There is little mention there of moral rights. Because of the nature of the area, no distinction is made between copyright for authors and the rights for performers. The issue of how much artists earn from copyright is generally ignored. It seems in this sector that most writers assume that the interests of creators and performers are aligned with those of publishers, sound recording makers, broadcasters and so on. These special characteristics, Towse argues, mean that careful consideration has to be made of any proposed alternatives to the current copyright laws that may be required because of technological change of a digital or Internet origin. What are the specific alternatives in the case of culture and heritage? Subsidies or grants to artists are some of the ways of overcoming market failure in cultural production that have been suggested as alternatives to copyright law. But do artists need copyright? There appears to be strong economic evidence that the main benefits of copyright are enjoyed by what Towse calls the 'humdrum' side of the cultural industries rather than the creators. Top stars may benefit from the distribution of royalties, but these revenues appear not to trickle down to the less successful, and they receive relatively little through the copyright system.

However, unlike some industries, artistic motivation may not be due solely to financial rewards and economic rights, but also to moral rights. Where to from here with copyright and the arts? Towse suggests, 'Economists may have to venture out of their usual eeries to investigate these things. If they don't, they should be far more careful in following the line that what is good for Sony is good for the world of art'.

Taking the case of cultural economics further, the fifth paper by D. Marinova (Murdoch University) and M. Raven (Murdoch University) considers the issue of intellectual property rights for indigenous knowledge and the people who generate and 'own' (but often subsequently lose) them. This is an area that is typically ignored in the mainstream literature, although the financial implications of indigenous knowledge have not been ignored by, for example, major pharmaceutical companies. The paper examines how the mainstream patents system, using as their example the US Patent and Trademark Office, fails to recognize indigenous input, which is typically holistic and not easily codified. They then consider, via a range of examples, alternatives to such a system that they regard as more 'sustainable', where this presumably means also incentive compatible. A particular case of 'indigenous intellectual accreditation' created by a partnership between Mt Romance (an Australian sandalwood company), Aveda (a US-based multinational cosmetics corporation) and the Kutkabubba community (represented by the Songman Circle of Wisdom) is presented. Marinova and Raven discuss how accreditation here allows the indigenous people to be recognized as owners of the land and gives them a share of the profits made from the contemporary use of the pure sandalwood oil.

In the sixth paper, B. Verspagen (Eindhoven Centre for Innovation Studies) considers the issue of intellectual property rights for university research and, in particular, university patenting. This is an area that many of the readers might find particularly interesting. Universities typically receive significant public funds either directly or indirectly through grant-related research. They receive these funds, in the main, to undertake 'socially useful research' in the quest for 'socially useful knowledge'. Under these public good type conditions, one would typically assume that this knowledge should be part of the intellectual commons, not one over which exclusive property rights are sought. However, what about incentives and the rights of the employees? Yet again, however, the intervention of a legal precedent, this time the Bayh-Dole Act in the USA, leads to incentives and outcomes that pure economics might not predict. The Bayh-Dole Act permits universities to register patents based upon research that was or is federally funded. The Verspagen paper considers the economic logic behind Bayh-Dole and the effects the Act has on universities and the knowledge they develop.

Would Bayh-Dole be a good thing for Europe to imitate? Verspagen considers this question in the second part of his survey. At the theoretical level the model of Aghion and Tirole (1994) suggests that university ownership of patents would lead to more of an incentive for investment in knowledge creation if the university is engaged in a public–private Research Joint Venture (RJV). With such ventures common in Europe, Verspagen concludes that university-owned patents might reduce (potential) market failures. New data are also examined on patent inventors in six European countries to consider initially the extent of university patenting. So should Europe follow the USA or not? As ever, there are arguments in favour and against! Verspagen notes that the European university and innovation system is different to that in the USA. Some universities currently permit their employees to register patents in their own name, while others do not. In conclusion, therefore, there is a plea for more research in the area before anything is changed. 'Muggling along' may be better than using the wrong model!

The seventh paper by K. Carlaw (University of British Columbia), L. Oxley (University of Canterbury), D. Thorns (University of Canterbury), M. Nuth (University of Canterbury) and P. Walker (University of Canterbury) explores the debates surrounding whether or not we have now moved into a new knowledge economy and/or knowledge society and, if so, whether this shift is as significant and as far reaching as the industrial revolution. In particular, they consider what we might mean by a knowledge economy/society. It soon becomes clear to them (and us) that we do not have a clear understanding of what we 'actually' mean by a knowledge economy, in the sense of defining how it does/might differ from anything we have had before and whether the future will be 'that different' from the past. They take a historically grounded approach to the issues raised, and their contribution provides an excellent broad overview from which to consider some of the other contributions in this compilation. Furthermore, the appendices provide a wealth of background on what has currently been written on the knowledge society, knowledge economy, information economy, digital economy, knowledge-based economy, weightless economy, goldilocks economy, knowledge-driven economy, new economy, internet economy, network society, post-industrial society and finally 'wisdom'.

The authors have economic and sociological backgrounds and bring, via their contribution, a unique perspective on the issues of intellectual property, knowledge and economic growth. From the economic perspective, economic theory provides potential answers to part of the puzzle on defining and ultimately measuring the size, composition and consequences of the knowledge society, with 'modern growth theory' recognizing the crucial importance of 'knowledge embodied in human beings', human capital, as an engine for growth and the role of intellectual property. However, this economics-based literature, though generally well grounded in theory, is typically too narrowly defined to consider social issues, and hence is not well placed to consider the knowledge society.

From a sociological perspective, the knowledge society is, to some, the latest form of accumulation to become a significant part of economic wealth generation. This work is a mix of technological/economic 'determinism'. The knowledge society leads to the 'emergence of new forms of economic production and management' (Castells, 1996). To others, however, knowledge is an enabling concept leading to a culture of innovation, which creates the knowledge society. Recent analysis of social inclusion, social connectedness and social cohesiveness leads to an increased emphasis on education, human capital theories and schemes to re-connect those who have 'fallen out of the system' and arguments around dependency. However, the current state of sociological thinking on the contours of the knowledge 'society' remains rather indistinct, and certainly lacks robust measures.

What the authors seem to conclude on the 'current state of knowledge' on the knowledge society is that it comprises a range of partial, typically discipline specific and determined, limited views, thoughts and concepts. No robust measures of its size, and importantly, contours exist, and hence no rigorous, scientific analyses of its effects on well-being have or could have been undertaken. We simply do not know who are the winners and losers in the knowledge society because we cannot seek to address such questions without the relevant data, and those data need to be created via informed theorizing.

The penultimate paper is by S. Hoti (University of Western Australia) and M. McAleer (University of Western Australia), who examine how country risk affects innovation, with an application to foreign patents registered in the USA. Hoti and McAleer argue that innovation can occur at a national level under a wide range of settings. Trends in the registration of patents have frequently been used to describe a country's technological capabilities, and have acted as a proxy for innovation. The USA has consistently been a destination for registering patents by innovative American and foreign companies, as well as by individuals who have aspired to commercialize new technologies. Consequently, the patents registered by the US Patent and Trademark Office (PTO) represent an excellent source of information regarding technological strengths and market ambitions for countries. It is also argued that the leading innovative countries internationally have several common traits, including economic, financial and political stability, which are reflected in various measures of country risk.

Country risk broadly refers to the economic and financial conditions and political stability of a country, and is an overall measure of country creditworthiness, indicating the capacity of a country to service its foreign financial obligations based on its economic, financial and political performances. The purpose of the paper is to examine, for the first time, the relationship between the economic, financial and political country risk ratings and innovation, as measured by a country's registered patents. Much of the research on granted patents in the USA has examined snapshot images representing the patent activities for a particular time period, based on a single-year or aggregated annual information base. While broader, the country risk literature does not seem to take into account measures of innovation as determinants of country risk.

Although there are numerous measures of country risk by the various country risk rating agencies, they use different methods of deriving country risk ratings. In particular, all of these agencies fail to accommodate measures of innovations in their rating system. Hence, the authors argue that it is important to analyze the relationship between country risk and innovation. Higher innovation reflects higher technological capabilities and growth opportunities in a country, which, in turn, leads to higher country risk ratings or creditworthiness. On the other hand, higher country risk ratings lead to higher foreign investment and capital flowing into a country, which, in turn, leads to higher growth and technological advancement, and hence higher innovation. This finding should be particularly important for less-developed countries, which need high country risk ratings to attract foreign investment to promote economic growth and innovation. One way of improving country risk ratings is for countries to increase their efforts in technological innovation.

Concluding the special issue is the paper by S. Hoti (University of Western Australia), M. McAleer (University of Western Australia) and D. Slottje (Southern Methodist University and FTI Consulting). Using the famous examples of Coca Cola and Microsoft, Hoti, McAleer and Slottje argue that brand names and trademarks carry incredible economic power and prestige. There is increasing recognition by world bodies that intellectual property, whether manifested in patents, trademarks, copyrights or trade secrets, is highly valuable and must be protected like any other asset. This recognition has resulted in robust intellectual property enforcement that would have been unheard of as recently as one decade ago. Notorious dens of intellectual property piracy such as China, India and Brazil have begun to realize that, as their own economies mature, the intellectual capital being created domestically within each country is valuable and must be protected.

Focusing on piracy issues and protection of intellectual property is becoming a central focus of diplomacy and trade talks internationally, with most nations having a significant stake in how this problem is resolved. The USA is an interesting natural laboratory as patent, trademark and copyright litigation battles have been raging domestically for some time. The authors describe some of the trends and intellectual property litigation activities that are occurring in the USA, where intellectual property enforcement is taken very seriously. They also discuss the four main forms of intellectual property assets, the legal remedies that are available to enforce the property rights inherent in each type of intellectual property asset, the basic damages theory relating to each form of intellectual property, and how damages may be calculated when each type of asset is presumed to be infringed.

The concurrent phenomena of growing worldwide recognition of the true value of intellectual property assets, increasing patent protection through litigation, the attendant demands made by patent holders for royalties on patented intellectual property and strengthened copyright enforcement and trademark recognition initiatives have begun to create interesting economic situations. Technological advances have caused the relative prices of some consumer electronics to fall, while royalties on these goods have risen. An important fact is that the increased recognition of the value of intellectual property has led to stronger enforcement of intellectual property protection, an increase in intellectual property litigation, and growing policy actions that are focused on how that protection should be manifested. As a consequence, intellectual property issues are beginning to have a significant impact on how firms behave and interact with each other, and how countries behave with respect to the safekeeping of their respective intellectual property portfolios.

3. Epilogue

The papers presented in this special issue consider, both from a micro, case study perspective and a more macro, economy level lens, issues related to the creation and dissemination of knowledge. Although moral issues to 'create' may be the major incentive in the arts, in many or most other areas of innovation financial implications typically dominate. In these circumstances, it is crucial to understand fully the 'landscape' in which we operate. Change that landscape, either with new technologies or new legal frameworks, and understandably (*ex post*, at least) behaviours may or will change.

The papers brought together in this special issue demonstrate this latter point clearly. Changing the legal issues surrounding patent infringement (Hausman and Leonard) changes the incentives to infringe; changing the technology (digital and Internet) changes the ability to prosecute and chase infringers (Liebowitz and Watt); changing the ability for publicly funded organizations to register patents changes the innovation incentives (Verspagen). In short, changing the legal setting changes the behaviour regarding intellectual property. Litigation relating to intellectual property is here to stay, and is exploding with a vengeance (Hoti, McAleer and Slottje).

Acknowledgements

The first author wishes to acknowledge the financial support of the Australian Research Council, and the second author the Royal Society of New Zealand, Marsden Fund.

References

Aghion, P. and Tirole, J. (1994) The management of innovation. *Quarterly Journal of Economics* I109: 1185–1209.

Carlaw, K., Oxley, L., Thorns, D., Nuth, M. and Walker, P. (2006) Beyond the hype: intellectual property and the knowledge society/knowledge economy. *Journal of Economic Surveys* 20: 633–690.

Castells, M. (1996) *The Rise of the Network Society*. Cambridge, MA: Blackwell.

Foss, N. J. (2002) Economic organization in the knowledge economy: an Austrian perspective. In N. J. Foss and P. G. Klein (eds), *Entrepreneurism and the Firm: Austrian Perspectives on Economic Organization*. Cheltenham, UK: Edward Elgar.

Hausman, J. and Leonard, G. (2006) Real options and patent damages: the legal treatment of non-infringing alternatives and incentives to innovate. *Journal of Economic Surveys* 20: 493–512.

Hoti, S. and McAleer, M. (2006) How does country risk affect innovation? An application to foreign patents registered in the USA. *Journal of Economic Surveys* 20: 691–714.

Hoti, S., McAleer, M. and Slottje, D. (2006) Intellectual property litigation activity in the USA. *Journal of Economic Surveys* 20: 715–729.

Liebowitz, S. and Watt, R. (2006) How to best ensure remuneration for creators in the market for music? Copyright and its alternatives. *Journal of Economic Surveys* 20: 513–545.

Marinova, D. and Raven, M. (2006) Indigenous knowledge and intellectual property: a sustainability agenda. *Journal of Economic Surveys* 20: 587–605.

Mokyr, J. (2003) *The Gifts of Athena: Historical Origins of the Knowledge Economy*. Princeton, NJ: Princeton University Press.

Ramello, G. (2006) What's in a sign? Trademark law and economic theory. *Journal of Economic Surveys* 20: 547–565.

Towse, R. (2006) Copyright and artists: a view from cultural economics. *Journal of Economic Surveys* 20: 567–585.

Verspagen, B. (2006) University research, intellectual property rights and European innovation systems. *Journal of Economic Surveys* 20: 607–632.

2

REAL OPTIONS AND PATENT DAMAGES: THE LEGAL TREATMENT OF NON-INFRINGING ALTERNATIVES, AND INCENTIVES TO INNOVATE

Jerry Hausman and Gregory K. Leonard

1. Introduction

Patent damage awards have become an increasingly important feature of business strategy in the USA over the past 20 years. While jury awards in excess of $100 million were relatively rare before 1990, they are now quite common. These large awards usually arise when damages have been calculated using a lost profits approach. Increased competition from an infringer can cause a patent holder to lose profits in several ways. By far the most important source of lost profits is the sales that the patent holder lost to the infringer. Absent the infringement (often termed the 'but-for' world), the patent holder would have made some or all of the sales that the infringer made. The damages associated with these lost sales are the incremental profits that the patent holder would have made on the sales. A second important source of lost profits is what is often called 'price erosion'. Here, the increased competition from the infringer can lead to decreased prices and thus decreased profits. These two sources of lost profits can both occur in a given situation and may often interact with each other.[1] Other sources of lost profits damages include the patent holder's lost sales of 'convoyed sales' (sales of unpatented products sold in conjunction with the patented product) and lost 'learning by doing' opportunities that would have led to lower marginal costs and thus higher profits for the patent holder in the absence of the infringement.

The US patent statute states that a patent holder whose patent has been infringed is entitled to at least a 'reasonable royalty' as damages. Thus, in the event that lost profits damages are not awarded, damages are calculated by using a reasonable royalty approach.[2] Damages calculated under a reasonable royalty approach are typically (but not always) less than the damages calculated under a lost profits approach.

The legal framework under which patent damages are calculated changed substantially after the decision by the US Court of Appeals for the Federal Circuit

(CAFC) in a case called *Grain Processing* in 1999. Perhaps the most important question in the typical lost profits analysis is determining the fraction of the infringing sales that constitute lost sales to the patent holder. The answer to this question usually depends on the set of non-infringing substitute products to which the customers of the infringing product could have turned in the but-for world where the infringing product was not available to them. Prior to *Grain Processing*, the case law as a legal matter generally restricted the set of non-infringing substitute products to include only products that were actually sold in the marketplace. For example, an infringer could claim that it would have continued to sell a non-infringing product that it had actually been selling and that this product would have captured some of the infringing sales, which would tend to limit the patent holder's lost sales. However, the infringer could not claim that it would have developed and introduced some new non-infringing product in the but-for world and that this product would have captured some of the infringing sales. *Grain Processing* eased this restriction on the set of non-infringing substitutes available in the but-for world by allowing an infringer to claim that it would have offered a non-infringing product that, while not actually sold in the marketplace, was technically feasible at the time and could have been made commercially available relatively quickly. The *Grain Processing* decision then went further and concluded that, in the particular case at issue, the plaintiff was not entitled to lost profits because the infringer's non-infringing product would have been identical from the point of view of customers (though more costly to the infringer). Damages were therefore calculated on a reasonable royalty basis only.

The *Grain Processing* decision has led to an enormous amount of law review articles and additional commentary.[3] We do not attempt to review this outpouring of articles. However, we are unaware of any article considering a factor that we see as an important economic consideration: the grant of a 'free option' by the *Grain Processing* decision to the infringer. Free options can have large economic incentive effects on rational economic decisions. We find that the grant of a free option is contrary to the basic framework of the patent system in the USA.

While it is widely appreciated how *Grain Processing* has made it more difficult for patent holders to claim lost profits damages, it is less well understood how *Grain Processing* has affected the incentives of companies to risk litigation by using patented technology (without a license) rather than to avoid infringement by using an economically inferior non-infringing technology. Whether the patent is valid and infringed is not known until the litigation takes place. A patent only provides the patent holder with the right to sue for infringement. A court decides whether the patent is valid and infringed.

Consider a firm facing a decision between these two alternatives. If it chooses to risk litigation and use the patented technology, it retains the option to switch to the non-infringing technology if the patent is later found to be valid and infringed. Of course, it will be liable for damages for the period of infringement. If, on the other hand, the firm chooses to use the non-infringing technology, it will not have the opportunity to learn whether the patent is valid and infringed.[4] Thus, by choosing the patented technology, the firm keeps its options open, although at the risk of having to pay damages once the uncertainty regarding validity and infringement is resolved.

The *Grain Processing* decision has the effect of substantially decreasing this risk by decreasing the size of the damages award. If the patent is found to be valid and infringed, the firm can argue under *Grain Processing* that it *would have* switched to the non-infringing technology in the but-for world, thereby effectively making the switch retroactively. The *Grain Processing* decision thereby makes the option essentially free. By providing potential infringers with increased option value if they use the patented technology, *Grain Processing* reduces the deterrence effect of litigation and therefore encourages infringement. As a consequence, the returns to research and development are negatively affected and the incentives to innovate are decreased. These effects of *Grain Processing* are the first subject of this paper.

We also address the conclusion of the *Grain Processing* decision that lost profits were inappropriate because the infringer could have offered an essentially equivalent non-infringing product in the but-for world, albeit at a higher cost of production. As we demonstrate below, this conclusion is not economically correct because the infringer would have had economic incentives to increase its price in this situation. As a result, the patent owner would have had greater sales and profits in the but-for world than in the actual world. We conclude that lost profits should not necessarily be precluded even if the infringer could have provided a non-infringing version of its product in the but-for world.

2. Background on Calculation of Patent Damages Under US Law

2.1 *Reasonable Royalty*

Under US law, one of the methods used to determine the appropriate reasonable royalty is an analysis of the outcome of a 'hypothetical licensing negotiation' between the patent owner as a willing licensor and the infringer as a willing licensee, which is assumed to have taken place at the time of first infringement.[5]

An economic approach to analyzing the hypothetical negotiation is to determine the bounds of the Edgeworth Box, that is, the minimum royalty the patent holder would accept (while still being better off than without a license) and the maximum royalty the infringer would be willing to pay (while still being better off than without a license). A negotiated royalty necessarily must fall between these upper and lower bounds, which define the 'bargaining range'.

The maximum royalty rate that the infringer would have been willing to pay is a function of the incremental profits that it would expect to earn by licensing the patents at issue as compared to not licensing. An important consideration is whether there exist any non-infringing 'design-arounds' and the costs of implementing and using these design-arounds as compared to using the patented technology. For example, suppose that a design-around exists, but would cost a certain amount to implement, would require greater ongoing marginal costs of production as compared to what could be achieved with the patented technology and would lead to a lower-quality product (and thus lower sales and a lower price) as compared to what could be achieved with the patented technology. In that case, the infringer would be willing to pay a royalty up to the increase in profits associated with the cost savings, the increased sales and the increased price (but no more) in order to license the patented technology.

The minimum royalty that the patent holder would be willing to accept to grant a license is a function of the losses that it would sustain by licensing as compared to not licensing. For example, if the patent owner would lose other licensing opportunities when it licensed the infringer, the patent owner would demand a royalty that at least replaced the profits that these lost licensing opportunities would have generated. If the patent owner would lose sales to the infringer, the patent owner would demand a royalty that at least compensated for the loss of profits on these sales.

Once the bargaining range has been established, economic factors are used to estimate where within the bargaining range an agreement would result.[6] In addition, courts in the USA have adopted a list of economic and business factors called the *Georgia Pacific* factors that are used to aid in determining the amount of the reasonable royalty.

2.2 *Lost Profits*

From an economist's point of view, the purpose of a lost profits damages award in a patent case is to compensate the patent holder for the profits on sales that it lost as a result of the infringement.[7] In order to determine the amount of profits that the patent holder lost, the first step is to determine the level of profits that the patent holder would have achieved had the infringement not occurred, that is, in the world as it would have been absent the infringement. This scenario is often called the but-for world. Damages are equal to the difference between the but-for profits and the actual profits of the patent holder.

As discussed above, higher profits for the patent holder in the but-for world could have resulted from, among other things, greater sales or a higher price. In calculating the but-for profits, it is important to account for any additional costs the patent holder would have incurred to make the additional sales. For example, the incremental costs required to produce and sell the additional units (including the cost of capacity expansion if needed) must be accounted for when calculating the but-for profits.

In attempting to ascertain whether an award of lost profits should be made, US courts often refer to four so-called 'Panduit factors', all of which must be satisfied for an award of lost profits:[8]

(1) demand for the patented product;
(2) absence of acceptable non-infringing substitutes;
(3) manufacturing and marketing capability to exploit the demand;
(4) the amount of profit that would have been made.

Panduit factor (1) requires a demonstration that customers of the infringing prod-uct would have bought the patented product in the but-for world where the infringing product would not have been available to them. In many situations, the patented product will not capture all of the sales of the infringing product because some demand will go to competing non-infringing products. An estimate of the amount of substitution can be obtained using econometric methods that measure the cross-elasticity of demand if the necessary data are available. The basic economic idea is that the price of the infringing product is increased to its 'virtual price' where its demand is zero, and the share of its sales to the patent owner's product and other competing products is determined from the econometric model.[9]

Panduit factor (3), which asks whether the patent holder had sufficient manufacturing and marketing capability to make the additional sales in the but-for world, usually comes down to the ability of the patent holder to expand its current operations by adding an additional shift at an existing manufacturing plant to expand output or to invest in additional manufacturing capacity. This factor may not be as important in industries such as software and other products where an output increase is relatively easy to undertake, as compared to manufacturing industries such as chemicals.

Panduit factor (4) requires that an estimate of the patent holder's incremental profit on the additional sales be calculated. As mentioned above, it is important to consider all of the potential incremental costs associated with the additional sales. Typically the incremental costs can be calculated based on existing cost data from the patent holder.

We now turn to Panduit factor (2), which concerns the absence of non-infringing substitutes. This factor is the main focus of this paper. In principle, it comprises both a demand-side consideration (substitute non-infringing products already on the market) and a supply-side consideration (substitute non-infringing technologies that the infringer could have used). On the demand side, however, US courts do not require that no non-infringing substitutes exist for an award of lost profits. Especially in an economic situation consisting of differentiated products, the relevant economic (and legal) question is not whether any non-infringing substitute product exists, but instead how much the demand of the infringing product would shift to the patent-holder's product as opposed to the non-infringing substitute products. We discussed above econometric techniques that permit estimation of the substitution among these competing products.

The more difficult economic question arises on the supply side. If the use of the patented technology was not available to the infringer, what techniques could it have substituted in place of using the patent-holder's technology? In the but-for world, this determination may be quite difficult because often no real-world observations of production exist absent infringement. At one extreme, the infringer might have exited the market in the but-for world because no substitution would have been possible. This situation sometimes arises in the pharmaceutical industry because a patent may cover the chemical compound that causes a given drug to work. In this situation, it may be impossible for the infringing firm to manufacture a competing drug without violating the patent.

At the other extreme, an infringer may claim it could have costlessly 'invented around' the patented technology and produced the identical product at the same cost as using the patented technology. Questions regarding the economic rationality of this claim arise because the infringer rationally should have shifted to the alternative technology rather than risking having to pay patent damages. This question aside, a further problem exists ascertaining whether the alternative technology could have been used, because it often was not actually used in real-world operations. Courts are often reluctant to credit the use of an alternative technology by the infringer when the infringer did not actually use or actively investigate the substitute technology. Otherwise, it may be extremely difficult to determine whether claimed behaviour in the but-for world has a factual basis.

However, two situations do exist where it may be reasonable to assume the use of an alternative non-infringing technology in the but-for world. First, the infringer may claim that in the but-for world it would have adopted the same technology used in an existing non-infringing substitute product. Where the patent is a production process patent, the cost of production using the non-infringing technology is typically higher than using the patented technology, so that lost profits would still likely result because of less price competition. We discuss this fact further below. Alternatively, where the patent involved product features, use of non-infringing technology would likely lead to a product without all of the features of the patented product. Here, both lost profits from lost sales and price erosion may occur leading to lost profits by the patent holder.

A closely related situation may occur when the infringer has previously used a non-infringing technology and subsequently adopted the infringing technology. In the but-for world, the infringer can claim that it would have continued to use the non-infringing technology. However, because the infringer would adopt the infringing technology only if it led to increased profits, again the older non-infringing technology would either be higher cost or lack some of the features of the infringing product. In either situation, lost profits would arise from either lost sales or price erosion or both.

2.3 The Grain Processing Decision

2.3.1 History of the Litigation

The *Grain Processing* case lasted 18 years and went to the CAFC three times – a story worthy of a latter day Dickens. Grain Processing and its infringing competitor American Maize sold large quantities of maltodextrins, which are food additives with food properties such as binding and viscosity and preserve food properties at low temperatures.[10] Food processors use maltodextrins in products such as drinks, cereals and frozen foods. Grain Processing owned a patent, 'Low D.E. Starch Conversion Products', which patented maltodextrins with particular attributes and processes for their production. Grain Processing manufactured and sold maltodextrins since 1969.

American Maize began selling maltodextrins in 1974. American Maize sold a particular maltodextrin, Lo-Dex 10, over the entire period that Grain Processing owned the rights for the patent at issue. However, American Maize used four different production processes over the time period to produce Lo-Dex 10. From 1974 to 1982, American Maize used a particular process that was found to infringe Grain Processing's patent by the Court of Appeals for the Federal Circuit (CAFC).[11] In 1982, American Maize changed its process, but Grain Processing claimed that the new process also infringed its patent. The CAFC found that the new process also infringed the patent. American Maize was enjoined from continuing to use either of the infringing processes.

American Maize developed a third process to manufacture Lo-Dex 10. The District Court found that American Maize's customers judged this new product to be equivalent to the product from the first two processes. American Maize used the third process over the period 1988–1991. However, in 1990, Grain Processing once again claimed that the new process infringed its patent. While the District Court did not find infringement, the CAFC found that the new process did infringe the patent.

American Maize tried a fourth time and developed yet another process to manufacture Lo-Dex 10. The District Court found that it took American Maize only 2 weeks to develop this new process. However, this new process had higher cost than the preceding processes. Grain Processing did not challenge this new process and American Maize used the process for 6 months in 1991 until the patent expired.

2.3.2 *Damages Claims in Grain Processing*

Regarding American Maize's third process, Grain Processing claimed lost profits based on lost sales. The District Court denied lost profits and granted a reasonable royalty of 3%, rather than the 28% asked for by Grain Processing.[12] The basis of the Court's decision to deny lost profits was Grain Processing's failure to satisfy Panduit factor (2): absence of acceptable non-infringing substitutes. The District Court ruled that American Maize 'could have produced' a non-infringing substitute using the fourth process that it developed in 1991. While American Maize did not actually manufacture and sell the non-infringing product until the final 6 months prior to patent expiration, the District Court decided that its availability in the last 6 months of the patent's lifetime 'scotches [Grain Processing's] request for lost-profits damages.' The District Court ruled that buyers found that the infringing and non-infringing products were equivalent. The District Court stated that 'no one argues that any customer cared a whit about the products' descriptive ratio.' Thus, the District Court set the 3% reasonable royalty rate based on an estimate of the cost difference between the non-infringing process and the third (infringing) process.

Grain Processing appealed the District Court's decision, claiming that it should have received lost profits, which presumably would have considerably exceeded the royalty based on the 3% royalty rate. Grain Processing's main claim was that the District Court's decision was based on 'a noninfringing substitute that did not exist during, and was not developed until after, the period of infringement'.[13] The CAFC reversed the District Court's decision, ruling that to qualify as an acceptable non-infringing substitute the product or process must be 'available or on the market at the time of infringement'. The CAFC remanded the case to the District Court for further determination of lost profits. On remand, the District Court again denied lost profits to Grain Processing. It found that the non-infringing process was actually available during the period of infringement. The District Court claimed that American Maize could have adopted the non-infringing process in 1979 but did not do so because it was a more expensive process. The District Court found the products to be equivalent independent of the manufacturing process and therefore found a failure of the Panduit factors, which it interpreted as requiring 'economically significant demand for a product having all . . . attributes' of the patented product. The District Court found that such a demand did not exist because market demand could have been met hypothetically by the non-infringing process. Because Grain Processing and American Maize were the only two manufacturers of this type of maltodextrins, if American Maize were not in the market, Grain Processing would have gained most of the sales made by American Maize. Thus, lost profits likely would have been substantial based on lost sales.

The CAFC affirmed the District Court's opinion, stating that the non-infringing product was an 'acceptable substitute for the claimed invention'. The CAFC ruled that '. . . a fair and accurate reconstruction of the "but for" market also must take into account, where relevant, alternative actions the infringer foreseeably would have undertaken had he not infringed. Without the infringing product, a rational would-be infringer is likely to offer an acceptable noninfringing alternative, if available, to compete with the patent owner rather than leave the market altogether. The competitor in the "but for" marketplace is hardly likely to surrender its complete market share when faced with a patent, if it can compete in some other lawful manner'.[14]

The CAFC considered the question that it took American Maize over 12 years to develop a non-infringing process to manufacture maltodextrin. The CAFC found that if an alleged alternative is not on the market during the period in which the patent owner claims damages, 'a trial court may reasonably infer that it was not available as a non-infringing substitute at that time'. The burden then switches to the infringer who has to demonstrate that the non-infringing substitute was in fact available during the infringement period. The CAFC stated that 'mere speculation or conclusory assertions will not suffice to overcome the inference. After all, the infringer chose to produce the infringing, rather than non-infringing, product'. Here the CAFC agreed with the District Court that economic reasons were the 'sole reason' that American Maize used the infringing process because it cost less to use. Furthermore, both the CAFC and the District Court found that the 'substantial profit margins' on Lo-Dex 10 were sufficient to conclude that American Maize would have used the more costly non-infringing process without increasing its prices. The CAFC decided that American Maize could have used the higher cost non-infringing process throughout the period beginning in 1979, even though it did not actually use the process until 1991.

3. Options and the US Patent System

The US patent system, which dates to the 18th century, was based on the British system. The basic idea is that a patent confers upon the holder the property right to exclude the use of its patented product or process for a given period of time.[15] In return for the period of exclusivity, the patent holder has to describe the nature of the patented invention so that, after the expiration of the patent, the product or process will enter the public domain where it can be used for free by the public.

If an infringer uses the patent without a license to do so, it is subject to monetary damages to compensate the patent holder for the use of its property. In *Grain Processing* the infringing company, American Maize, made an infringing use of the patent until the last 6 months of the lifetime of the patent. Because both the District Court and CAFC found 'substantial profit margins' on the American Maize product, we find it reasonable to conclude that a duopoly situation likely existed with no close substitute for the products at issue. Thus, in the absence of American Maize from the market it is likely that the patent holder Grain Processing would have made even greater profit margins because it would have been in a position of considerable market (monopoly) power with no close substitutes to constrain the price. However, instead American Maize infringed the patent and made 'substantial profit margins'. In our view, the *Grain Processing* decision gives infringers such as American Maize a 'free option'.

3.1 *Financial Options and Real Options*

Options are a significant factor in financial markets and in economic decision making. An option gives the right, but not the obligation, to engage in the purchase or sale or a financial instrument or real property. A call option on a stock gives the owner the right to buy a share of the stock at a specified exercise price on or before the option's expiration date. A put option gives the owner the right to sell a share of the stock at a specified exercise price on or before the expiration date. For example, an Intel call option for $25 might give the owner the right, but not the obligation, to purchase 100 shares of Intel stock at $25 per share on or before the expiration date, say December 31, 2006. If Intel's stock exceeds $25 on the expiration date the option will be exercised. Otherwise, it will expire without being exercised. Options are valuable. For example, on May 12, 2006, with Intel stock at about $19, a call option with an exercise price of $17.50 and an expiration date of June 30, 2006 sold in the market at a price of $1.80; a call option with an exercise price of $20 and the same expiration date sold for only $0.35.

Real options are closely associated with financial options. Real options involve 'real' assets instead of financial assets. Thus, real options involve the opportunity but not the obligation to modify a project. Some common examples are the option to expand a project, the option to abandon a project or the option to modify a technology used in a project. Real options are valuable for a firm because having an option increases flexibility if circumstances change. Thus, a firm making an investment decision will often spend extra funds to maintain flexibility because the future is always uncertain. The ability to better adapt to future uncertain outcomes is often worth the extra expenditure. Indeed, a leading finance textbook discusses this flexibility real option under the name of 'production options'.[16]

While we have stressed the value of options, government regulation can often grant 'free options' to certain firms. For example, under the US Federal Communications Commission's (FCC) application of the Telecommunications Act of 1996, incumbent owners of telecommunications networks were required to rent their networks elements (e.g. loops) to new entrants on the basis of a monthly contract. Thus, while the investment in a telecommunications network is typically very long-lived and irreversible, often called a sunk and irreversible investment, the FCC permitted the new entrant to stop renting the network at any time without advance notice. Thus, the FCC gave the new entrant the right, but not the obligation, to continue to rent the network elements. The FCC conferred this benefit upon new entrants often for free, because the new entrants were not required to sign a long-term contract or take on any obligation to continue renting the network element. Hausman (1997, 2002, 2003) termed this type of regulation a 'free option'.[17] Because a free option is the transfer of value from one party to another, it will have consequences on economic incentives. As explained by Hausman, grant of a free option will have negative economic consequences on investment by the incumbent provider because a portion of the value of its investment has been transferred to the new entrant. This outcome occurred in the USA, and the FCC has now changed its policy so as not to require incumbents to rent network elements from their new investment in telecommunications networks.[18]

3.2 *Options and Grain Processing*

We now apply a real options analysis to the decisions in the *Grain Processing* case. To keep the analysis straightforward, we will ignore the last 6 months of the damage period before patent expiration when American Maize adopted a non-infringing production process. Thus, we assume that throughout the period American Maize used a production process that infringed Grain Processing's patent. We further assume that American Maize never used a non-infringing process, but such a process was known and available for American Maize to adopt throughout the period. When Grain Processing sues for patent infringement and claims lost profits for damages, American Maize will be able to claim that it could have used the non-infringing process throughout the period, although in actuality it never adopted the non-infringing process. We further assume, as actually happened, that the courts will deny lost profits because Panduit factor (2) is not satisfied. Instead, Grain Processing will only receive a reasonable royalty in the event that the patent is found valid and infringed. Thus, if the patent is found by the Court to be either invalid or not infringed then American Maize need pay no damages to Grain Processing. Alternatively, if the patent is found to be valid and infringed American Maize must pay no more than a reasonable royalty.

We analyze this situation in the context of a stylized model. A firm can choose between two technologies: technology 1, which may infringe a patent, and technology 2, which is non-infringing. The firm's per period profits are π_1 if it uses technology 1 and π_2 if it uses technology 2, with $\pi_1 \geq \pi_2$. There are two periods. If the firm has chosen technology 1, at the end of period 1 it is determined whether the patent is valid and whether technology 1 infringes the patent (we assume that the costs of this determination, i.e. litigation costs, are zero).[19] The probability that the patent is valid and infringed by the first technology is θ. If the patent is found to be valid and infringed, the firm must switch to technology 2 in period 2 and it must pay damages in the amount D. For the purposes of this model, we assume that there is no discounting.

If the firm chooses technology 2, its total expected profits over the two periods are $2\pi_2$.[20] If the firm chooses technology 1, its total profits are $\pi_1 + \pi_2 - D$ if the patent is found to be valid and infringed and $2\pi_1$ if the patent is found invalid or non-infringed. Thus, if the firm chooses technology 1, its total expected profits are

$$\theta(\pi_1 + \pi_2 - D) + (1 - \theta)2\pi_1 = 2\pi_1 - \theta(\pi_1 - \pi_2) - \theta D \qquad (1)$$

The firm will choose technology 1 if

$$2\pi_1 - \theta(\pi_1 - \pi_2) - \theta D \geq 2\pi_2 \qquad (2)$$

or, rearranging, if

$$\frac{2 - \theta}{\theta}(\pi_1 - \pi_2) \geq D \qquad (3)$$

Thus, if the damages award D is sufficiently large, it will deter the firm from choosing the potentially infringing technology 1.

This model has the economic characteristics of a real option. In the investment context, real options considerations arise when the investment decision is at least partially irreversible (i.e. some investment costs are sunk) and if the decision to invest can be delayed while uncertainties are resolved.[21] Under these conditions, there is a value to waiting to sink costs until the uncertainties are resolved. This value derives from retaining flexibility (an option) to avoid sinking costs if the uncertainties resolve in an adverse fashion. In the model described above, by choosing technology 1, the firm retains the flexibility to switch to technology 2 if, when the uncertainty is resolved, the patent is found to be valid and infringed. This option is lost if the firm chooses technology 2 at the outset, a decision assumed to be irreversible.

One cost of retaining the option is that the firm will have to pay the damages award D in the event that the patent is found to be valid and infringed. Indeed, as seen above, in principle D can be sufficiently large to make maintenance of the option unprofitable. We now turn to the question of how the value of using technology 1 and retaining the option is affected by the *Grain Processing* decision.

As discussed above, *Grain Processing* has made it more difficult to prove lost profits damages, which are typically larger than reasonable royalty damages. Suppose that $D = \pi_1$. Prior to *Grain Processing*, a damages award of this magnitude was a possible outcome in the situation where the potentially infringing firm and the patent owner were the only suppliers of the product in question. In that case, the patent owner would argue that, in the but-for world where the infringing product was not on the market, it would have made all of the infringing sales itself. If the patent owner's price was essentially the same as the potentially infringing firm's price, the patent owner's profits on these additional sales (i.e. its lost profit damages) would be equal to the potentially infringing firm's profits on these sales and damages would be $D = \pi_1$.[22] With the damages award at this level, the firm may or may not choose technology 1, depending on whether inequality (3) is satisfied. For a relatively small profit differential $\pi_1 - \pi_2$ and relatively high patent strength value θ, it is likely that inequality (3) will not be satisfied and the firm will be deterred from choosing potentially infringing technology 1.

After *Grain Processing*, the potentially infringing firm could claim that an award of lost profits damages is inappropriate because it could have switched to technology 2 at the outset to avoid infringement. In that case, damages would be calculated on a reasonable royalty basis. As discussed above, the largest the reasonable royalty could be is the upper end of the Edgeworth Box, or the infringing firm's maximum willingness to pay. The maximum royalty that the infringing firm would be willing to pay each period to obtain a license to use the patented technology is $\pi_1 - \pi_2$ because for any royalty greater than this amount, the infringing firm would prefer to switch to technology 2 rather than take a license to the patent. Thus, under *Grain Processing*, $D \leq \pi_1 - \pi_2$. But, this inequality implies

$$D \leq \frac{2 - \theta}{\theta}(\pi_1 - \pi_2) \qquad (4)$$

because $0 \leq \theta \leq 1$. Inequality (4) therefore implies that the firm will necessarily choose technology 1. In other words, the firm will not be deterred from choosing technology 1 by the prospect of having to pay the reasonable royalty damages award resulting from application of *Grain Processing*. Put another way, *Grain Processing* increases the value of the option inherent in choosing technology 1 to the point where it becomes essentially 'free' – the firm would be irrational to turn it down.

3.3 *Example of the Change in Option Value Due to Grain Processing*

To illustrate how much of a difference *Grain Processing* makes to the value of choosing the potentially infringing technology, we performed calculations that approximate the case facts in *Grain Processing*. There are assumed to be 13 years until patent expiration. The infringer's revenue each year is $100 and the profit margin when using the patented technology is 50%. Each year there is some probability that a finding of patent validity and infringement will occur, conditional on it not having occurred already. This 'hazard rate' is assumed to be constant each year at 0.1 so that we assume an exponential density function.[23] If a finding of validity and infringement occurs, the infringer must pay damages for past infringement and switch to the alternative non-infringing technology for the remaining years; the profit margin for these years is reduced to 47% (to reflect the cost increase associated with using the non-infringing technology). The infringer discounts the future at a 6% rate.

We calculate the expected present discounted value as of year 0 of the infringer's cash flow stream under two scenarios. In the first scenario, damages after a finding of validity and infringement are calculated under a lost profits approach. We assume in this case that the patent holder's lost profits damages are equal to the profits that the infringer actually made. This assumption is reasonable if, in the but-for world, the patent holder would have made all of the infringing sales at the same price and profit rate as the infringer. In this scenario, the expected present discounted value of the cash flows to the infringer would be $325.

In the second scenario, we assume that damages after a finding of validity and infringement are calculated under a reasonable royalty approach because of the application of Panduit factor (2) under *Grain Processing*. In particular, damages are assumed to equal 3% of the infringing revenues. In this scenario, the expected present discounted value of the infringer's cash flows is $425. Thus, the value to the infringer of choosing to use the patented technology increases by 31% due to *Grain Processing*. This change in values would be expected to have a significant effect on an infringer's decision whether to use the patented technology or avoid infringement through use of the non-infringing technology.

3.4 *Changes in the Incentives of Firms to Engage in Research and Development*

We have demonstrated how *Grain Processing* has substantially increased the incentives of firms to choose potentially infringing technologies rather than non-infringing technologies. In principle, this change in incentives can lead to greater amounts of litigation as patent owners are faced with more frequent cases of potential infringement.

Grain Processing also has changed the incentives of firms to engage in research and development (R&D). The smaller damages awards and the increased incentives on the part of potential infringers to infringe dampen the returns to R&D. As a consequence, the incentives to invest in R&D are weaker. This outcome may undermine the original goals of the US patent system.[24]

4. Lost Profits if the Infringer Adopts a Non-Infringing Alternative Technology in the But-For World

Up until now, we have taken as given one of the underlying assumptions of the *Grain Processing* decision: that, having adopted the non-infringing alternative technology in the but-for world, American Maize would have retained its sales and the patent owner Grain Processing would have made no additional sales. This assumption underlies in part the conclusion in *Grain Processing* that damages should be based on a reasonable royalty approach rather than lost profits.

However, the assumption that American Maize would have retained all of its sales in the but-for world is inconsistent with well-established economic theory. If American Maize had switched to the non-infringing process, its marginal costs in the but-for world would have been higher by an amount approximately equal to 3% of the price. The *Grain Processing* decision assumes that American Maize would have absorbed the additional marginal costs and held its price at the same level it charged in the actual world. But this course of action would not be optimal in most models of competition. Instead, American Maize's optimal response to an increase in its marginal costs would be to increase its price. This increase in American Maize's price would, in turn, lead to increased sales, an increased price and increased profits for Grain Processing. In other words, contrary to the conclusion of the *Grain Processing* decision, Grain Processing did sustain lost profits damages even under the assumption that American Maize would have turned to the alternative non-infringing process in the but-for world.

We will demonstrate the extent of lost profits sustained by the patent owner in the context of two basic models of competition: Nash–Bertrand with differentiated products and Cournot with homogeneous products.[25]

4.1 Nash–Bertrand Differentiated Products

For simplicity, we assume the case of two firms, each selling one product, although the results generalize to N firms, with each selling multiple products. The patent owner is firm 1 and the infringer is firm 2. The demand faced by firm i ($i = 1,2$) is $Q_i(p_1, p_2)$. The marginal cost faced by firm i is c_i.[26] The firms simultaneously set prices in a one-shot game. Firm i chooses p_i to maximize profits

$$(p_i - c_i)Q(p_i, p_j) \tag{5}$$

taking p_j as given.

We examine the resulting Nash equilibrium. The first-order condition for firm i is

$$(p_i - c_i)\frac{\partial Q_i(p)}{\partial p_i} + Q_i(p) = 0 \tag{6}$$

The system of two equations of form (6) implicitly define the Nash equilibrium prices as functions of the costs of both firms.

Suppose now the cost of the infringing firm 2 increases because it has to adopt the more costly alternative, the non-infringing process. By differentiating first-order condition (6) for firm 2 with respect to c_2 (while holding p_1 constant), we can obtain the derivative $\frac{\partial p_2}{\partial c_2}|_{p_1}$, that is, the change in firm 2's optimal choice of price resulting from the decrease in its marginal cost:

$$\frac{\partial p_2}{\partial c_2}\bigg|_{p_1} = \frac{\frac{\partial Q_2}{\partial p_2}}{(p_2 - c_2)\frac{\partial^2 Q_2}{\partial p_2^2} + 2\frac{\partial Q_2}{\partial p_2}} \tag{7}$$

The numerator is negative and non-zero and the denominator is negative by firm 2's second-order condition. Thus, $\frac{\partial p_2}{\partial c_2}|_{p_1} > 0$, which establishes that firm 2 would have the incentive to increase its price in response to the increase in its marginal cost rather than hold its price constant.

Equation (7) describes the change in firm 2's pricing incentives holding constant the price of firm 1. However, the increase in the marginal cost of firm 2 also gives firm 1 the incentive to increase its price. Thus, in equilibrium both prices change due to the increase in the marginal cost of firm 2. The change in the equilibrium price of firm 2 can be determined by differentiating the first-order condition (6) for firm 2 with respect to c_2 without holding firm 1's price constant.[27] We obtain

$$\left(\frac{\partial p_2}{\partial c_2} - 1\right)\frac{\partial Q_2}{\partial p_2} + (p_2 - c_2)\left[\frac{\partial^2 Q_2}{\partial p_2^2}\frac{\partial p_2}{\partial c_2} + \frac{\partial^2 Q_2}{\partial p_2 \partial p_1}\frac{\partial p_1}{\partial c_2}\right]$$
$$+ \frac{\partial Q_2}{\partial p_2}\frac{\partial p_2}{\partial c_2} + \frac{\partial Q_2}{\partial p_1}\frac{\partial p_1}{\partial c_2} = 0 \tag{8}$$

Note that Equation (8) includes the term $\frac{\partial p_1}{\partial c_2}$, which is the change in the equilibrium price of firm 1 caused by a change in firm 2's cost. Equation (8) can be rearranged to take the following form:

$$\frac{\partial p_2}{\partial c_2}\left(2\frac{\partial Q_2}{\partial p_2} + (p_2 - c_2)\frac{\partial Q_2}{\partial p_2^2}\right) + \frac{\partial p_1}{\partial c_2}\left(2\frac{\partial Q_2}{\partial p_1} + (p_2 - c_2)\frac{\partial^2 Q_2}{\partial p_2 \partial p_1}\right) = \frac{\partial Q_2}{\partial p_2} \tag{9}$$

The term inside the first parentheses on the left-hand side of (9) is negative by the second-order conditions for firm 2's maximization problem. The second term on the left-hand side of (9) is positive if the firm's prices are strategic complements. Thus, the equilibrium prices are increasing in c_2. The magnitude of the increase in price for a given increase in c_2 depends on the slope and curvature of the two demand curves.

The change in the profits of firm 1 as a result of the increase in c_2 can be determined to first order by differentiating firm 1's equilibrium profit function

$$\pi_1(c_2) = (p_1(c_2) - c_1)Q_1(p_1(c_2), p_2(c_2)) \tag{10}$$

with respect to c_2 (where we have suppressed the additional dependence of the equilibrium profit function on c_1). This differentiation yields

$$\frac{\partial \pi_1}{\partial c_2} = \frac{\partial p_1}{\partial c_2}Q_1 + (p_1 - c_1)\frac{\partial Q_1}{\partial p_1}\frac{\partial p_2}{\partial c_2} + (p_1 - c_1)\frac{\partial Q_1}{\partial p_1}\frac{\partial p_2}{\partial c_2} \tag{11}$$

The first two terms are zero due to the envelope theorem. The third term demonstrates that firm 1's equilibrium profits increase when c_2 increases, and that, to first order, this increase in profits is equal to the increase in firm 1's quantity sales resulting from the increase in firm 2's price, multiplied by firm 1's pre-existing per unit profit margin.

As a concrete example, consider the case of linear demand where the demand functions take the form

$$Q_i = \alpha - \beta p_i + \gamma p_j \tag{12}$$

where $\beta \geq \gamma > 0$. In that case equation (9) simplifies to

$$\frac{\partial p_2}{\partial c_2}(-2\beta) + \frac{\partial p_1}{\partial c_2}\gamma = -\beta \tag{13}$$

and the corresponding equation derived from differentiating the first-order condition (6) for firm 1 with respect to c_2 is

$$\frac{\partial p_1}{\partial c_2}(-2\beta) + \frac{\partial p_2}{\partial c_2}\gamma = 0 \tag{14}$$

Solving these two equations for $\frac{\partial p_i}{\partial c_2}$ yields

$$\frac{\partial p_2}{\partial c_2} = \frac{2\beta^2}{4\beta^2 - \gamma^2}, \quad \frac{\partial p_2}{\partial c_2} = \frac{\beta\gamma}{4\beta^2 - \gamma^2} \tag{15}$$

Thus, in the boundary case where $\beta = \lambda$, for each \$1 increase in c_2, p_2 would increase by \$0.67 and p_1 would increase by \$0.33. The fact that p_2 increases more than p_1 implies that firm 1 would gain market share after an increase in c_2.

We will now calibrate the parameters to approximate the *Grain Processing* case facts and calculate the lost profits that firm 1 sustains as a result of the infringement by firm 2, assuming that in the but-for world firm 2 would utilize the alternative non-infringing technology (i.e. under the assumptions of the *Grain Processing* decision). When both firms are using the patented technology, we assume equal costs ($c_1 = c_2 = 50$). The parameters are chosen ($\alpha = 100$, $\beta = 2$ and $\gamma = 2$) so that each firm sells $Q_i = 100$ at a price of $p_i = 100$. The firms therefore split the market evenly when both use the patented technology. Each firm has profit $\pi_1 = 5000$.

If the infringer, firm 2, is forced to use the non-infringing technology, its costs rise to $c_2 = 53$. In that case, the equilibrium prices are $p_1 = 101$ and $p_2 = 102$ and the equilibrium quantities are $Q_1 = 102$ and $Q_2 = 98$. The profits of the patent holder, firm 1, increase to $\pi_1 = 5202$. Thus, the patent holder sustained lost profits even if the infringer would have used the non-infringing technology in the but-for world.

Damages in these circumstances would be calculated using a hybrid lost profits–reasonable royalty approach. In addition to the lost profits of \$202, a reasonable royalty of \$3 (3% of the \$100 selling price) would be applied to the 98 infringing units that did not represent lost sales to the patent owner. Thus, total damages would be \$496. This damages award would substantially exceed the reasonable royalty-only damages award of \$300 (\$3 royalty on 100 infringing units).

4.2 *Cournot*

Denote inverse market demand by $P(Q_1 + Q_2)$, where Q_i is the quantity supplied by firm i. Again we assume constant marginal costs c_i. The first-order condition for firm i is

$$\frac{\partial P}{\partial Q}Q_i + (P(Q_1 + Q_2) - c_i) = 0 \tag{16}$$

The two first-order conditions implicitly define the equilibrium quantities, which are functions of the marginal costs. To determine the effect of a change in c_2 on the equilibrium quantities, we differentiate (16) with respect to c_2 and rearrange to obtain

$$\frac{\partial Q_1}{\partial c_2} = -\frac{\partial Q_2}{\partial c_2} \frac{\frac{\partial p}{\partial Q} + Q_1 \frac{\partial^2 p}{\partial Q^2}}{2\frac{\partial p}{\partial Q} + Q_1 \frac{\partial^2 p}{\partial Q^2}} \tag{17}$$

Because the numerator and the denominator of the second term of equation (17) are both negative, we have that sign($\frac{\partial Q_1}{\partial c_2}$) = −sign($\frac{\partial Q_2}{\partial c_2}$), and under the usual conditions $\frac{\partial Q_1}{\partial c_2} > 0$. Thus, an increase in the infringer's cost will cause the patent holder to expand its output while the infringer contracts its output.

In the case with linear demand $P = \alpha - \beta Q$, we have $\frac{\partial Q_1}{\partial c_2} = \frac{1}{3\beta}$. We now calibrate the linear demand case to the facts of the *Grain Processing* case. As before, we assume that, when both firms are using the patented technology, they have equal costs ($c_1 = c_2 = 50$). The parameters are chosen ($\alpha = 200$ and $\beta = 0.5$) so that each firm sells $Q_i = 100$ at a price of $P = 100$. The firms therefore split the market evenly when both use the patented technology. Each firm has profit $\pi_i = 5000$.

If the infringer, firm 2, is forced to use the non-infringing technology, its costs rise to $c_2 = 53$. In that case, the equilibrium price increases to $P = 101$ and the equilibrium quantities are $Q_1 = 102$ and $Q_2 = 96$. The profits of the patent holder, firm 1, increase to $\pi_1 = 5202$. Thus, again, the patent holder sustained lost profits even if the infringer would have used the non-infringing technology in the but-for world. Also, the total (hybrid) damages award of $490 (the $202 lost profits damages plus the $288 reasonable royalty damages on the 96 infringing units that the patent holder would not have made in the but-for world) again substantially exceeds the $300 damages award that would result from a reasonable royalty-only approach.

5. Conclusion

Patent litigation has become an increasingly important consideration in business strategy. Damage awards in patent litigation are supposed to compensate the patent owner for economic harm created by infringement. The *Grain Processing* decision has decreased the expected value of damages from infringement by conferring a 'free option' on the infringer. The infringer is permitted to claim that in the but-for world it would have adopted a non-infringing technology, if such a technology exists. The infringer does not actually have to practice the technology; the existence of the technology is sufficient. This free option transfers economic value to the infringer and transfers economic value away from the patent holder. Thus, it decreases the economic incentives to innovate, which is one of the primary goals of the US patent system.

We also demonstrate that the conclusion of the District Court with respect to the absence of lost profits is contradicted by most models of firm behaviour and profit maximization. When a firm's costs increase, it typically will increase its price. Thus, if the infringer were to adopt the higher-cost non-infringing technology, prices would typically increase and the patent holder would both increase its price and gain greater sales. Calculation of lost profits in most economic models, plus a reasonable royalty on those infringing units that do not represent lost sales to the patent holder, will then exceed the cost difference between the infringing low-cost technology and the non-infringing high-cost technology multiplied by the sales made by the infringer. From this calculation the hybrid lost profits and reasonable royalty damages award will typically substantially exceed a reasonable royalty-only damage award. Thus, we conclude that the Court's decision that no lost profits existed if the infringer were assumed to have adopted the non-infringing technology is inconsistent with most economic analysis. The economic basis for the *Grain Processing* decision is at odds with most models of profit maximization by firms acting in an economically rational manner.

Acknowledgement

We thank Ketan Patel and Kelly Paulson for research assistance.

Notes

1. See, for example, *Minnesota Mining & Mrg. Co. v. Johnson & Johnson Orthopedics, Inc.*, 976 F.2d 1559, 24 USPQ2d 1321 (Fed. Cir. 1992). As the first author pointed out in that case, in the but-for world absent price erosion, a decreased quantity would be sold at the higher price.
2. A hybrid approach is often used as well in situations where not all of the infringing sales represented lost sales to the patent holder. In that case, a lost profits approach is used to calculate damages on the infringing sales that represent lost sales to the patent holder and a reasonable royalty approach is used to calculate damages on the remaining sales.
3. We do not review this commentary here. Much of it is in student-edited law reviews. An interested reader can find the material using either Westlaw or Lexis in a university library.
4. It is possible that the patent holder would sue some other infringer and the validity of the patent would be determined in that litigation. However, the question of infringement would often still remain.
5. Thus, the assumption is made that a license would always result from the hypothetical negotiation. A similar framework is used in numerous other countries to determine royalty damages after infringement has occurred.
6. In principle, the Edgeworth Box can be empty, in which case the infringer cannot pay the amount lost by the patent holder and still be profitable. This situation can occur, for example, when the patent holder is a significantly lower-cost producer than the infringer.
7. This approach is consistent with the US Supreme Court approach to damages as 'The difference between [the patent owner's] pecuniary condition after the infringement, and what his condition would have been if the infringement had not occurred'. *Aro Mfg Co. v. Convertible Top Replacement Co.,* 377 U.S. 476, 84 S.Ct. 1526.
8. *Panduit Corp. v. Stahlin Brothers Fibre Works, Inc.* 575 F.2d 1152, 197 USPQ 726 (6th Cir. 1978). See also *Rite-Hite Corp. v. Kelley Co., Inc.*, 56 F3d 1538, 35 US2d 1065 (Fed. Cir. 1995)

9. See, for example, J. Hausman and G. Leonard (2005).
10. The details of the case are taken from the final Appeals court decision, *Grain Processing Corp. v. American Maize-Products Co.*, 98-1081, US Court of Appeals for the Federal Circuit.
11. The original district court decision (the lower court) found that American Maize did not infringe. This decision was reversed by the CAFC. Absent exceptional circumstances the CAFC is the final decision in patent litigation because the Supreme Court only very rarely reviews patent decisions.
12. *Grain Processing Corp. v. American Maize-Products Co.*, 893 F. Supp. 1386, USPQ2d (N.D. Ind. 1995). The trial was a bench trial (no jury), so Judge Easterbrook decided the case.
13. *Grain Processing Corp. v. American Maize-Products Co.*, 108 F, 3d 1392 (Fed. Cir. 1997).
14. *Grain Processing Corp. v. American Maize-Products Co.*, 98-1081, US Court of Appeals for the Federal Circuit.
15. Strictly speaking, a patent gives the holder the right to sue to exclude an infringer. The court may find that the patent is invalid.
16. See R. Brealey *et al.* (2005, p. 262, Ch. 22, pp. 597ff).
17. See J. Hausman (1997, 2002, 2003).
18. For a discussion of this outcome see J. Hausman and G. Sidak (2005).
19. Litigation costs can be included by deducting them from profits.
20. We assume that the firm cannot choose technology 2 in period 1 and then switch to technology 1 in period 2 because, in a more general model, the firm would be continuously subject to an infringement lawsuit.
21. See A. Dixit and R. Pindyck (1994, p. 6.)
22. The patent owner might additionally claim price erosion damages. In that case, $D > \pi_1$ is possible.
23. We could change the constant probability assumption to allowing an increasing or decreasing hazard over time using a Weibull distribution. Other distributions would allow for a non-monotonic hazard. However, the general form of the results does not depend on the particular distribution chosen.
24. See, for example, J. Hausman and J. MacKie-Mason (1988) for a discussion of how economic returns to patents interact with the US patent system's goal of increasing innovation.
25. J. Bulow and P. Pfleiderer (1983) showed how a monopolist optimally changes its price in response to a marginal cost change. J. Hausman and G. Leonard (1999) showed how marginal cost efficiencies resulting from a merger lead to lower prices in the context of several models of competition.
26. We assume that the marginal costs are constant over the relevant range of output.
27. For a general approach to comparative statics in this type of situation, see A. Dixit (1986).

References

Brealey, R., Myers, S. and Allen, F. (2005) *Principles of Corporate Finance*, 8th edition. New York: McGraw Hill.
Bulow, J. and Pfleiderer, P. (1983) A note on the effect of cost changes on prices. *Journal of Political Economy* 91: 182–185.

Dixit, A. (1986) Comparative statics for oligopoly. *International Economic Review* 27: 107–122.

Dixit, A. and Pindyck, R. (1994) *Investment Under Uncertainty*. Princeton, NJ: Princeton University Press.

Hausman, J. (1997) Valuation and the effect of regulation on new services in telecommunications. *Brookings Papers on Economic Activity: Microeconomics*: Washington, DC: Brookings Institution.

Hausman, J. (2002) The effect of sunk costs in telecommunication regulation. In J. Alleman and E. Noam (eds), *The New Investment Theory of Real Options and its Implications for Telecommunications Economics*. Boston, MA: Kluwer.

Hausman, J. (2003) Regulated costs and prices in telecommunications. In G. Madden (ed.), *International Handbook of Telecommunications*. Northampton, MA: Edward Elgar.

Hausman, J. and Leonard, G. (1999) Efficiencies from the consumer viewpoint. *George Mason Law Review* 7: 707–727.

Hausman, J. and Leonard, G. (2005) Competitive analysis using a flexible demand specification. *Journal of Competition Law and Economics* 1: 279–301.

Hausman, J. and MacKie-Mason, J. (1988) Price discrimination and patent policy. *Rand Journal of Economics* 19: 253–265.

Hausman, J. and Sidak, G. (2005) Did mandatory unbundling achieve its purpose? Empirical evidence from five countries. *Journal of Competition Law and Economics* 1: 173–245.

3

HOW TO BEST ENSURE REMUNERATION FOR CREATORS IN THE MARKET FOR MUSIC? COPYRIGHT AND ITS ALTERNATIVES

Stan J. Liebowitz and Richard Watt

1. Introduction

Digital technologies, particularly the Internet, have had profound effects on the way the business of music is managed. Music performers and writers, as well as the companies and individuals that produce, publish and distribute musical compositions, are increasingly worried that the onslaught of technology is seriously interfering with their ability to charge end users for their creations. The important cost savings that these technologies can bring to distribution and storage activities have had a serious downside in the challenge they impose on the ability of creators to receive remuneration for their work.

Remuneration for creators of musical compositions usually relies on the provisions afforded by copyright – a legal regime that is supposed to define the rights controlled by creators and their delegates. Copyright law, of course, does more than this. By stipulating statutory remedies in cases of infringement, copyright law also provides for a level of enforcement of the established rights; that is, copyright not only defines the right of ownership but it also provides some protection of this right.

It is becoming increasingly clear, however, that in the face of digital copying, copyright is not functioning as well as it once did. The main problem is not so much in the definition of the set of rights to be allocated to creators,[1] but rather with the enforcement, or protection, of these rights. The costs of policing infringing behavior are escalating as copying is done outside of organized markets by anonymous strangers, as the copied items are almost perfect substitutes for the original good, and as the very act of copying becomes practically costless. In such an environment, copyright loses its effectiveness as a property right.[2]

Inasmuch as copyright is concerned with imperfect markets, contracting issues, incentive mechanisms, and possible externalities, the study of copyright has been an increasingly popular subject of discussion in the economics literature. Over the past

25 years economists and others have scrutinized many aspects of the relationship between copyright and the production, distribution and consumption of information goods.[3]

The current topic of the day is the impact of file sharing on the music industry. Music has captured the attention of economists for several reasons – because the music industry is undergoing a massive transformation due to transformations in its business model, because music is an international market of substantial economic size (particularly as measured by the importance that music plays in the psyche of man), and because what is happening in the music industry is seen as a likely harbinger of most forms of entertainment, such as movies, computer software, videogames and the like. Many economists have noticed the impending problem; some have argued that with sufficient alterations copyright can meet the challenge while others have argued that copyright should be abandoned altogether since remuneration can be adequately guaranteed by other means. In this paper we attempt to review this literature.

The paper continues as follows: in the next section we give a very short outline of the traditional economic theory of copyright as a remuneration and incentive mechanism for creation. We include within that section an analysis of the literature, now rather extensive, that considers the characteristics that copyright should have if it is indeed to properly address the remuneration and incentive issue. In Section 4 we look at the particular case of the market for music. Concretely, we review the literature that considers the effects of copying of music on the legitimate market. This literature clearly highlights the possible shortfalls of the copyright regime as a mechanism under which creators receive recompense. Then, in Section 5 we consider the literature that discusses possible alternative mechanisms for providing remuneration and incentives to creators. Finally, Section 6 concludes.

2. The 'Paradox of Creation' and the Basic Economics of Copyright[4]

The economics of copyright can be summarized as a particular case of private provision of a public good (see Demsetz, 1970). Once a copyrightable creation exists, there is a serious problem in that its consumption is non-rivalrous, in the sense that the product does not get used up upon consumption. For this reason efficient consumption requires that any consumer whose value for the good outweighs the (often very low) costs of delivery should be allowed to consume the good – *assuming that the intellectual property itself already exists*. The price that assures efficient consumption is a price that is no higher than the delivery cost. A price that covers only delivery cost, however, guarantees that the total revenue is insufficient to provide any recompense to the original creator for the (most likely high) initial costs of creation (Arrow, 1962).[5] Thus a sort of conundrum can exist – efficient consumption precludes efficient production.

In a competitive world without any ownership rights of the intellectual property, the price would be driven down to the costs of delivering the intellectual product to the consumer (which would include the cost of producing any physical embodiment of the intellectual product). Assuming that failure to provide compensation to creators will lead to an inefficiently small production of creative works (and thus inefficiently small consumption of the works not created); such a result would not be socially desirable.

The solution provided by copyright is to award the creator a means of appropriating a sufficient portion of the willingness to pay of consumers for there to be enough incentive for the creative process to go ahead. Copyright is supposed to provide such a mechanism, by establishing the right of the copyright owner to legally exclude free-riders (those who would deliver the intellectual product with no payment to the creator), and this in turn allows the copyright owner to charge a price greater than the delivery cost of the intellectual product. Thus, copyright considers a social balance; the social gain that is derived from the enjoyment of creative goods must be balanced against the inefficiencies that pricing above marginal cost implies. How this is done in practice is often associated with the drawing of an arbitrary 'line in the sand', due both to the inherently theoretical nature of the measures being traded off and to the obvious information problems involved in trying to construct an efficient copyright system (the consumer willingness to pay and the true costs of creation are often not known). Indeed, as Posner (2005, p. 59) states:

> Unfortunately, economists do not know whether the existing system of intellectual property rights is, or for that matter whether any other system of intellectual property rights would be, a source of net social utility, given the costs of the system and the existence of alternative sources of incentives to create such property.

Nevertheless, in spite of not having come to concrete answers one way or the other, economists have certainly attempted to address the issues of characterizing an optimal copyright law, and they have also given quite some thought to the issue of alternative sources of incentives. We will now go on to consider this literature in general.

3. The Optimal Structure of Copyright Law

The early literature that emerged discussing the issue of the optimal structure of copyright law from an economic point of view questioned the very need for any type of legal protection system (see Plant, 1934; Hurt and Schuchman, 1966; Breyer, 1970). Written in an epoch in which digital concerns were an unforeseen effect that was still well into the future, this literature appeals to such aspects as the benefits of lead time and stock-piling to dissuade unauthorized copying and distribution of written material (books), as well as to the non-pecuniary motives of creators.

The underlying conclusion of some of these papers is that some protection might be required but the protection from being first was sufficient so that no additional protection in the law was necessary. However, the issues surrounding the distribution and sale of books was very soon to be complicated by new copying technologies that significantly reduced the lead time. These early papers also focused on commercial-scale copying and not the private copying that has come to dominate discussions in the more recent decades (photocopying, copying of music to tape cassettes, digital copying of music from and to CDs, and of course, downloading of music and films over the Internet).

Of particular note, perhaps with the early literature, is the issue of the costs associated with copyright protection. The literature clearly identifies the fact that increased copyright protection limits access to socially valuable creations. But furthermore, Plant (1934) also notes that copyright law might lead to an inefficient allocation of resources, in terms of what is now known as 'rent seeking'. Rent seeking presumes that above-normal rents are to be found in an activity, in this case, copyright. The mere existence of a 'copyright monopoly', however, does not imply that any monopoly profits are to be gained, as pointed out by Kitch (2000).[6] Nevertheless, the possibility of short-term rents or windfalls is often noted for incomplete property rights controlled by the government, as Posner describes the classic treatment (2005, p. 59); '. . .by enabling pricing in excess of marginal cost, intellectual property rights attract resources into the creation of such property that may have a larger social product in alternative uses in which, however, they would generate only a competitive return for producers'.

In 1989, Professors William Landes and Richard Posner of the University of Chicago published a seminal paper modelling the economic analysis of copyright law (Landes and Posner, 1989). In their paper, Landes and Posner make a distinction between the economics of copying (which studies the impact of the availability of copies on the demand for originals, and on the welfare of creators and of society in general),[7] and the economics of copyright *per se* (which studies the impact of legal copyright protection on the production of, and subsequent access to, creative works). Landes and Posner identify a clear benefit of copyright protection – it addresses the market failure issue of free-riding on creative effort, allowing creators to receive payment, and thereby providing an incentive for more creative products to exist. On the other hand, Landes and Posner identify at least four costs to copyright – the social costs of restricting access to consumers (a *static* effect, found in each period in which protection ensues), the increased costs of second-generation creation (a *dynamic* effect, affecting the inter-temporal sequence of creative activity[8]), the 'rent seeking' resource allocation problem alluded to above, and the transactions costs of maintaining the system (mainly protection and enforcement costs). The literature on the economics of copyright has attempted to identify the correct balance between these costs and benefits.

Almost all of the subsequent literature (and indeed, some papers that predate Landes and Posner by a few years) on the balance of the costs and benefits of copyright protection have attempted, in one way or another, to arrive at an 'optimal' configuration of copyright (see, for example, Novos and Waldman, 1984; Pethig, 1988; Besen and Kirby, 1989; Koboldt, 1995; and more recently Yoon, 2002). Basically, the argument assumes that copyright is adequately enforceable (as most models assume that property rights are enforceable), and so the creator is indeed able to reduce copying to the extent that he can sell to a legitimate demand curve at a price that exceeds marginal cost. Given that, the objective is then to attempt to identify the set of parameters that define a socially optimal balance of the costs and benefits of the grant of copyright.

Since the true product demand, the temporal pattern of demand, and the supply curves for creation are impossible to locate,[9] no fully convincing paper on the optimal level of protection has yet been written. However, most papers that have addressed this issue conclude that an 'optimal' balance of the effects will imply a level of protection that is neither infinite nor zero.[10]

The issue of whether or not copyright law does confer monopoly power of any real consequence has been debated in the literature. Of course, the right granted is still a property right, and so the 'monopoly power' that copyright grants is really no more than the monopoly that we hold over any private possessions (on this issue, see Liebowitz, 1981; Easterbrook, 1991). Any inherent monopoly power must reside in the product with the property right, not in the property right itself. Second, the models typically assume that copyright law allows the creator to sell as a monopolist to a legitimate demand curve, but does not exclude the possibility of free entry. Third, some unauthorized copying still occurs, and so legitimate copies (normally called 'originals') may have to compete with illegitimate copies. Thus market power, as economists typically know it, may be severely eroded, and it is possible that the appropriate setting may be one of monopolistic competition (see Yoo, 2004). Finally, in the case of copyright, without the grant of copyright there is a clear danger that far too little creation will exist, so the 'deadweight loss' from equating marginal cost to a downwards sloping marginal revenue is productive, to use the terminology of Liebowitz and Margolis (2005). That is to say, we should not really compare social welfare under copyright with the social welfare that would occur under an ideal situation. Instead, we should compare it to the best social welfare that can actually be achieved, and if copyright is the best solution, the deadweight losses associated with generating payments required to compensate the author are not social losses at all.

Aside from the costs of limiting access, the literature has also mentioned, although to a lesser extent, the fact that a system of copyright protection implies its own set of transactions costs,[11] the costs of administering and enforcing the copyright that is granted. The transactions costs of enforcement were explicitly noted by Landes and Posner, as were the 'lobbying' costs associated with rent-seeking activity as different groups appeal to the authorities for legislative change. Also present are the costs associated with negotiating, writing and enforcing contracts for the subsequent exchange or transfer of intellectual property (see Cheung, 1970). It is also worth noting here that the existence of copyright collectives – large groups of copyright holders who administer their intellectual property together – is based mainly on a transactions costs savings argument (see Hollander, 1984; Smith, 1986; Besen et al., 1992).

When taking into account all of the costs and benefits conferred by copyright law, there remains the question of exactly what are the 'optimal' parameters to apply (for an interesting selection of papers, mostly unpublished, on this general issue, see Farrell, 1994; McCain, 1994; Thorpe and Rimmer, 1995; CPB Netherlands Bureau for Economic Policy Analysis, 2000; Siebrasse and McLaughlin, 2001). In particular, however, the question of the best duration of copyright has been hotly debated over the years. Of course, we have already mentioned some of the early literature (Plant, 1934; and more recently Boldrin and Levine, 2002. See also the historical perspective on this issue in David, 1993) that suggested that there was really no need for legal copyright protection at all (and so the optimal duration was in fact whatever being first provided). This contrasts with another group of papers that argue that not only should copyright exist, but there are arguments to support it lasting forever (Turnbull, 1998; Landes and Posner, 2002). In any case, the alterations in the duration that legal systems provide add more fuel to the academic debate, and invariably lead to a flourishing of new papers on the issue of the optimal duration of copyright protection – in particular see Ginsburg *et al.* (2000), Akerlof *et al.* (2002) and Liebowitz and Margolis (2005).

Much of this literature focuses on the theoretical aspects of copyright, such as the possible impact of laws that create changes far in the future whose present value would appear to be exceedingly small. What is lacking are detailed empirical analyses. There is at least a trickle of such analyses with Rappaport (1998), Liebowitz and Margolis (2005) and a more thorough examination by Baker and Cunningham (2006).

4. The Effectiveness of Copyright Law in the Market for Music

In spite of copyright law protecting the interests of creators and authors during its term, copyright infringement is clearly present, and indeed is currently at levels that are extremely troublesome (Liebowitz, 2006a). A large and unanticipated increase in copyright infringement could be taken as evidence that that copyright law is not functioning as intended, and thus the design of the system might need to be addressed.

The main questions to be considered are whether or not the current level of copyright infringement is significantly eroding creation,[12] and whether or not such erosion (assuming it exists) is socially inefficient or not. There are several possible ways in which infringement might be socially efficient (see, for example, Watt, 2004, for a brief mention of some of these), and might even have a positive effect upon the amount of secondary creation that takes place. First, of course, we have the fact that, since private infringement takes place at prices below the legitimate market price, it allows consumption by individuals that have a willingness to pay below the market pricing allowed by copyright. In this way, infringement reduces the consumption deadweight loss, and if infringement were only engaged in, say, by those with values below market pricing, society as a whole would gain.

Second, as far as the erosion of creative works is concerned, if copying were to affect all creators proportionally, then the first to defect to alternative employment would be those earning the lowest economic rents – those artists whose value outside of music is very close to their value as musicians. The social value of the loss of such creators might not be high. Third, it is clear that copying networks such as file sharing might constitute a method of free advertising for as yet unheralded artists without record contracts, and such copyright infringement, by promoting such networks, may create a positive impact for newcomers, since the costs of distribution are so much cheaper. Of course, some of the lost revenues come from record companies who have fewer resources to pay for those acts that mostly turn out to be dry holes, so a decline in revenue due to copying networks will be expected to have a corresponding decrease in new acts that otherwise would have landed a record contract.

Finally, the most likely scenario is that the groups of artists that are hardest hit (both in absolute and relative terms) by copyright infringement are those with super-star status and incomes. However, these individuals are likely to be earning large economic rents so the effect of lost dollars to these artists might have little impact on their creative works.

In any case, it is extremely difficult to correctly and convincingly answer the types of questions that are of interest as far as the relationship between infringement and creation is concerned, and indeed the literature has not yet made any truly rigorous attempt to address them. However, much attention has been paid to the very closely related issues of exactly how much of an effect copyright infringement has upon the legitimate market, especially for the case of musical compositions.

The first aspect of infringement that was seriously considered in the economics literature was the calculation of the degree to which infringement represented lost sales of originals. That this was considered to be worthy of study was mainly due to the outcries of copyright holders (for example, the record industry – see the data in the IFPI Report on Piracy (2003)), with claims that infringement represents lost sales almost as great as the total legitimate trade itself.[13] As was clearly shown in a quite general theoretical setting by Besen and Kirby (1989), since copies are priced below originals, many consumers of illegitimate copies would not likely consume originals even if copies were not available (see also the analysis in Watt, 2004).

Reliable estimates of the proportion of copies that represent lost sales are difficult to come by, but the early literature (before online file sharing and downloading were an issue) suggested that for the case of music the figure was closer to 40% (see, for example, Mannering, 1994, who gives a figure of 38%, and Warner Communications Inc., 1982, which rounds it off to 40%). Besen (1987) cites research done by Alan Greenspan for the Recording Industry Association of America in which it is estimated that about 40% of home taping of pre-recorded music represented displaced legitimate sales, and research done by G. Davis for the International Federation of Phonogram and Videogram Producers suggests that 25% of home taping of LP records represented lost sales of originals.

The early literature on the effects of copying on the pre-recorded music industry is often represented by two papers – Belinfante and Davis (1979) and Widdows and McHugh (1984). Both of these papers conclude that piracy and copying of music had only a small negative effect upon sales and profits of the music industry, and one that was considerably smaller than had been claimed by music industry officials. Indeed, these two papers found that other factors, such as demographic change and the general state of the economy were more likely than piracy to have caused the downturn in sales of the latter part of the 1970s.

Modern treatments of the effects of physical copying upon the demand for music are more difficult to come by, as modern authors have concentrated much more on the case of downloading and file sharing (see below). However, quite recently Hui and Png (2003) estimate that, worldwide, about 6.6% of the CD copying that takes place in for-profit counterfeit markets represents lost sales in the legitimate market.

Physical copying of music has also been examined recently using experimental data. For example, Maffioletti and Ramello (2004) shed light upon the microeconomic behaviour of potential consumers of copied CDs using an experiment with a population of 188 Italian university students, using both hypothetical and real choices. In their paper, Maffioletti and Ramello find that, first, the mean willingness to pay for a legitimate CD is typically below the market price (between about 60% and 80% of the full market price). This result, if true, would imply that very few of their students actually would purchase any CDs, which seems slightly strange in a world where most students would be expected to have collections of CDs.[14] The second result was that the mean willingness to pay for a copied (i.e. illegitimate) music CD, while significantly greater than 0, is only about a third to one half of the willingness to pay for a legitimate CD.[15] If these results reflected the entire population of potential purchasers, they would imply that the recording industry underestimates the elasticity of its demand curve and would likely benefit from lower prices.

Also, recently, Bounie et al. (2005) have made an attempt to provide the separation of the substitution and complementary effects using survey data from French university students. They find much interesting evidence relating to stated CD purchases, MP3 files, and the size of CD collections. They also suggest the novel idea of using the answer to a question about how many MP3 files are deleted from hard drives as a measure of the degree of sampling. Their statistical analysis shows that overall, using file sharing networks and having more MP3 files lead to a decline in CD sales. This is particularly true for the larger subgroup that does not delete MP3 files. For the smaller group identified as 'samplers', the impact of downloading files on CD sales is ambiguous, which, as we explain below, is as theory predicts.

4.1 Examining the Impacts of File Sharing

For the interesting case of digital file sharing for music, a recent literature has emerged. This literature was initiated, in a modest way, at the Napster trial, in which the plaintiff commissioned a study (see Fine, 2000) to estimate the effect of online file sharing upon the sales of physical music on CDs. The study, which compared point-of-sale data in brick and mortar record stores located within a small radius of universities in the USA (since it was considered that university students were more likely to engage in downloading than the rest of the population), and compared sales to the overall sales of CDs at retail both before and after Napster was available. The study found that from the first quarter of 1999 (Napster did not exist) to the first quarter of 2000 (Napster did exist), while nationwide sales of CDs grew by some 6.6%, sales near universities dropped by 2.6%. Thus it might seem that the study provides some evidence for a negative effect upon sales being caused by downloading. However, the study found very similar results in the period from 1998 to 1999 when Napster did not exist, casting serious doubt on how to interpret these results. One possibility was simply that college students were more likely to order CDs online during this period so that sales in local stores fell, but not because of file sharing. It was also the case that in the first quarter of 2000 Napster was still very small, being only one seventh the size it would reach in the first quarter of 2001.

As is often the case, the economic impact of Internet downloading and file sharing can have various theoretical impacts. There are four possible impacts that have been discussed in the literature:

1. First, downloading can be an activity that substitutes for legal sales due to digital media providing a very high degree of substitutability of the two products. The impact of this substitution is unambiguous and it is difficult to imagine that the substitution effect is not fairly large when the copy is a good substitute for the original.

2. Second, it is possible that some file sharing and downloading is motivated by sampling (trying before one buys), and the ability by consumers to purchase more precisely targeted products can alter the legitimate sales, although in uncertain ways. Analysts have tended to focus on the positive possibility of sampling, leading them to a more positive view of it than they should have. In fact, sampling will rotate the demand for CDs clockwise, raising the value of early CD purchases but lowering the value of later purchases because there is little time left to listen to additional CDs, say, because the early CD purchases were listened to so intently. In fact, empirical work is needed to determine whether the typical impact of sampling on sales is positive or negative.

3. There is a set of models based on network effects (Conner and Rumelt, 1991; Takeyama, 1994), which suggest that network effects might alter the impact of copying on sellers of originals. This has been applied to music by Gayer and Shy (2005). The basic intuition is that purchasers of CDs might have higher values for CDs depending on the number of other people listening to music, implying a positive network effect for music listening. Whether there are such network effects is unknown. If there were such network effects, and if file sharing increased the overall music listening among those who otherwise were unlikely to purchase CDs but who still provide positive network effects to those who do, then the demand for CDs on the part of purchasers would increase. Given the rather restrictive conditions required for this process to work, and given the fact that radio has always been a freely available source of music, it seems problematic that file sharing could increase music listening

and generate positive network effects sufficient to increase demand to any significant extent.

4. One final possible factor involved with copying is indirect appropriability, which is discussed in more detail in Section 5 of this paper. Indirect appropriability allows the seller of originals to target alterations in the price of originals because the value of the copies is indirectly transmitted to the seller by way of higher valuations from those making copies. As discussed in Liebowitz (2002), indirect appropriability does not seem capable of having any impact on file sharing. The reason is that neither of the two conditions, which would allow indirect appropriability to work, hold – there is great variability in the number of copies made from each original, and it is not possible to identify those originals that have copies made and charge higher prices for them.

Given the theoretical analysis it is not surprising that most empirical work finds a negative impact of file sharing on sales of sound recordings.

The papers that have examined the impact of file sharing can be categorized by result and by methodology. By results the classification is quite simple. There is one study (Oberholzer and Strumpf, 2004) that claims to find a zero impact, although an outside reading of both versions of their paper could lead one to conclude that they actually find a positive relationship. All the other studies find some degree of negative relationship between file sharing and sales of sound recordings. These latter studies can be classified into those which find that file sharing caused some portion of the decline but not the entire amount and other studies that are consistent with file sharing causing the entire decline, or more, as explained below. Since many studies have a range of results, this latter distinction will be made apparent when the studies are categorized by methodology, an endeavour to which we now turn.

4.1.1 *Using Countries or Cities as the Unit of Analysis*

There are several papers that take this approach. The idea is straightforward enough: compare changes in sales of sound recording in different geographic locations over time using some measure, such as the share of Internet users, to proxy for the impact of file sharing across these regions.

Liebowitz (2006b) examines how the change in the sales of CDs in 99 US cities is impacted by file sharing as proxied by Internet access, and several demographic variables. Using Internet access as a proxy for file sharing (but after removing the impact of Internet usage on generic entertainment activities) he finds that cities with high levels of file sharing have had considerably larger decreases in CD sales than other cities over the period 1998–2003. The coefficients are of sufficient size to support a conclusion that file sharing could explain the entire decline in sales plus an implicit growth in sales that never materialized. Peitz and Waelbroeck (2004) use data from 16 countries for the period 1998–2002. They find a 20% decline in the sales of music for the world due to file sharing. Zentner (2005) uses international cross-section data from a very large number of countries during the period 1997–1998 to 2001–2002. He finds a worldwide decline of 15% and a US decline of 30%. Since neither of these papers present direct evidence of how these declines compare with actual declines we do not know how to translate this result into a share of the total decline. Nevertheless, these numbers are quite large and generally in the vicinity of the entire decline in many countries.

The difficulties with the geographic approach used by these authors include the fact that there are many factors that differ across geographic areas that are difficult to account for in these regressions. In some instances these areas have different levels of organized piracy, speak different languages, and have very different levels of per capita income, CD sales, Internet use, and stereo equipment. For example, CD writers make downloaded music much better substitutes for the purchase of a CD. In countries (or cities) where there are fewer CD writers per computer, downloading will have a smaller impact on sales. Statistics on the number of CD writers are frequently difficult to come by, thus potentially clouding any analysis. Attitudes towards piracy are also likely to differ by geographic area, which is another difficult variable to control for. Finally, the sizes of the data sets are usually quite small because the number of geographic areas with data on file sharing/Internet use is not large.

4.1.2 *Using Records as the Unit of Analysis*

There are two papers using this approach – one by Oberholzer and Strumpf (2004) and a dissertation at Harvard by Blackburn (2004). Both observe CD sales in the United States. Oberholzer and Strumpf were allowed access to actual downloads logs on a server that was part of a file-sharing system, whereas Blackburn used data provided by Big Champagne. Oberholzer and Strumpf have the advantage of having actual downloads but the disadvantage of having information from only a single small part of the file-sharing world. Blackburn's data are based on the entire industry but do not directly measure downloads – instead, it is based on the number of files available on hard drives for individuals to download. Both papers assume that their samples are representative of the entire market and provide some evidence to support this view. Both papers then match their estimates of music downloads to the recordings where the songs appeared and then both papers use data from SoundScan to compare the downloads of CDs to the sales of CDs. Nevertheless, these two papers come to diametrically opposed conclusions.

Each paper finds that for the average CD, file sharing has a negligible impact. Of course, it is incorrect to give each CD equal weight if the purpose of the analysis is to determine the overall impact of file sharing on CD sales since a small number of popular CDs are responsible for the lion's share of industry sales. Blackburn interacts a measure of prior artist popularity with his measure of downloading and finds that file sharing has a positive impact on relatively unknown artists, but more importantly, has a strong negative impact on CDs from more popular artists, leading him to conclude that file sharing has a large negative impact on record sales. Oberholzer and Strumpf used two different techniques to determine how their measured impact differed by type of album. In the original version of their paper they divided their sample into quartiles based on how successful the album was in the market, and found that file sharing had a small, insignificant negative impact on the less successful albums but a fairly large positive impact that was on the border of significance for the more successful albums. Their newer version of the paper removes the tables providing details of the regression results by quartiles. Instead, the authors use an interaction term (based on prior popularity) similar to that of Blackburn and produce a result strikingly at odds with their prior analysis: now the more popular artists are negatively impacted by file sharing, although, contrary to Blackburn's results, they are not significant.

There is a potential fallacy of a composition problem and also seriously difficulties with simultaneity. The reader is referred to Liebowitz (2005a) for a detailed discussion of these issues.

4.1.3 *Using Surveys*

There are several papers based upon surveys. Both Hong (2004) and Michel (2005) use data from the US Consumer Expenditure survey. Rob and Waldfogel (2006) use data based on a survey of American college students and Zentner (2006) uses data based upon a survey of consumers in several European countries.

All of these studies conclude that file sharing is harmful to record sales. Michel finds that file sharing caused a decline that seems small except that it was larger than the actual decline that occurred over his period of measurement while Hong finds that file sharing causes a decline less than half of the measured decline. Zentner finds a decline in the likelihood of purchase, which does not easily translate into a quantity of lost sales. Nevertheless, he provides an estimate of sales loss of approximately 8% from what they would have been as of 2002, but his results are based on seven European countries and it is not clear whether this change is larger or smaller than the actual change that occurred.

Rob and Waldfogel (2006) find that each downloaded album reduces legitimate sales by at least 0.2 albums (and a much larger amount if their instrumental methods are correct), which is a large enough result that it could explain the entire decline in record sales depending on the amount of file sharing that has actually occurred. They also suggest that file sharing might have a net benefit to society if one ignores the negative consequences of reduced production of creative works caused by lower revenues to the industry.

Surveys can be misleading because respondents may not be representative of the entire population, or they may not know the answers to questions asking for detailed information about purchases, or because they are unwilling to answer questions honestly. Given the highly politicized nature of file sharing, it would not be surprising if respondents tried to minimize their reported reduction in CD purchases. If so, results based on such surveys would be likely to understate the true impact on sales.[16]

Zentner and Rob and Waldfogel have direct information about MP3 downloading in their data, whereas Hong uses Internet access as a proxy and Michel uses computer ownership. The two studies with direct measures of downloading attempt to overcome a potential simultaneity problem (due to the fact that those individuals who are most interested in music tend to be heavy purchasers as well as heavy downloaders) with instrumental variables although Rob and Waldfogel report a negative relationship even before attempting to control for simultaneity using instrumental variables.

5. Alternatives to Legal Copyright Protection

Parallel to the literature on the economics of copyright, an important series of papers has appeared that considers the ability of creators to appropriate revenue from the market with no appeal at all to copyright law *per se*. This literature has suggested many ways in which this may be done (see Varian, 2005, pp. 134–136, for a short description of most of them), each of which we will now discuss in turn, and how they pertain to the particular case of music.[17]

Before beginning, however, we should always bear in mind that these suggested alternatives are a type of second-best solution, in the sense that the existence of copying and file sharing might render the first-best (copyright) unworkable. If any of the alternatives were in fact first-best we would have expected them to have been used well before copying became an issue. Digital transmission of copyrightable media, via Internet or even on physical formats, is a superior technology for the delivery of information goods, but it also provides the basis for programs that allow and encourage the erosion of property rights, perhaps even to the point of eliminating any semblance of property right. Without secure property rights market economies cannot function (and non-market economies function very poorly), and that is equally true for the functioning of individual markets.[18]

To begin with, it is important to note that while very closely related, the issues of the optimal structure of copyright law on the one hand and the alternatives to it on the other are often approached in different ways. Concretely, the study of the optimal structure of copyright law almost invariably considers the social trade-off associated with property rights in creative goods, and incorporated into the analyses are the trade-offs associated with creation taking place. Thus the economic analysis of copyright law typically attempts to provide for sufficient incentives for the creator to create, but only just.[19]

On the other hand, most (but not all) of the literature concerning the possible alternatives provides free access to consumers, eliminating the under-consumption problem associated with copyright. The main question for welfare analysis for these models then becomes solving the problem of finding mechanisms that generates the proper set of creative works. There is no attempt to suggest that these mechanisms provide only enough payment, perhaps because, being focused on actual conditions, they eschew the notion of perfection as even being remotely reachable.

Quite generally, the types of non-copyright mechanisms that have been discussed in the literature slot into three general headings: (i) mechanisms that ameliorate the difficulties caused by copying, i.e. manners in which copyright holders can take financial advantage of certain aspects of copying, (ii) mechanisms that attempt to reduce or eliminate copying, and (iii) mechanisms that are independent of the amount of copying (that replace copyright). We will discuss each of these options in turn.

5.1 Mechanisms that Ameliorate Negative Impacts of Copying

5.1.1 Indirect Appropriation

As already mentioned, one strand of literature suggests that when copying is a possibility, then strategies involving re-pricing of the product may be available to creators to extract rents from the market. The seminal paper in this literature is Liebowitz (1985),[20] in which it is shown that the emergence of the photocopying technology may well have benefited rather than hurt publishers of academic journals. The idea is indeed simple; the ability to copy originals has two effects – it reduces the number of originals sold (a substitution effect between originals and copies), but it provides possible *indirect appropriation* – that is, it may increase the willingness to pay for each original (since more use can be made of it). When price discrimination is possible, or when there is little variability in the number of copies made from each original the additional value that consumers place on originals due to the ability to copy can be appropriated by the sellers.

Indirect appropriability provides a strategy under which copying may actually be of benefit for creators of originals, but the necessary conditions for it to work may often not be present. For example, it requires that the originals that will be subject to copying be clearly identified, and there be some transmission of value from those receiving the copies to those purchasing originals. Indeed, Liebowitz himself (Liebowitz, 2002, 2003) has argued that indirect appropriability is very unlikely to play an ameliorative role in digital file sharing for several reasons. First, there is no transmission of values since the copier and lender have no relationship with one another. Second, the seller of originals cannot identify which will be used to make copies. Third, there is a great variability in the number of copies made from each original. Besen and Kirby (1989), Johnson and Waldman (2005) and Liebowitz (2005b) have also shown that specific market characteristics, which seem to describe file sharing, may ensure that copying always harms creators.

Notwithstanding the possibility that indirect appropriability may not work, there is a small but influential literature, led by Professors David Levine and Michele Boldrin, that asserts that market mechanisms based on appropriate pricing strategies (read, indirect appropriability) will always be an efficient remuneration mechanism (see Boldrin and Levine, 2002). The assumption throughout this literature is that this remuneration will also always suffice as an adequate incentive for creation, and so this literature sees no place for copyright law, except for the first copy. The thesis of Boldrin and Levine is based squarely upon the neoclassical theory of economic growth, and the efficiency of the market mechanism. It is, however, difficult to see how the market failures implied by the public good aspects of copyrightable creations are addressed in those models, if indeed they are.

5.1.2 *Network Externalities*

A network externality exists whenever the willingness to pay of any one user of a product is influenced by the number of other users of the same product. Classic examples of network externalities are telephones and fax machines, while computer operating systems (the more users of a common platform, the greater is the value of that platform due to a greater selection of software) and fashion fads are still other examples.[21]

Copyrightable intellectual property is often thought of as being an example of network externalities (see Scotchmer, 2005, chapter 10, for a good general treatment of the case of network externalities in intellectual property). For the case of some software the network effects are clear. It is also possible that there are positive network effects for music in that the more popular a particular artist becomes (where 'popularity' is measured by the number of people who listen to the artist's music, whether or not they actually paid for an original recording) the greater might be the willingness to pay to listen to that music (for example, as measured by the price that can be charged for concert tickets) independent of the consumer's autarky valuation of the product.

It is clearly the case that in the presence of positive network effects, since copying can increase the user base, which in turn might increase the willingness to pay for originals on the part of some users, which it might turn out that copying can work in the copyright holder's favour (see Takeyama, 1994, for a well-known formal model that captures this type of network effect).[22]

Network effects might be important to the music industry as a whole, or not, although it is clear that they are important for individual creative works that benefit from faddish behaviour. What is not clear is whether file sharing increases network effects, if there are any, since consumers had a free alternative in radio before file sharing and there is as yet no evidence whether file sharing actually increases the consumption of music in a manner that might impact network effects. More, or even some, work on this topic is necessary before we can make any strong statements about network effects, music and copying.

5.1.3 *Bundling with Physical Complements, Advertising and Informational Complements*

It is not uncommon to see two items marketed together. Economists use the term 'bundling' to describe this type of practice. As examples of bundling of complementary products, we often see pre-recorded music on CDs sold along with non-copyable (or at least more difficult to copy) items such as the artist's autograph, fan club membership, or some other type of relevant merchandise (posters, tee shirts, options for concert tickets, etc.). More recently, it is becoming common to see easily copyable CD ROMs or DVDs being sold along with much more difficult to copy items such as newspapers. Such bundling makes copies less good substitutes and thus weakens the substitution effect.

In a similar vein, but an unbundled one, it is sometimes suggested that the music industry is really a set of complementary activities and that the advent of copying requires a readjustment of the relative prices of the complements. For example, most recording artists also give concert tours. Tours are thought to help sell CDs.[23] For this reason the price of tours might be set below its individual profit-maximizing level in order to increase sales of CDs. If concerts and CDs were strong complements then one strategy to solve the copying problem would be to raise the price in the non-copyable concert market and lower the price in the CD market. This type of strategy has been suggested by Ku (2002). The problem with these suggestions is that we do not know whether many of these products are even substitutes or complements (e.g. concerts and sound recordings, radio and sound recordings). Further, in order for this strategy to work they need to be very strong complements, on the order of the manner in which left and right shoes are used together. Otherwise, the lost revenues from the market beset with copying cannot be made up in the other market. Of course, we would expect market players to be able to discover this superior strategy on their own. It is also the case that this new strategy would be expected to lead to a solution inferior to the original market organization since it was not chosen prior to file sharing and if it were superior we would have expected it to have evolved on its own in the many decades prior to file sharing.

There is a second type of bundling that can provide some benefit to copyright owners from unauthorized copying – bundling advertising with copyable goods (see Bakos and Brynjolfsson, 1999). The more copies of a given film that circulate, the greater is the value of certain types of advertising that can be inserted in the film. For example, BMW provided vehicles for recent James Bond films, and clearly the more viewers there are of the film, the more can be charged to BMW for this advertising. Thus in this case copying, which might increase (perhaps greatly) the number of viewers, could provide a lucrative source of revenue for the owners of the copyright in the film. Of course, if this had been a superior revenue generation device we would have expected to see the market voluntarily moving in that direction before the advent of file sharing since it was perfectly possible to give away free music or movies before the advent of Napster. Again, the fact that we did not see this behaviour is strong evidence that it was not profit maximizing before file sharing altered the nature of the market.

In a different dimension, we have seen a new business model in software (the Open Source Software movement) that has achieved a great deal of attention far in excess of its current market share. There are suggestions (Fisher, 2004) that this might be a model that can apply to other copyright markets. Yet the staying power of open source is as yet unknown. Neither is the underlying business model fully understood. Although there is a mythology surrounding open source claiming that it is a completely different production process (many more individuals involved in coding and bug fixes), recent research into the creation of open source software suggests that it closely resembles production in more traditional software markets and if anything, the creation of open source software is actually more concentrated (Mockus et al., 2002, 2003; Asundi et al., 2006). Even the claim that creators of open source do it for reasons contrary to normal markets is questionable since many of the individuals providing the lion's share of the work are apparently paid to do so by large corporations. The benefits to firms that provide support for the creation of open source comes from the possibility of selling complementary goods, such as hardware, support contracts, or advertising.[24]

Finally, a very interesting case of informational bundling occurs when new artists attempt to advertise themselves via widespread circulation of their creations. The idea is very similar to the reason why record companies often pay radio stations to play new records (this is known as 'payola'; see Liebowitz, 2004, and Coase, 1979) – the more people hear these records, the more likely it is that the records will become popular, and thus the more lucrative becomes the market for them once they are released to the general public. In the case of unknown artists, the more widely they can get their initial creations heard, the more likely it is that they will have a financially rewarding future.

The unknown recording artist example is a case of inter-temporal advertising – facing an unknown opportunity cost in the present (the cost of allowing one's creations to be freely copied) in order to allow for a better future market. However, exactly the same thing occurs for different types of copyrightable products. For example, there are often free versions of software or books with reduced functionality available over the Internet with the more complete versions for sale elsewhere. This strategy of offering different versions of a single item of copyrightable property, with quality differences between versions, is often known simply as 'versioning'. The freely available low-quality versions are supposed to act as advertising for the more expensive high-quality version.[25]

It needs to be kept in mind, however, that although free samples may be beneficial for new market entrants, it is never a profit-maximizing policy for entire markets unless there is some complementary good that is sold at a positive price, which covers the losses on the free good. Even if file sharing helps establish a new musical group, say, it is likely that the sales generated by that new group come at the expense of some other established or up-and-coming group, and that it would be incorrect to generalize this benefit that accrues to a single entity to the entire industry.

These new models are worthy of serious examination. Nevertheless, although the above stratagems provide theoretical possibilities of revenue generation in lieu of traditional copyright, unless we are willing to suppose that the market has failed to find the best model, even over many decades, a supposition we are not willing to make, we must assume that these are inferior to the prior mechanisms chosen by the market that have lasted for generations.

It is possible that the unprecedented degree of copying caused by file sharing has tilted the market so that one of these models will now be superior to the more traditional models. But we need to remember that it is only superior under the new, inferior situation faced by copyright owners. The new result would still be inferior to the old, from the perspective of copyright owners. If, however, some change in the market other than the weakening of property rights led to a repositioning of strategies, then the new models would likely be considered superior.

5.2 *Mechanisms that Reduce Copying*

5.2.1 *Strategic, or Limit, Pricing*

Limit pricing is traditionally a strategy for a dominant firm to employ so as to reduce incentives for competitors to enter. It generally requires that price be set at a level such that after the entrance of a competitor, assuming there is some minimum efficient scale required to enter, the price would fall to an unprofitable level. Both the entrant and incumbent would suffer these losses, but since the entrant knows this in advance, entry becomes far less attractive.

One might try to apply such reasoning in copyright markets, where the 'entrant' is the copier. One problem is that limit pricing is not likely to be a successful strategy when the entrant has lower costs. If the incumbent tries such pricing the incumbent will incur greater losses than the entrant.

In a similar vein, organized copyright infringement usually prices its product at a level that provides profits while also selling at a considerably lower price than authorized copies, and although firm evidence on these facts is difficult to come by, the surveys by Maffioletti and Ramello (2004) point to considerably lower consumer valuations for copies. Thus, it is often argued (see, for example, the model in Watt, 2000) that there is a great deal of scope for legitimate producers to reduce their prices, thereby squeezing out piracy by price competition,[26] rather than turning to a legal devise like copyright law to maintain high prices.

It is not clear that such models provide a rational defence for copyright owners against the onslaught of copying. Some portion of the literature seems to feel that limit pricing is in fact a viable tactic, which implicitly assumes that the advantages to the copier are small. It is not at all uncommon in the literature to find models such that any harm to creators caused by copying is merely the reduction in the producer's surplus and this only occurs when the price lies above the marginal cost of production, at least for the inframarginal units (see, for example, Belleflamme, 2002).

But the cost advantages to a producer of counterfeits are much greater than normally acknowledged. There are at least four important costs that are neglected in such models that are ignored at our peril. The first is the direct cost associated with the payment to the author by the book publisher or record company, which is the one cost that is most likely to be acknowledged. Second are the costs associated with the losses incurred by the majority of books, records, and movies, which must be quite large since there are many more unsuccessful than successful works. Third, there are the costs associated in wading through the large number of possible musical groups that are not given recording contracts and manuscripts that are not purchased. Fourth, there are the costs of advertising and promoting the works, costs that the copier is perfectly capable of free-riding upon.

To the extent that any focus is given to cost disadvantages held by legitimate firms, only the payments to the creator of the single product are generally noted as a differential cost that must be covered. Because these models do not include the high costs of finding and funding the numerous failures nor for promotion costs, any policies based on such models would lead to less variety and choice than we currently have. Record studios would be forced to take fewer chances and would only give record contracts to artists with a very high likelihood of success. Bruce Springsteen, as one example, would not likely have been allowed to record *Born to Run*, his make-or-break breakout third album, coming as it did after the poor performance of his first two albums.

Economists who fail to count these other expenses short-change their analysis and are likely to derive unrealistic conclusions. Exactly how low legitimate products can be priced while still allowing for the required monetary incentive for creation, and for finding new creations, is a very difficult question that has yet to be properly addressed. Nor is it likely that we are capable of addressing it. Normally, we rely on competition, or competition law, to ensure that prices are kept at a sufficiently low level, not on government fiat to decree the correct price.

An instructive variant of these models of limit price setting is given by Varian (2005).[27] There, a monopolist must decide on the price to charge for his good, where consumers have two options – to purchase a unit of the good from the monopolist, or to join together in a 'sharing syndicate' and purchase a communal unit that is then shared among them. Clearly, the sharing syndicate is a close analogy to a situation in which copying occurs; for example, it can be thought of as being analogous to a group of file sharers of music MP3 files. The sharing, however, is a form of indirect appropriability. It is not difficult to see that the optimal size of each sharing syndicate is determined by the price that the copyright owner charges (it is assumed that no price discrimination is possible, so individuals are charged the same price as a syndicate). It is also not difficult to show that the copyright owner will always have the option to price the product such that the optimal sharing syndicate size is exactly 1, that is, no sharing at all happens. However, such a possibility may not be optimal for the seller (or for society) – rather, it may be worthwhile for the seller to set a price such that some, but a limited amount, of sharing occurs in the final equilibrium and to spend fewer resources finding new creative talent. This really says little more than if the copyright owner were to sell at a price that did not cover the cost of paying, finding, and promoting creators, i.e. the competitive price, there would be no incentive for any competitors to enter the industry. The bottom line of the sharing models of the type expounded by Varian is that it is costly to reduce sharing, and this cost needs to be taken into account when setting the final price at which originals are to be sold.

Whether or not the trade-offs that exist in the pricing of the different formats for pre-recorded music are really properly understood in the real world is at best unclear. For example, take the case of the pricing of music CDs and music on cassette tapes. Although the former are by far the major format for pre-recorded music, cassette tapes still exist and are still sold with the same content as CDs. However, CDs are sold at much higher prices than are cassettes, although it might be the case that the costs of production of a CD are below those of a cassette. It would appear these days that blank write-once CDs are less expensive than blank cassettes (although that was not always the case), but it is not known whether the master-slave machines to produce CDs (which record at speeds faster than playback) are more or less expensive than master-slave machines to produce cassettes, which also record at faster speeds (which lowers the fidelity of the playback for cassettes but not for CDs). Nor do we know anything about packaging costs. Thus, we do not know whether tapes are sold more cheaply to engage in a form of price discrimination to cover possibly lower costs. It is clear that a full and proper study of the production costs and the price elasticity of demand for pre-recorded music in different formats would be most enlightening as to how these products can be (and have or have not been) optimally priced in a market in which copying exists.

5.2.2 *Digital Rights Management Systems*

The objective of limit pricing strategies is to attempt to reduce the price of originals in order that they can effectively preclude copies from coming to the market, a stratagem that seemed unlikely to be a happy solution for copyright owners. Other strategies exist with the objective of increasing the cost of copies, so that originals may once again compete with them on a more level playing field while still preserving the ability of copyright owners to pay for creative aspects of the industry.

Legal protection under copyright law can be thought of as one such option, since the possibility of litigation against copiers must be considered when the decision to copy or not is taken. Another option that makes copying more expensive is the use of anti-copying devices and mechanisms. For the case of digital media, these anti-copying mechanisms take the form of code and encryption written on the same device as the intellectual property and that prevents copying from taking place, or that requires some form of payment before a copy can be made. This is what is known as a digital rights management system (DRM).[28] For the case of pre-recorded music CDs, the possibility of distribution on non-copyable disks exists, but in many countries this type of DRM vitiates some common consumer behaviours, such as the right of private copy and the defence against infringement known as 'fair use' (Scotchmer, 2005, p. 216). Of course, we also need to re-examine the purpose of fair use, which was often thought to be largely motivated because the costs of these transactions would be greater than the benefit from the transaction, thus making any transacting impossible. DRM holds the promise of substantially decreasing these transaction costs. If it did so, there may no longer be any justification for fair use, or at least some components of fair use.

Not only is DRM controversial due to the possibility that it may interfere with previously allowed behaviours, but there is also fear that it may lead to an inefficient and resource wasting technology race that typically ensues when hackers work at breaking through DRM, and other programmers work to strengthen them (Watt, 2000). Of course, this same concern exists for every form of theft protection, including locks, alarms, doors, security guards and the like. Whether the situation will be worse in the case of copyright is yet to be determined.

On the other hand, copyrights are currently costly to protect using more traditional systems (at least for the case of copyrights in digital products like music) such as legal protection. The deterrent effect of lawsuits seems small, apparently due to the general (and correct) perception of a very tiny probability of actually being caught (Maffioletti and Ramello, 2004).[29] It is perfectly possible that the use of DRM is a more efficient way of reducing copying than is the law; however, we have not yet seen this technology at work and thus a proper economic analysis of this cannot yet be carried out.

The power of the DRM technology is yet to be tested in these markets. Such technology appears to be quite successful in the case of satellite television, fairly successful in the case of DVDs, and unsuccessful in the case of CDs. It is almost certain that current CDs will need to be scrapped before a useful DRM technology can be put to use in the sound recording business since it provides no room for computer codes except those that are easy to defeat and/or likely to cause negative publicity.[30] [31]

5.3 *Mechanisms to Replace Copyright*

The previous two subsections discussed mechanisms under which copyright holders can either eliminate or reduce copying, or reduce the harm from copying. There is, however, a third set of options, somewhat unrelated among themselves except for the fact that they are attempts to solve the problems of copying in other ways.

5.3.1 *Taxes on Copying Devices*

Almost any type of copying requires some sort of physical support (blank CDs and DVDs, MP3 players, computer hard disks, etc.), or at least a physical copying or 'replay' technology (software, CD and DVD burners, photocopiers, MP3 players, Internet connections, etc.). Since copying is entirely dependent upon these physical complements, it has often been suggested that it is fair to place a tax, or levy, on the sale price of these devices, with the objective of generating funds from which to compensate copyright holders for lost royalties from copying. Clearly, then, the more copying that goes on, the more blank supports will be sold, and the greater will be the revenue that is collected via levies. Thus, taxes on blank supports and technologies are one method with which to attempt to overcome the deleterious impacts of copying, although taxes have their own well-researched set of negative consequences.

If copying were a minor problem, taxes such as these could be considered a minor supplement to traditional copyright revenues, and that is how they were considered until recently. Now, however, they are often analyzed as complete replacements for the copyright system and that is why this section is listed under the heading of copyright replacement.

Each of the blank supports and copying technologies can, of course, be used for purely legitimate activities (storing and retrieving documents and graphics created by oneself, storing and retrieving legitimately purchased copyrighted material, etc.). Since the media taxes are paid by all users, independent of the use that is made, this is really nothing more than a means of passing the externality from copying onto users of these technologies who do not engage in copying of copyrighted material.[32]

There are circumstances where media taxes may provide a second-best solution to the problems of copying. Clearly, if rampant or massive copying cannot be controlled through normal market mechanisms then the media tax could indeed be an alternative manner in which royalty payments can be made. In reality, this interpretation of media taxes is very much akin to the use of blanket licensing by copyright collectives – one pays for the right to use a great many copyrights, although one will in all likelihood only ever use a small subset of the entire repertory.[33]

Recently, Oksanen and Valimaki (2005) have argued strongly in favour of media levies as an alternative compensation system, basing their analysis upon the particular case of the online music market in Finland. The extremely rapid advance of digital copying and sharing leads Oksanen and Valimaki to conclude that levies are perhaps the *only* viable solution to copyright compensation in the future.

Netanel (2003) takes a somewhat different view of the issue, making a clear distinction between copying for commercial purposes (piracy) and copying for non-commercial purposes. He states:

> ... unlike commercial piracy ... the noncommercial sharing and reworking of cultural expression in P2P networks is a phenomenon to be celebrated, not repressed. It is fundamentally speech, not theft. The key is to find a means to compensate authors and copyright holders efficiently, without impeding P2P file sharers' expressive activity. (Netanel, 2003, p. 83)

The 'key' that is proposed by Netanel is that non-commercial sharing should be countered by a levy charged upon Internet connections (a 'Noncommercial Use Levy'), which would be used to compensate copyright holders for copying of a strictly non-commercial nature. The underlying concept is to propose a system that, while denying copyright holders proprietary control over non-commercial file sharing and remixing, would entitle them to compensation for such uses.

This replacement of the market with a system based on taxes reaches its fullest expression in the work of Fisher (2004) who provides the flesh to hang on skeletons such as that put forward by Netanel. Fisher would prefer that revenues come from income taxes but would accept taxes on complementary goods. He also proposes a form for the regulatory devices needed to determine the distribution of the proceeds of such taxes (surveys of usage, such as that created by Neilsen for television in the United States, although it would require far more detail and a much larger sample since it would cover numerous copyright industries and many thousands of products). Unfortunately he is largely silent on the very thorny issue of determining the appropriate amount of revenues to be generated by such taxes, which is the strongest of several criticisms made in Liebowitz (2005c).

On balance, and considering the particular case of the music market, it would seem that the use of media taxes and levies is a possible way to provide compensation for creators if more traditional market mechanisms fail to do the job. However, determining the correct amount of any such tax is a completely separate issue that does not provide for an easy solution. It is clear that this solution is one that should only be seriously examined after other avenues have proven fruitless. Additional work in this area would, of course, be most welcome.

5.3.2 *Outright Sale (Buy-Outs) Instead of Royalty Payments*

The concept of rewarding creative efforts by granting the creator a limited monopoly (copyright) that would then provide the creator with the ability to turn downstream users into customers is really quite a novel idea. During the renaissance, as is very well known, a large number of extremely creative individuals (artists, playwrights, etc.) were employed under a system of patronage. Such a system is akin to the outright sale of the rights to a creation even before the creative efforts are exerted, something like a commission. It appears that the motivation for the patron was one of status more than financial gain. It is certainly possible to go back to such a system but since there has been no legal restriction on its use we can take its decline in popularity to indicate that the copyright system that evolved to take its place had superior characteristics. As copyright declines in value, however, it is possible that billionaires will commission numerous musical works to replace the decline brought about by file sharing although the authors of this paper find this an unlikely prospect.

A form of buy-out is in force today. Recording contracts specify that the creators of sound recordings make some minimum number of recordings (often seven) before the contract loses force. And these contracts also provide advances against royalties. So the record companies play the same role as patrons used to, except that they try to make a profit from these activities. In the patron system the amount of copying that goes on afterwards would not have been of concern if the patron was not in the business of selling copies.

Up-front sale of rights, or buy-outs are considered a valid option throughout the patent literature (see Kremer, 1998, for a well-known reference),[34] but it is unclear that they would be a solution to the problem of copying. Kremer's solution was to hold auctions for intellectual products where the bidders would occasionally receive the item but where the government would get the item most of the time. The government would then put the product in the public domain, removing any under-consumption inefficiency. Private individuals would randomly receive the product so as to induce serious bidding; otherwise the amounts of the auction paid by the government will not resemble market values, which is an important consideration if the system is to promote efficiency.

Two problems arise with this type of system as applied to copyright, with the second being critical. Bidders have little incentive to put out the effort to correctly value the product when they have little chance of winning. More importantly, for the case of file sharing, bidders will have very low value for the product if file sharing is rampant and so such auctions would not be able to reveal the value of highly copied products such as sound recordings.

5.3.3 *Voluntary Contributions and Auctions (Bidding for Content)*

A small, largely unpublished, literature exists that suggests that copyright holders can achieve compensation by appealing to voluntary contributions from consumers (see, for example, Nadel, 2002, and Woodhead, 2000). This basically amounts to reliance upon 'tipping' as a source of revenue. Of course, tipping has long been known in the economic theory literature to be a seemingly irrational act, unless inter-temporal concerns are invoked – no one (with positive marginal utility for money) should ever give a voluntary tip unless by doing so it is thought that future service will be enhanced. Of course, the expectation is that the tipee knows who has been a high tipper and rewards that individual with superior service.

The case of creation of copyrightable material is a poor example where tipping would seem likely to work. The same performance occurs for all consumers, so no individual tipper gets the individual benefit of a better performance from a tip. Instead, everyone has complete anonymity in the process, providing a very strong incentive to free-ride. There is no doubt that some fans will be willing to pay and that some funds will be generated. But there is every reason to believe that this system will lead to far lower revenues than traditional copyright. After all, any copyright creator could have tried this in the past, and few have. The best-known instance where it was tried was Stephen King writing a novel chapter by chapter. If enough contributions came in he would continue the novel, so he provided stronger motivations than a completed work would have. Nevertheless, he gave up on the project when the revenues were not forthcoming at the rate he had hoped.

5.3.4 *Public Funding: Rewards and Prizes*

Finally, we come to the option of providing recompense to creators of copyrightable intellectual property via rewards and prizes, rather than by the grant of copyright. This type of system has long been touted as a reasonable alternative incentive mechanism for creative endeavours, at least for the case of innovation and patentable creations (see Wright, 1983, and Shavell and Van Ypersele, 2001, for classic references). There are many examples of great creations in history that were the direct result of a competition with a monetary prize for the winner (see Scotchmer, 2005, chapter 2), and so it is reasonable to at least consider if rewarding creation via prizes is a valid alternative to copyright in modern society.

In reality, it is difficult to think of a situation in which copyrightable creativity can be effectively rewarded by a publicly organized prize system, since copyrightable creation is not normally the result of thinking towards the solution of particular problems, such as could be posed as the challenge in a contest. However, there is certainly no reason why artists (and authors) who prove themselves to be successful cannot, as some sort of prize for this contribution to the stock of cultural goods, receive public funding in exchange for allowing their future creations to fall directly into the public domain. This seems very similar to the tax system mentioned above since taxes are government funding. If there were to be a difference it might be that artists would be put on the public payroll and asked to create their wares.

Probably the closest example to something like this would be the arts departments in public universities. Some, including us, recoil in horror at the thought of our creative industries resembling the output of those institutions.

6. Conclusions

Aside from a general introduction to the topic of the economic theory of copyright, in this paper we have considered the published literature concerning two very important, and rather interrelated, aspects of the market for music. First, we were interested in studying exactly how copying has affected the final demand for music on legitimate markets. Second, we have considered the possible alternatives to the grant of copyright that could be used by the music industry to compensate artists and creators.

These two questions are interrelated because of copyright infringement, or 'piracy', in the market for pre-recorded music. Currently, the financial interests of creators are supposed to be protected by copyright, which deems copying without paying a royalty to be illegal. However, illegal or not, copying certainly occurs, and so we are faced with a situation in which copyright law is proving inadequate for its stated purpose, namely that of providing compensation and incentives for creation. Thus our interest in the effects of infringement upon legitimate sales stems from the need to know the true extent to which copyright law, as a mechanism for ensuring compensation and the correct incentives for creation, is failing.

We can find plenty of evidence that economic harm is indeed being done, in spite of the fact that new artists are emerging and existing artists continue to produce new recordings. This is not surprising as long as file sharing does not completely destroy the industry. Therefore, it would seem that some incentive to create still exists, in spite of the failure of copyright law to fully protect against copying.

The task of comparing the current situation with one in which copying did not exist is, however, a counter-factual argument that is very difficult to perform. Thus we can only state that although creative efforts in the realm of music are going ahead in spite of the existence of copying, the magnitudes of the estimated losses due to copying are likely to cause serious dislocations in the market.

How that affects social welfare depends on the value of these copies to the individuals that consume them and the value of the creative works lost to the decline in industry revenues, something that seems virtually impossible to know.

Our second question, that of the possible alternatives to copyright law, basically takes as granted that an alternative is in order, and looks at what the economics literature has had to offer. We have noted that all of the possible alternatives are likely second-best solutions to the problem of efficient creation and distribution of information products, where the market failure based on copying renders the first-best solution unworkable.

There are many theoretical options, but not all of them necessarily have any practical value. The possibilities that seem most likely to provide some ameliorative impact are DRM and taxes on blank supports. If there are better business models (using bundling) the industry should be able to discover these on its own and perhaps some economists can make some money helping to show them the way. Theories based on network effects, on tipping, or auctions seem most unlikely to provide useful guidance. Nevertheless, some of these alternatives are debateable to say the least, in the sense that they may or may not be politically and legally feasible, mainly due to the adverse effects that they imply for the rights of others (above all, music consumers and non-copiers).

Notes

1. Of course the proper division of the total set of allocatable rights between the creator and society in general (via fair use) has also been hotly debated in the literature. See, for example, Gordon (1982) and Posner (1992).
2. The difficulty in enforcement is only one of many issues concerning copyright that could be addressed although it is currently undergoing the most dramatic alterations. Ever since Arrow's seminal contribution (Arrow, 1962), the 'paradox of disclosure' has been widely cited – the fact that in order to properly assess the willingness to pay for intellectual property involves disclosure of the very property that is intended to be later purchased, thereby reducing the posterior market value. Gans *et al.* (2002) cite several other interesting problems in the effective marketing of intellectual products.
3. Independently to the 'utilitarian' argument for copyright, the rationale for copyright based on moral and natural rights has also been examined – see, for example, Becker (1993) and Gordon (1993). Still others have argued for copyright based on such aspects as the importance of free expression – see Fisher (1988) and Netanel (1996).
4. Informative treatments of the basic economics of copyright abound. For example, the interested reader could consult Landes and Posner (1989), Besen and Raskind (1991), Watt (2000, chapter 1), Cooter and Ulen (2003), and Landes and Posner (2003). Gordon and Bone (2000) is also a most invaluable text, and includes an extensive list of references.
5. The costs of creation are limited to the costs of the creator which include the opportunity cost as a central component. See Shapiro and Varian (1999, p. 3) for a short explanation of the cost structure of information products.
6. Also, it is often argued that by allowing a price above marginal cost, copyright confers monopoly power on the creator, and so there is an associated dead-weight loss to society as access to the protected creation is restricted. But free entry into these markets will prevent most creators from earning monopoly rents.
7. The seminal papers on the economics of copying are Liebowitz (1981), Liebowitz (1985) and Johnson (1985). See also the more recent paper by Belleflamme (2002).
8. Dynamic efficiency refers to the cumulative nature of creative efforts – when creators build upon existing creations. The issue of cumulative creation is also a hot topic in the economics of patent, where the basic issues are identical to the case of copyright. See Scotchmer (1991) for the seminal paper on this topic.
9. This is simply because we are faced with a huge asymmetric information problem – we do not know the creator's utility function, or her opportunity costs, and neither do we know the willingness to pay of each individual consumer, or even the aggregate willingness to pay of the entire consumption sector. Hopefully, such empirical issues as these will be the subject of rigorous study in the near future.
10. The few exceptions are those that argue for complete lack of need for copyright in favour of market based solutions (e.g. Boldrin and Levine, 2002). This literature will be reviewed more fully below.

11. Of course, the case for copyright to exist can also be justified on the existence of transactions costs. By allocating entitlement to authors (who are few) rather than users (who are many), copyright is designed to save on transactions costs of allowing exchange to take place, a familiar aspect of many other workable exchange systems (Holderness, 1985). This rationale for copyright is based on the idea that it is much easier for authors to create and then sell a work to potential users than it is for users to get together to convince authors to write a work. This has been discussed by Gordon (1992a), (1992b) and (1992c), among others.

12. In the early literature on copyright, much was said of the non-pecuniary motive for creation (see, for example, Plant, 1934, and Hurt and Schuchman, 1966). Clearly, if creation is not motivated by monetary recompense, then infringement may not crowd out creation at all, and may even clearly stimulate it. The more modern view of the rationale for copyright is firmly based upon the monetary motives behind creation.

13. Even more impressive figures can be found for the case of software copyright infringement (see, for example, the 8th Annual BSA Global Software Piracy Study, published as Business Software Alliance 2003, in which the piracy rate (the percentage of installed software that does not have a valid user license) in the USA is 24%, and in Vietnam it is 95%).

14. Although, admittedly, CD collections can be the result of gifts and discount price purchases.

15. Maffioletti and Ramello also report other findings concerning the perceived probability of being caught copying, and the perceived illegality of copying.

16. In the United States this would be particularly true for surveys conducted after the much publicized and unpopular lawsuits brought against individual file-sharers by the recording industry.

17. For a general discussion concerning when legal mechanisms are or are not superior to other alternatives, see Galini and Scotchmer (2002).

18. One should not mistake a new technology which has the impact of removing property rights with a superior technology that replaces an inferior incumbent. File sharing is similar, in many ways, to a hypothetical 'physical matter transporter', such as the transporter in the 'Star Trek' series. Such a transporter, if it existed, might be used to replace many inferior shipping techniques, such as trucks and railroads. If, however, the transporter were mainly used by individuals to remove products from stores and place them into private homes without payment, this would not be a case of a superior technology replacing an inferior one. Instead this would be a clear market failure based on the inability to protect property rights and, carried to its extreme, might lead to the dissolution of the advanced economy.

19. The level of copyright protection that maximizes social welfare must meet the participation condition of the creator. As we have pointed out above, copyright protection also increases in some instances the costs of creation and this should be accounted for as well.

20. This paper builds on earlier work by Liebowitz (1981).

21. Of course, a network externality may also work in a negative direction – for example, the case of traffic congestion on a highway, where additional users impose an externality cost on all others.

22. See also, for example, King and Lampe (2003), and Farrell (1994) who argues that the existence of network externalities is a valid reason why copyright law should be weakened.

23. Tours might increase CD sales because attendees are more interested in the music after hearing a concert. Alternatively, tours might increase sales due to the publicity surrounding the tour even if most of the additional sales come from individuals not attending the concert. In this latter case it is conceivable that concerts are actually a substitute for CD sales on the part of concert goers. In the former case raising the concert price might work as hoped. In the latter case it will not.

24. For example, Microsoft (among many others) offers free access to e-mail software, with a free individual account to anyone who wants one under hotmail.com. However, users of this service must endure the advertising banners that appear unsolicited as the software is used.

25. And it can be a good strategy too. For example, Lawrence Lessig offers his book 'Free Culture' as a pdf file for free on his website, and yet the hard-print version of the book maintains a privileged place among the best sellers on Amazon.com.

26. This is a possibility whenever copies have a transactions cost – direct costs of copying, inconvenience costs, and the implicit cost of consuming an inferior item.

27. See also the models in Bakos *et al.* (1999), and Varian (2000). Furthermore, Scotchmer (2005, pp. 219–23) offers a short model that captures most of the salient elements of sharing clubs.

28. Scotchmer (2005, chapter 7, section 3) offers a short introduction to DRMS as a protection mechanism for intellectual property.

29. Penalties paid by infringers sued by the RIAA are reportedly in the range of $3000 and it is claimed these penalties largely cover the costs of the prosecutions, although if true we would expect to see prosecutions ramped up to a much larger scale than the current number of 15,000 that have occurred over the last few years.

30. The transition to a new hardware technology is usually motivated by some technical improvement that the user wishes (portability with cassettes, scratch free quality with CDs). In this case it is not clear that there is any new valuable gain so the audio industry might need to try bundling players with a group of CDs (say 6) that makes the price of a player almost zero, while also claiming some audio advantage, of course.

31. The Sony BMG 'Rootkit' fiasco, in November of 2005, whereupon putting a CD in a computer drive caused a virus-like product to be put on the hard-drive, resulting in enormous bad publicity, a botched product recall, and various lawsuits, is a case point.

32. Other problems can emerge also. For example, in Spain the copyright collective SGAE negotiated a media levy with the producers of blank CDs (i.e. not a regulatory measure introduced by law) that was to be charged at point of sale and then passed on to copyright holders via the collective. As soon as one blank support producer reneges on this deal (in order to then sell at a lower price than its competitors), then all blank CD producers will be forced to renege in order to stay in business. Thus this system can be seen to be a type of prisoner's dilemma that implies its eventual inoperability.

33. Of course, the restriction to a blanket license has also not gone without critique. See, for example, Besen and Kirby (1989) for a good account of how copyright collectives function, and also Kernochan (1985), and Tournier and Joubert (1986), for legal discussions on the use of blanket licensing.

34. Also, Llobet *et al.* (2000) show how buy-out clauses can be an integral part of an efficient mechanism for rewarding cumulative creation.

References

Akerlof, G. *et al.* (2002) Amici curiae in support of petitioners. *Eldred* v *Ashcroft*, No. 01-618.

Arrow, K. J. (1962) Economic welfare and the allocation of resources for invention. In K. J. Arrow (ed.), *The Rate and Direction of Inventive Activity* (pp. 609–625). Princeton: Princeton University Press.

Asundi, J., Kazman, R. and Arunachalam, V. S. (2006) Examining change contributions in an OSS project: the case of the Apache Web Server Project. Working Paper, Center for the Analysis of Property Rights and Innovation.

Baker, M. J. and Cunningham, B. M. (2006) Court decisions and equity markets: estimating the value of copyright protection. *Journal of Law and Economics* forthcoming.

Bakos, Y. and Brynjolfsson, E. (1999) Bundling information goods: prices, profits and efficiency. *Management Science* 45: 1613–1630.

Bakos, Y., Brynjolfsson, E. and Lichtman, D. (1999) Shared information goods. *Journal of Law and Economics* 42: 117–155.

Becker, L. (1993) Deserving to own intellectual property. *Chicago-Kent Law Review* 68: 609–629.

Belinfante, A. and Davis, R. (1979) Estimating the demand for record albums. *Review of Business and Economic Research* 14: 47–53.

Belleflamme, P. (2002) Pricing information goods in the presence of copying. In W. Gordon and R. Watt (eds), *The Economics of Copyright: Developments in Research and Analysis* (pp. 26–54). Cheltenham, UK and Northampton, MA: Edward Elgar.

Besen, S. (1987) New technologies and intellectual property: an economic analysis. *RAND* Report No. N-2601-NSF.

Besen, S. and Kirby, S. (1989) Compensating creators of intellectual property: collectives that collect. *RAND* Report No. R-3751-MF.

Besen, S. and Raskind, L. (1991) An introduction to the law and economics of intellectual property. *Journal of Economic Perspectives* 5: 3–27.

Besen, S., Kirby, S. and Salop, S. (1992) An economic analysis of copyright collectives. *Virginia Law Review* 78: 383–411.

Blackburn, D. (2004) Online piracy and recorded music sales. Working Paper, Department of Economics, Harvard University.

Boldrin, M. and Levine, D. (2002) The case against intellectual property. *The American Economic Review* 92(2): 209–212.

Bounie, D., Bourreau, M. and Waelbroeck, P. (2005) Pirates or explorers? Analysis of music consumption in French Graduate Schools. Paper presented to the Annual Congress of the Society for Economic Research on Copyright Issues, Montreal. Available at http://www.serci.org/documents.html.

Breyer, S. (1970) The uneasy case for copyright: a study of copyright in books, photocopies, and computer programs. *Harvard Law Review* 84: 281–351.

Business Software Alliance (2003) *Eighth Annual BSA Global Software Piracy Study, 2003.* Available at http://www.bsa.org/globalstudy/

Cheung, S. (1970) The structure of a contract and the theory of a non-exclusive resource. *Journal of Law and Economics* 13: 49–70.

Coase, R. (1979) Payola in radio and television broadcasting. *Journal of Law and Economics* 22(2): 269–328.

Conner, K. and Rumelt, R. (1991) Software piracy: An analysis of protection strategies. *Management Science* 37: 125–39.

Cooter, R. and Ulen, T. (2003) *Law and Economics.* Reading, MA: Addison Wesley, Longman.

CPB Netherlands Bureau for Economic Policy Analysis (2000) Copyright protection: Not more but different. CPB Working Paper No. 122. The Hague: CPB Netherlands Bureau for Economic Policy Analysis.

David, P. A. (1993) Intellectual property institutions and the panda's thumb: Patents, copyrights, and trade secrets in economic theory and history. In M. B. Wallerstein, M. E. Magee and R. A. Schoen (eds), *Global Dimensions of Intellectual Property Rights in Science and Technology* (pp. 19–62). Washington, DC: National Academy Press.

Demsetz, H. (1970) The private production of public goods. *Journal of Law and Economics* 13: 293–306.

Easterbrook, F. (1991) Intellectual property is still property. *Harvard Journal of Law and Public Policy* 13: 108–109.

Farrell, J. (1994) Arguments for Weaker Intellectual Property Protection in Network Industries. Working Paper No. 94-11, 1-14. Centre for the Study of Law and Society, University of California.

Fine, M. (2000) Soundscan Study on Napster Use and Loss of Sales. Available at http://www.riaa.com.

Fisher, W. W. (1988) Reconstructing the fair use doctrine. *Harvard Law Review* 101: 1659–1795.

Fisher, W. W. (2004) *Promises to Keep: Technology, Law, and the Future of Entertainment*. Palo Alto, CA: Stanford University Press.

Gallini, N. and Scotchmer, S. (2002) Intellectual property: When is it the best incentive system? *Innovation Policy and the Economy* 2: 51–78.

Gans, J., Williams, P. and Briggs, D. (2002) Intellectual Property Rights: A Grant of Monopoly or an Aid to Competition? Intellectual Property Research Institute of Australia Working Paper No. 07/02. Available at http://www.ipria.org.

Gayer, A. and Shy, O. (2005) Copyright enforcement in the digital era. *CESifo Economic Studies* 51(2–3): 477–489.

Ginsburg, J. C., Gordon, W. J., Miller, A. R. and Patry, W. F. (2000) Symposia: The constitutionality of copyright term extension: How long is too long? *Cardozo Arts & Entertainment Law Journal* 18: 651–737.

Gordon, W. (1982) Fair use as market failure: A structural and economic analysis of the Betamax case and its predecessors. *Columbia Law Review* 82: 1600–1657.

Gordon, W. (1992a) Asymmetric market failure and prisoner's dilemma in intellectual property. *University of Dayton Law Review* 17: 853–869.

Gordon, W. (1992b) On owning information. *Virginia Law Review* 78: 149–281.

Gordon, W. (1992c) Of harms and benefits: Torts, restitution and intellectual property. *Journal of Legal Studies* 21: 449–482.

Gordon, W. (1993) A property right in self-expression: Equality and individualism in the natural law of intellectual property. *Yale Law Review* 102: 1533–1609.

Gordon, W. and Bone, R. (2000) Copyright. In B. Bouckaert and G. Degeest (eds), *Encyclopaedia of Law and Economics,* Vol. 2 (pp. 189–215). Aldershot: Edward Elgar.

Holderness, C. G. (1985) A legal foundation for exchange. *Journal of Legal Studies* 14: 321–344.

Hollander, A. (1984) Market structure and performance in intellectual property: The case of copyright collectives. *International Journal of Industrial Organization* 2: 199–216.

Hong, S. H. (2004) The effect of digital technology on the sales of copyrighted goods: Evidence from Napster. Working Paper, Stanford University.

Hui, K. and Png, I. (2003) Piracy and the legitimate demand for recorded music. *Contributions to Economic Analysis and Policy* 2(1): article 11. Available at http://www.bepress.com/bejeap/contributions/vol2/iss1/art11.

Hurt, R. and Schuchman, R. (1966) The economic rationale of copyright. *American Economic Review* 56: 421–432.

IFPI (2003) *IFPI Music Piracy Report 2003*. Available at http://www.ifpi.org/site-content/library/piracy2003.pdf.

Johnson, J. and Waldman, M. (2005) The limits of indirect appropriability in markets for copyable goods. *Review of Economic Research on Copyright Issues* 2(1): 19–37.

Johnson, W. (1985) The economics of copying. *Journal of Political Economy* 93: 158–174.

Kernochan, J. (1985) Music performing rights organizations in the United States of America: Special characteristics, restraints and public attitudes. *Copyright* 11: 389–410.

King, S. P. and Lampe, R. (2003) Network externalities, price discrimination and profitable piracy. *Information Economics and Policy* 15(3): 271–290.

Kitch, E. W. (2000) Elementary and persistent errors in the economic analysis of intellectual property. *Vanderbilt Law Review* 53: 1727–1741.

Koboldt, C. (1995) Intellectual property and optimal copyright protection. *Journal of Cultural Economics* 19: 131–155.

Kremer, M. (1998) Patent buyouts: A mechanism for encouraging innovation. *Quarterly Journal of Economics* 113: 1137–67.

Ku, R. S. R. (2002) The creative destruction of copyright: Napster and the new economics of digital technology. *University of Chicago Law Review* 69: 263–324.

Landes, W. and Posner, R. (1989) An economic analysis of copyright law. *Journal of Legal Studies* 18: 325–363.

Landes, W. and Posner, R. (2002) Indefinitely renewable copyright. University of Chicago, John M. Olin Law and Economics Working Paper No. 154.

Landes, W. and Posner, R. (2003) *The Economic Structure of Intellectual Property Law*. Cambridge, MA: Harvard University Press.

Liebowitz, S. J. (1981) The impact of reprography on the copyright system. Copyright Revision Studies, Bureau of Corporate Affairs, Ottawa.

Liebowitz, S. J. (1985) Copying and indirect appropriability: Photocopying of journals. *Journal of Political Economy* 93: 945–957.

Liebowitz, S. J. (2002) Policing pirates in the networked age. Cato Policy Analysis No. 438. Available at http://www.cato.org/pubs/pas/pa438.pdf.

Liebowitz, S. J. (2003) Back to the future: Can owners appropriate revenues in the face of new copying technologies? In W. Gordon and R. Watt (eds), *The Economics of Copyright: Developments in Research and Analysis* (pp. 1–25). Northampton, MA and Cheltenham, UK: Edward Elgar.

Liebowitz, S. J. (2004) The elusive symbiosis: The impact of radio on the record industry. *Review of Economic Research on Copyright Issues* 1(1): 93–118.

Liebowitz, S. J. (2005a) Pitfalls in measuring the impact of file-sharing on the sound recording market. *CESifo Economic Studies* 51(2–3): 435–473.

Liebowitz, S. J. (2005b) Economists' topsy-turvy view of piracy. *Review of Economic Research on Copyright Issues* 2(1): 5–17.

Liebowitz, S. J. (2005c) MP3s and copyright collectives: A cure worse than the disease? In W. Gordon, L. Takeyama and R. Towse (eds), *Developments in the Economics of Copyright: Research and Analysis* (pp. 37–59). Cheltenham, UK and Northampton, MA: Edward Elgar.

Liebowitz, S. J. (2006a) File-sharing: Creative destruction or plain destruction. *Journal of Law and Economics* 49(1): 1–28.

Liebowitz, S. J. (2006b) Testing File-Sharing's Impact by Examining Record Sales in Cities. Working Paper, University of Texas at Dallas.

Liebowitz, S. J. and Margolis, S. E. (2005) 17 Famous economists weigh in on copyright: The role of theory, empirics and network effects. *Harvard Journal of Law and Technology* 18(2): 435–457.

Llobet, G., Hopenhayn, H. and Mitchell, M. (2000) Rewarding Sequential Innovators: Prizes, Patents and Buyouts. Working Paper 0012, CEMFI.

Maffioletti, A. and Ramello, G. B. (2004) Should we put them in jail? Copyright infringement, penalties and consumer behaviour: Insights from experimental data. *Review of Economic Research on Copyright Issues* 1(2): 75–89.

Mannering, F. (1994) Assessing the impacts of audio home copying restrictions. *Quarterly Journal of Business and Economics* 33: 30–41.

McCain, R. A. (1994) The Case for Minimal Protection of Intellectual Property Rights: Game Theoretic and Cost of Transaction Perspectives. Paper presented at the International Conference on the Economics of Intellectual Property Rights. Venice, October.

Michel, N. (2005) The Impact of Digital File Sharing on the Music Industry: A Theoretical and Empirical Analysis. Paper presented to the Annual Congress of the Society for Economic Research on Copyright Issues, Montreal. Available at http://www.serci.org/documents.html.

Mockus, A., Fielding, R. T., and Herbsleb, J. (2002) Two case studies of open source software development: Apache and Mozilla. *ACM Transactions on Software Engineering and Methodology* 11(3): 309–346.

Mockus, A., Weiss, D. M., and Zhang, P. (2003) Understanding and Predicting Effort in Software Projects. Proceedings of the 25th International Conference on Software Engineering (ICSE '03). Portland, USA.

Nadel, M. S. (2002) Questioning the Economic Justification for (and thus Constitutionality of) Copyright Law's Prohibition Against Unauthorized Copying: §106. Paper presented at the Annual Congress of the Society for Economic Research on Copyright Issues. Northampton, MA: Available at http://www.serci.org/documents.html.

Netanel, N. W. (1996) Copyright and a democratic civil society. *Yale Law Journal* 106: 283–387.

Netanel, N. W. (2003) Impose a noncommercial use levy to allow free peer-to-peer file sharing. *Harvard Journal of Law & Technology* 17: 1–84.

Novos, I. and Waldman, M. (1984) The effects of increased copyright protection: An analytic approach. *Journal of Political Economy* 92(2): 236–246.

Oberholzer, F. and Strumpf, K. (2004) The Effect of File Sharing on Record Sales: An Empirical Analysis. Working paper.

Oksanen, V. and Valimaki, M. (2005) Copyright levies as an alternative compensation method for recording artists and technological development. *Review of Economic Research on Copyright Issues* 2(2): 25–39.

Peitz, M. and Waelbroeck, P. (2004) The effect of internet piracy on music sales: Cross-section evidence. *Review of Economic Research on Copyright Issues* 1(2): 71–79.

Pethig, R. (1988) Copyrights and copying costs: A new price theoretic approach. *Journal of Institutional and Theoretical Economics* 144: 462–495.

Plant, A. (1934) The economic aspects of copyright in books. *Economica* 1: 167–195.

Posner, R. (1992) When is parody fair use? *Journal of Legal Studies* 21: 67–78.

Posner, R. (2005) Intellectual property: The law and economics approach. *Journal of Economic Perspectives* 19(2): 57–73.

Rappaport, E. (1998) Copyright Term Extension: Estimating the Economic Values. Congressional Research Service, CRS Report for Congress. Available at http://countingcalifornia.cdlib.org/crs/pdf/98-144.pdf.

Rob, R. and Waldfogel, J. (2006) Piracy on the high C's: Music downloading, sales displacement and social welfare in a survey of college students. *Journal of Law and Economics* 49(1): 29–62.

Scotchmer, S. (1991) Standing on the shoulders of giants: cumulative research and patent law. *Journal of Economic Perspectives* 5(1): 29–41.

Scotchmer, S. (2005) *Innovation and Incentives*. Cambridge, MA: MIT Press.

Shapiro, C. and Varian, H. (1999) *Information Rules: A Strategic Guide to the Network Economy*. Boston: Harvard Business School Press.

Shavell, S. and van Ypersele, T. (2001) Rewards versus intellectual property rights. *Journal of Law and Economics* 44(2): 525–548.

Siebrasse, N. and McLaughlin, J. D. (2001) Contested Markets and the Optimal Breadth of Copyright Protection: The Example of Surveyors' Plans of Survey. Available at http://www.spatial.maine.edu/tempe/siebrasse.html.

Smith, D. A. (1986) Collective administration of copyright: An economic analysis. *Research in Law and Economics* 8: 137–151.

Takeyama, L. (1994) The welfare implications of unauthorized reproduction of intellectual property in the presence of demand network externalities. *Journal of Industrial Economics* 17: 155–166.

Thorpe, J. and Rimmer, S. (1995) An economic approach to copyright reform. *Australian Intellectual Property Law Bulletin* 8(10): 125–128.

Tournier, J. and Joubert, C. (1986) Collective administration and competition law. *Copyright* 3: 96–103.

Turnbull, S. (1998) Should ownership last forever? *Journal of Socio-Economics* 27(3): 341–363.

Varian, H. R. (2000) Buying, sharing and renting information goods. *Journal of Industrial Economics* 48(4): 473–488.

Varian, H. R. (2005) Copying and copyright. *Journal of Economic Perspectives* 19(2): 121–138.

Warner Communications, Inc. (1982) Estimate of loss due to home taping: Tapers' reports of replacement. Internal Document.

Watt, R. (2000) *Copyright and Economic Theory: Friends or Foes?* Cheltenham, UK and Northampton, MA: Edward Elgar.

Watt, R. (2004) The past and the future of the economics of copyright. *Review of Economic Research on Copyright Issues* 1(1): 151–171.

Widdows, R. and McHugh, R. (1984) Taxing purchases of home tape recorders and supplies to compensate for copyright infringements: An econometric analysis of the role of economic and demographic factors. *Journal of Consumer Affairs* 18: 317–325.

Woodhead, R. (2000) Tipping – A Method for Optimizing Compensation for Intellectual Property. Available at http://tipping.selfpromotion.com.

Wright, B. D. (1983) The economics of invention incentives: Patents, prizes and research contracts. *American Economic Review* 73: 691–707.

Yoo, C. (2004) Copyright and product differentiation. *New York University Law Review* 79: 212–280.

Yoon, K. (2002) The optimal level of copyright protection. *Information Economics and Policy* 14: 327–348.

Zentner, A. (2005) File sharing and international sales of copyrighted music: An empirical analysis with a panel of countries. *Topics in Economic Analysis & Policy* 5(1): Article 21. Available at http://www.bepress.com/bejeap/topics/vol5/iss1/art21.

Zentner, A. (2006) Measuring the effect of music downloads on music purchases. *Journal of Law and Economics* 49(1): 63–90.

4

WHAT'S IN A SIGN? TRADEMARK LAW AND ECONOMIC THEORY

Giovanni B. Ramello

1. Introduction

A sign is anything that stands for something else.[1] Words, for example, are signs used to represent objects, experiences, states of mind and much more.

Human communities are loaded with signs, as are interactions between individuals. Signs are necessary instruments for social existence that perform a variety of functions. A sign is a container whose significance can be extended in different directions: it can have a literal meaning, that is to say a direct and straightforward interpretation, as well as a series of more complex and indirect complementary meanings which contribute in different ways to the communication process, broadening its scope. Religion provides an excellent example of this: the drawing of a fish, which has of course the direct and universal meaning of denoting an inhabitant of the sea, to followers of the Paleochristian religion also represents, by a complex association of ideas, a reference to God.[2] A similar mechanism of indirect association occurs for the star (of David), which in the Hebraic religion identifies the religion itself.

Signs emerge from any process of interaction between individuals, including the specific case of economic interactions. In particular, we note how at a certain point in human history, signs began to be used in markets specifically to answer the needs of trade. This ushered in the era of the trademark, which from its gradual beginnings rapidly gained momentum with the industrial era, and is today crucial to the existence of a market economy as we know it.

A trademark is a sign used within economic activities by a producer or vendor to identify a particular product or service. In other words, it is a 'distinctive sign' that enables offerings of goods or services to be – more or less consistently – differentiated, and consequently enables consumers to distinguish between different goods and recognize their provenance. These attributes make trademark an extremely powerful economic device.

However, although the law and marketing literature devoted to the role of trademark law and the use of branding[3] is fairly homogeneous and well consolidated, the application of economic analysis to this same topic has instead been fragmentary, with different approaches leading to different results. There are in fact at least three distinct and poorly communicating lines of study that have examined the role of trademark law from different economic perspectives. The first is the so-called law and economics perspective, under which trademark is viewed as a tool for pursuing efficiency. The second approach looks at the effects of trademark on market structure, focusing specifically on practices aimed at maximizing the profits of the owners of the rights, that question, at least in part, the efficiency argument. Finally, the third approach – as yet only roughly sketched out – attempts to examine trademark as an entity in its own right that can be treated as both an asset and a commodity.

The present contribution will undertake to summarize the existing literature, and suggest some directions for further research.

The paper is organized as follows: Section 2 provides a definition of trademark, briefly presenting its origins and characteristics. Section 3 summarizes the economic theory connected with the Chicago Law and Economics tradition, which interprets trademark law as an economic device aimed at producing efficiency. Section 4 extends the analysis by introducing the literature, which describes the further dynamic effects of trademark on the market structure, while Section 5 focuses on the progressive process of unbundling marks from production and products. Finally, Section 6 contains the concluding remarks.

2. Definition and Origins of Trademark

A trademark is a sign – a logo, a name, a word, a symbol or a combination thereof – used by a producer or vendor to distinguish a particular product or service. Examples of this are the words Coca-Cola, Walkman, No.5 (for a perfume) and the Nike 'swoosh' logo.

Because creating distinctiveness is the primary attribute and function of a trademark, producers can in practice superimpose the use of different trademarks in order to better achieve this effect. In the case of Coca-Cola, for example, not only is the name protected by trademark law, but also the distinctive copperplate logo style (purportedly based upon the handwriting of the company's founder Frank M. Robinson), the shape of the bottle, the colour combination and much more. Individual elements such as these can be protected using either a single trademark, or several trademarks together (Blakett, 1998).

Strictly speaking, trademark says nothing, or nearly nothing, about the composition or characteristics of the product: it simply identifies its origin, that is to say the maker of the good. However, purchasers can still glean information about the quality of the good from their own past experience or that of others (Economides, 1988, 1998). Viewed in this way, trademark is therefore a sign that resolves an information asymmetry problem (Riley, 1990), and this role is of course relevant to the economic analysis, and shall be discussed below.

So it is by virtue of its ability to convey information and facilitate purchase decisions that trademark is given legal protection. This is explicitly acknowledged by the modern statutes which confer legal protection to a trademark on condition of its being 'inherently distinctive', that is, able to directly fulfil its stated function.

The signs that possess this attribute can generally be divided into three categories: 'fanciful', 'arbitrary' and 'suggestive'. A trademark is termed 'fanciful' if it consists of novel signs that do not have any pre-existing meaning, as in the case of the words 'Exxon' or 'Xerox'. A trademark is considered 'arbitrary' when it does have a previous direct meaning, but in such a vastly different field that there is no possibility of confusion. Examples of this are the 'Apple' brand of personal computers, 'Quaker' breakfast cereals, and 'Diesel' casual wear. Finally, a trademark is termed 'suggestive' when it refers – even if indirectly – to some property of the product, as in the case of 'Frigidaire' for the refrigerators or 'Business Week' for a weekly news magazine devoted to the world of business.

On the other hand, if a trademark is not 'inherently distinctive' – meaning that the sign does not convey the requisite information and might even, on the contrary, elicit confusion – the owner receives legal protection only if the mark can be shown to have a 'secondary meaning' that directly associates it in the minds of consumers with the origin of the good. Examples of this are surnames used as the names of companies ('Ferrari', 'Armani', 'Levi's', etc.), descriptive terms such as 'All Bran' for whole grain breakfast cereals, and 'Digital' to indicate a maker of personal computers, as well as terms which originally referred to geographical locations such as 'Marlboro', 'San Francisco Chronicle', 'Paris Match', etc. (Economides, 1998; Landes and Posner, 2003).

The information-conveying function of trademark is thus specifically recognized by the law and given explicit protection when it facilitates the purchase decisions of consumers.

We cannot say exactly when trademarks first appeared on markets, though it is widely posited that 'trademarks have existed for almost as long as organized trade' (Blakett, 1998, p. 5). Progenitors of the modern trademark can be found in societies and cultures that are widely disparate, but share the common denominator of having developed sufficiently extensive roadway and communication systems. In fact, the development of long distance trade severs the direct and trust-based relationship that exists between producers and consumers. The latter, in particular, will no longer be able to determine the origin (and hence the expected quality) of the goods, unless a specific sign is introduced for this purpose: namely, trademark. Its function is therefore to encapsulate and represent the origin of products, and so also their quality and authenticity.

Some examples of the above mechanism are the production of pottery in ancient Greece, the Etruscan kingdom and the Roman empire, or the production of pottery and silk in Imperial China. In all these cases, trademarks became important elements for conveying information about the origin of the goods (Rogers, 1910; Schechter, 1925; Wilkins, 1992; Alford, 1995; Blakett, 1998). So from its inception trademark had the specific function of conveying information about particular productions, and was used by individual craftsmen or guilds to denote the origin of goods, and hence their quality of workmanship. However, the protection afforded them was limited, often arising from a 'privilege' – meaning a particular favour granted to an individual or category of producers by the sovereign – rather than from any systematic body of laws applicable to trade in general. As a consequence, legal protection was virtually non-existent and counterfeiting widespread (Alford, 1995; Blakett, 1998).

Notwithstanding this, trademark continued its inexorable advance with the expansion of markets and trade, and reached its maturity with the Industrial Revolution. The advent of mass production, which on the one hand extended the geographical range of production and consumption, on the other hand weakened the producer–consumer relationship owing to the information problem created by increased distance. In the case of extended distribution chains that often crossed national boundaries, a producer's reputation could no longer be maintained through any form of direct familiarity between buyers and sellers, and so trademark became a crucial element for the mediation of reputation-building.

Theoretically speaking a trademark does not need to be registered, because its validity can be established through use. And in fact, this method was common when trade covered more limited geographical areas, facilitating surveillance and reducing the likelihood of conflict with other producers adopting similar signs. Unregistered trademarks are often denoted by the symbol ™. Today, although registration is not compulsory, it does give owners some significant advantages, including a more secure right that does not require demonstrating prior use, greater ease of protection and virtually unlimited duration (except in the cases that will be discussed below). The symbol used to denote a registered trademark is ®.

The current regulatory trend is towards a strengthening of trademark protection, allowing the owner of an exclusive right over a sign to easily transfer use of that sign to a different market, whereas in the past, the same sign could be used by different vendors operating in distinct markets. This form of extended protection applies in particular to those trademarks that are designated 'famous' or 'strong' (Blakett, 1998).

3. Trademark and Efficiency

From a legal perspective, trademark is an exclusive right, that is to say a legal monopoly, which pursues the aim of creating new information. It is an intellectual property right attributed to the owner, at least in the first instance (though various possible extensions exist that will be discussed in Section 5) to provide an incentive to produce information that is not itself the good being exchanged (as is instead the case for patent and copyright), but rather an accessory element to the exchange of other products (Ramello, 2005).

In general, trademark conveys information relating to the quality of products and therefore facilitates and enhances consumer purchase decisions, while at the same time leveraging the reputation of producers to create an incentive for firms to produce goods or services of desirable quality, to the benefit of consumers and markets (Alchian and Allen, 1977; Landes and Posner, 1987; Economides, 1988, 1998; Lott, 1988; Menell, 1999).

This line of reasoning, widely accepted within the economic theory and the legal decisions of the courts (Beebe, 2005), was formalized by the theoretical contribution of Landes and Posner (1987, reviewed in 2003), and is as a whole informed by the so-called law and economics approach, which sees trademark as an incentive to create information, for the benefit of markets.

3.1 *Trademark as Information*

The premise being put forward, which appears to take on 'programmatic' contours (the adjective is Beebe's, 2004), is that 'trademark law, like tort law in general [. . .], can best be explained on the hypothesis that the law is trying to promote economic efficiency' (Landes and Posner, 1987, p. 265).

The underlying economic problem is information asymmetry as the cause of a market failure, described by Akerlof (1970) in the celebrated *Market for Lemons*. In the presence of uncertainty relating to the quality of goods, and in the absence of adequate and credible information, the consumer search cost to consumers in purchase decisions would escalate, while companies would have a greater incentive to mislead consumers as to the quality of the goods produced. The final outcome of such a situation is a reduction in both the average quality of products and the size of the market. Now, because the central problem in these cases is a divergence between social and private returns, an economic device can be introduced to redress their alignment and so maximize the social welfare. In other words, the optimal solution is to create an institution capable of 'counteracting the effects of quality uncertainty. [. . .An] example of an institution which counteracts the effects of quality uncertainty is the brand-name good' (Akerlof, 1970, p. 499).

Trademark therefore reduces both the information costs and, generally speaking, the transaction costs within a market, promoting the attainment of competitive equilibria. In its role as a 'distinctive sign', trademark can indirectly inform consumers as to the quality characteristics of the branded product, even when these are not directly observable.[4] At the same time, this mechanism creates an endogenous incentive for enterprises to avoid opportunistic behaviour and deliver a higher level of quality, in accordance with the precepts of the economic theory on 'reputation' (see Shapiro, 1982).

Therefore, from this perspective, trademark law has the additional effect of extending the liability regime of producers, thereby functioning as an *ex-post* market regulation system. In fact, as Akerlof has already noted (1970, pp. 499–500), '[b]rand names not only indicate quality but also give the consumer a means of retaliation if the quality [of a given producer] does not meet expectations'.

Further empirical studies have shown that the magnitude of trademark losses incurred by firms in the event of product recalls, airline crashes, deceptive advertising, fraud and the like is far greater than the actual value of damages caused. This would therefore appear to be not at a directly proportional compensation mechanism, but rather a penalising effect in which the value of losses incurred by the trademark holder may effectively exceed the damages caused (Jarrell and Peltzman, 1985). From this perspective '[t]he loss of trademark capital has the same effect as a penalty clause in deterring a promisor for breaching [a contract]. Unlike a penalty clause, however, the wealth loss borne by the promisor does not accrue to the promisee; thus it does not provide an incentive to induce breach' (De Alessi and Staaf, 1994, p. 480).[5] In this sense, therefore, trademark has the additional function of producing a 'deterrent' effect in markets. The workings of this deterrence are decentralized, that is, not enforced by any central body set up specifically for the purpose according to the 'command and control' method (in which case we would speak of *ex-ante* regulation), but rather by consumers who intervene more flexibly wherever they consider their rights to have been breached, according to the typical paradigms of liability mechanisms.

Overall, according to a consolidated body of law and economics literature, the combined adoption of *ex-ante* regulation and liability is able to not only promote efficiency but also to produce an optimal level of deterrence, which constitutes a public good (Shavell, 1987).

3.2 *Trademark and Hierarchies*

Looking instead at the supply side, the existence of trademark and branding can have specific effects on the 'hierarchy' adopted by producers, and consequently, facilitate the attainment of production efficiency (Williamson, 1985). We can therefore say that the countenance of today's economic activities has been profoundly affected by the existence of trademarks.

In certain cases, trademark has enabled the creation of vertically integrated firms. In fact, as pointed out above, if an increased distance between maker and buyer creates an information problem that can bring about a market failure (in the absence of trademark), the existence and effectiveness of trademark as a signal can conversely promote the creation of ever more extensive and decentralized production organizations, as compared with the previous system of local workshops and craftsmen. It is in fact difficult to imagine mass production without trademark to provide the 'information umbrella' necessary for protecting consumers. What is more, certain observers consider that the emergence of large scale firms thanks to the trademark leads to other functional advantages, such as achieving minimum efficient scales in the production of goods or information, access to capital markets, the ability to attract and train specialized personnel, and optimizing levels of R&D expenditure (Wilkins, 1992).

In other situations, trademark results in the creation of smaller, specialized production units organized as standalone firms. In this case, the property rights attributed by trademark law can contribute to lowering transaction costs in accordance with the so-called new property rights approach, comprehensively discussed by Hart (1995). Trademark is the glue, which averts opportunistic behaviour in these relationships, and permits the creation of vertical restraints. One example of such a relationship is franchising, which through use of trademark allows an upstream firm (the franchisor) to specialize in the production of certain goods and services, also including reputation-building, while the downstream firm (the franchisee) is able to specialize in distribution and cut some of the risks connected with operating on the market, obviously subject to certain contractual terms designed to maintain the value of the reputation acquired by the franchisor (Treece, 1968; Mathewson and Winter, 1985; Dnes, 1996).

If the production specialization made possible by trademark eventually enables firms to enjoy productive and informational economies of scale (the average information costs are decreasing in the quantity), by the same token it gives rise to economies of scope, as testified by the frequent production diversification of firms that rely heavily on trademark. This is a very common practice in those markets characterized by widespread recourse to so-called brand extension and brand stretching.

Such practices are essentially connected with the increasing returns to scope in the use of a trademark. Once a credible signal has been created, the firm can in fact use it to convey an equivalent amount of information about other, distinct products, and this, in line with the above arguments, can lead to the emergence of multi-product firms (Economides, 1998).

3.3 *Economic Features of Trademark Law*

In general, the efficiency-enhancing objective of trademark law can therefore be used to interpret the regulatory framework and the legal practices associated with it. Because the primary effect of trademark is informative, the distinctiveness of the sign becomes the central element for validating or negating its welfare-enhancing role, while the principles that govern its creation, enforcement and dissolution must be consistent with the above-stated efficiency criteria.

The underlying rationale is that the objective of any communication system is to minimize information costs. In other words, there is a sort of 'economics of signs and language' that regulates the appropriability of the semiotic universe. So that, for example, if a trademark is considered 'fanciful', there are no particular restrictions upon appropriability. The trademark is completely novel, and because it is possible to create *ex-novo* an infinite number of such words or signs, no information problem exists. The semiotic stock available to firms seeking to distinguish their products is potentially unlimited.

The same principle also applies in the case of 'arbitrary' and 'suggestive' trademarks, although as Landes and Posner (1987, 2003) point out, because these are refereed to existing signs, the available stock is more limited. In any case, given the vastness of the resource – *Webster's Third International Dictionary*, for example, lists 450,000 words – the supply elasticity of signs is still sufficiently great to not create any problems.

On the other hand, the efficiency balance is very different when the distinctiveness presumably affected by a trademark clashes with a pre-existing meaning, thereby compromising the informative function of the mark, or even contaminating the 'primary meaning' of the sign and its original informative worth to consumers. In this case, the criterion of 'secondary meaning' is used to verify the effectiveness of the signal and limit appropriability to those cases where the descriptive term has clearly taken on the function of denoting a specific product (e.g. 'All Bran' in the case of cereals). This restriction thus has the effect of averting rent-seeking appropriations that might attempt to transfer the 'primary meaning' of the sign to a specific product.

For the same reason, it is therefore not possible to use generic signs as trademarks (e.g. the term 'car' as the trademark of a car manufacturer). In fact the social cost of such an operation would exceed any informational benefits accrued to consumers by the trademark, because all other producers would incur the increased information costs of finding alternative expressions for identifying their products. Landes and Posner (2003) describe such a situation with the term 'language monopoly', which aptly captures the resultant inefficiency (see also Carter, 1990).

A similar efficiency criterion applies to the well-known situation of a trademark (whether fanciful, arbitrary or suggestive) that has entered the common language, to become a generic term denoting an entire category of products (consider, e.g. the trademarks 'aspirin', 'yo-yo', 'nylon', 'escalator', 'cellophane', 'thermos', 'kerosene', 'typewriter') (Economides, 1998). In this case, the specific information-conveying effect of the sign lapses in favour of its general connotation, and maintaining the trademark is no longer economically efficient because it would increase the overall communication costs between other producers and consumers. Therefore, the trademark is no longer protected.

It is interesting to note that, in this particular case, trademark works exactly in the same way as patent and copyright: it provides an incentive to create new information by attributing a temporary exclusive right over the information produced.[6] However – unlike patent and copyright, where this is the primary mechanism for exercise of the right – in trademark, it is a sort of outside option for those situations where the public information-conveying value of the trademark exceeds its private value (Ramello, 2005).

The above discussion provides an introduction to the debate on the 'duration' of trademark. In fact, although the duration of the right is theoretically infinite, in practice there exist a number of derogations to the property right designed to limit appropriability when the expected social costs exceed the benefits, as in the above example, or where there is no distinguishing effect – for example, in the absence of 'secondary meaning'.[7] A similar argument applies when a firm ceases trading, so that the distinguishing effect of its trademark no longer has any reason to exist.

Finally, it is once again the distinctiveness criterion that governs the enforcement of trademark law in the case of infringement or dilution. The former is the unauthorized use of the trademark or the use of a misleadingly similar trademark on the part of another firm. The general principle is always to avoid creating any confusion, in the minds of consumers, as to the origin of the goods. Penalties for infringement have the function of reinstating the trademark's informative value, disrupted by opportunistic behaviour. In fact, the infringer here acts as a free rider who takes advantage of the information created by the trademark owner to produce goods of a different (generally lower) quality, without incurring the costs of creating the trademark, and so misleading consumers. The final outcome is a lower average quality of goods, whether original or infringing, than there would have been under exclusive use of the mark, and a loss of credibility of the sign. In other words, there is a return to the original situation of a market without marks.[8]

The case of dilution is similar, though somewhat more complicated. In fact this is not a violation as such, but rather a theoretically legitimate behaviour that can nevertheless compromise, *lato sensu,* the distinguishing effect of a given trademark and is therefore forbidden by numerous national laws (Schetcher, 1927; Economides, 1998; Landes and Posner, 2003).[9] It should be noted here that the dilution objection is generally waived in the case of so-called famous or strong trademarks where the informative effect on consumers is very firmly established. What we are looking at here is therefore a sort of indirect violation.

We speak of 'dilution by tarnishment' when the same (or a similar) sign is used by both the owner of the famous trademark and another producer for different goods, but the latter makes a product of inferior value which diminishes the overall value of the sign. An example of this might be a manufacturer of land mines that uses Armani as a trade name. This could, by the workings of an indirect psychological mechanism, alter the reputation of the famous Armani name in consumer's minds, and degrade its connotations of quality (Lunney, 1999).

We speak of 'dilution by blurring' when the use of similar signs in two different markets diminishes the consumer's perception of the distinctiveness of the famous mark. For example, a firm that uses the trade name Martini to manufacture clothing would in a sense be appropriating some of the information conveyed by the Martini trademark – engaging in a form of indirect free riding – and so reducing the distinguishing effect of the mark. Because the assumption in these cases is that famous trademarks are associated with higher quality, which is the source of their stronger distinguishing effect (Landes and Posner, 1987, 2003), the absence of antidilution protection would, from a dynamic perspective, compromise investments in quality.

The concept of trademark dilution also implies the existence of a further effect of trademark that merits due consideration: the distinguishing effect of the sign, especially in the case of famous and strong trademarks, creates a complex psychological and economic dynamic that goes far beyond mere information-conveying value. This is a dynamic that can significantly alter the market structure and the behaviour of firms, as will be discussed in the following section.

4. Distinctiveness and Market Structure

The previous paragraph discussed some of the economic effects of trademark: the creation of information that facilitates exchanges, making it possible to increase the distance between production and consumption, promoting the emergence of certain types of productive organization, and exerting a deterrent effect. All of these arguments, taken together, portray trademark as a source of efficiency for the market. However, implementation of the right may also impact upon the market structure and the relational behaviours of firms and consumers, and such effects must be factored into the final efficiency balance.

In fact, the literature sources quoted thus far have always assumed, implicitly or explicitly, that the market will remain competitive. The information cost of trademark is for the most part treated as a production cost necessarily incurred to avert a failure of the competitive market, but which does not have any other significant effects on the choices of consumers (De Alessi and Staaf, 1994). In their contribution, Landes and Posner (1987, 2003) propose a perfect competition market model in which the (final) gross price to consumers comprises both the net price – that is, the money price paid out for the good – and its information costs.[10]

It follows that, for any given competitive gross price, the firm that can reduce the information costs of consumers through use of trademark will be able to command a higher net price for its goods. The demand curve remains horizontal, indicating that the various combinations of product quality and information provided by trademark are a single homogeneous good in the eyes of consumers. Now this will in effect be true in those situations where trademark has a purely informational role, so that the avoided or reduced search cost represents exclusively an opportunity cost to consumers (Pashigian and Bowen, 1994).

However, this simplification overlooks the twofold nature of trademark, as an indication of quality as well as origin, a fact which alters the behaviour of consumers and their relationship with the goods, as legal practice has also clearly shown (Lunney, 1999). In fact, whereas an indication of origin completes the good by adding information and averts a market failure in the presence of information asymmetry, an indication of quality instead gives firms a novel opportunity to establish a preferential communication channel with consumers, and influence their decisions.

Therefore, trademark can be said to produce two separate kinds of distinctiveness, operating on two different levels, and which it is useful to examine separately. The first is an 'absolute' informational effect that tells individuals about the existence and origin of a good identified by a particular trademark. The second is a 'differential' informational effect that causes consumers to perceive a particular trademark-protected good as different from all the others. This feature corresponds to the aptly termed legal definition of trademark 'strength', and refers to the impact that the sign has on consumers. When lawyers discuss trademark in court, they are principally concerned with its ability to distinguish itself from other trademarks, that is, to the 'differential distinctiveness' (Beebe, 2005).

If the differential distinctiveness effect prevails, that specific sign will take on for consumers a uniqueness that transforms it from a 'sign among signs' to a 'sign above other signs', a situation referred to as 'salience' or 'brand awareness' in marketing (Aaker, 1991; Ehrenberg and Barnard, 1997).[11]

These two levels of 'distinctiveness' are clearly defined on the semiotic plane, and not interchangeable. Failure to grasp their different economic effects may lead to representations and conclusions that do not reflect the reality (Beebe, 2004, 2005).

Consider, in this connection, the example of a consumer who walks into a shop and looks at a shelf of trademarked toothpastes. There are two possible perceptions that can be separately analyzed. One is that the consumer recognizes the existence of different kinds of toothpastes, that is, produced by different firms, but considers them to be interchangeable. In this case, the 'source distinctiveness' effect of trademark prevails and the market is essentially competitive. The second possibility is that the consumer perceives the various toothpastes but considers one particular brand (say, WHITE) to be superior, perhaps as a result of past experience, because a dentist said so, and so forth. If this second effect prevails, the product WHITE will to a certain extent – proportionate to the strength of differentiation – become unique and poorly substitutable by other products. This consequence depends on the degree of 'differential distinctiveness'.

The prevalence of one or the other effect is naturally not predetermined, but rather the net result of the workings of various mechanisms. This is consistent with the antitrust literature on the relationship between intellectual property rights and competition, which asserts that the rights do not necessarily produce market power. In our example, this would correspond to the first case, where 'source distinctiveness' prevails. Intellectual property rights are at source a legal monopoly, which does not necessarily translate into an economic monopoly (Anderson, 1998). Nevertheless, the prospect of an economic monopoly and its attendant supra-profits gives right-holders a strong incentive to adopt any behaviour that can enhance the (real or perceived) uniqueness of the product, making it poorly substitutable and so securing significant market power (Lunney, 1999; Nicita *et al.*, 2005; Ramello, 2005).

We can therefore say that the value of trademark resides in its 'selling power', dependent 'not merely upon the merits of the goods upon which is used, but equally upon its own uniqueness and singularity' which can be created and opportunely enhanced by the owner (Schechter, 1927, p. 831).

Trademark introduces the dimension of 'differentiation' into the market, leading to an endogenous modification of the market structure that is all the more pronounced as differentiation strategies become stronger, with the limiting case of the process being an economic monopoly, where the producer who succeeds in totally differentiating her or his product becomes the monopoly holder (Dixit, 1979; Singh and Vives, 1984).[12]

In other words, when there is a significant differentiation effect, demand for the good becomes downward sloping and trademark functions as a barrier to the entry of competitors.[13] Such a scenario suggests the risk of a different type of market failure which will also have an impact on the overall efficiency of the market. This is a problem that has been debated in the literature since the start of the 20th century (see Lemley, 1999; Lunney, 1999; Menell, 1999), but is still far from being definitively resolved – although some scholars consider it irrelevant since the pro-efficiency view of trademark has prevailed in legal practice (Landes and Posner, 1987, 2003). That said the economic analysis of the right could provide a truly useful contribution from a regulatory perspective, by pointing out the weak points of any particular law.

Although the question of the effects of perceived differentiation (i.e. identical products which are perceived as different and unique due to the effects of trademark) remains undecided, requiring as it does an evaluation of willingness to pay for semiotic content, there are nevertheless some undisputable negative effects arising from the rent-seeking practices that trademark holders may adopt in exercising the right.

One example is the well-known case of 'brand proliferation' in the cornflakes sector (Schmalensee, 1978), where the production of a wide array of differently branded products by a few firms, under conditions that included the existence of increasing returns in production, had the aim of reducing the potential profitability of the market to competitors to restrict their entry.

A similar strategy is being pursued today apparently without hindrance (despite the decades that have passed) by the owners of patented and branded pharmaceuticals, following the expiration of their patents. In fact the introduction of so-called pseudo-generic drugs on the part of these companies appears to be chiefly aimed at prolonging their market power by deterring the entry of generic drugs (Morton, 1999; Kong and Seldon, 2004).

Some observers have also noted a more subtle effect occurring in international trade that because of the asymmetrical distribution of trademarks in favour of richer nations, the effects of brand loyalty on consumers can to a certain extent be leveraged to transfer market power acquired elsewhere, thereby distorting the development of local industry sectors (Baroncelli *et al.*, 2005).

The general hypothesis which emerges is that the use of trademark creates inertia in the consumers of an incumbent firm, resulting in persistence of its market power and altering the competitive scenario so that it no longer resembles any form of the Schumpeterian 'innovation race' that certain contributions explicitly or implicitly assume (Schmalensee, 1982).

Consumer inertia is a crucial side effect of trademark, and can result in the erection of barriers to entry. Firms are well aware of these inertial effects, which are in fact the objective of creating brand loyalty, which seeks to endogenously generate and increase the switching costs of consumers to achieve lock-in (Aaker, 1991). Such practices have clear beneficial effects on the profitability of the firms that succeed in gaining market power; however, their ultimate social welfare effects are not so obvious (Klemperer, 1995).

5. The Unbundling Process: the Sign as Asset and Commodity

The emergence of brand loyalty indicates the establishment of a special relationship between distinctive signs and consumers, which transcends the purview of information to touch upon the emotive and psychological spheres, with some clearly desirable implications for firms. This is a topic area that the economic theory has as yet only touched upon, but with some interesting initial results.

In particular, certain authors have observed a sort of 'unbundling' taking place within different contexts, that is, the trademark gradually detaching itself from the product to take on a physiognomy and character in its own right, able to be exploited on the markets in various ways.

For example, adopting a supply side perspective and looking at the literature which studies firms as bearers of reputation, Tadelis (1999) shows how trademark makes it possible to convert the reputational inertia acquired by firms in the past into a tradable asset that can be exchanged on the market like any other resource. The result is the emergence of a market for intangible assets which have a clear role in production, on a par with that of tangible assets.

A part of the scientific literature has also started to examine the emerging practice of transferring the signs and the related signals created through trademark between different markets, with beneficial effects on the firms that are thus able to reduce their information costs and possibly extend their market power. This opens up the chapter of 'umbrella branding', a practice which takes the form of 'brand extension' when a trademark is transferred for use on another similar product, or of 'brand stretching' if the trademark is transferred to a very different product, and has recently also attracted the interest of industrial organization researchers (Luini and Mangani, 2002).[14]

Thus far, there has been no consistent economic evaluation of these practices, with the results in the literature pointing in different directions. For example, some contributions focus on the possibility of resolving multiple information asymmetries on disconnected markets through the creation of a single sign which is then adopted for different productions (Choi, 1998; Cabral, 2000). Others look instead to identify the optimal strategies for firms who decide to extend their production into different sectors, all this with the non-trivial observation that consumers can sometimes derive added utility from the purchase of a branded product, even when the brand in question originates in a very distant market and would thus be difficult to justify with the traditional quality arguments (Pepall and Richards, 2002). In such cases marketing scholars speak of 'brand equity', meaning the 'incremental utility' to the consumer or the 'value added' to a product by its trademark (Aaker, 1991, 1996; Keller, 1993; Rangaswamy et al., 1993; Yoo and Donthu, 1999). Nevertheless, the evaluation of the resultant welfare effects remains unclear.

Turning instead to address the problem of foreign counterfeiting, Grossman and Shapiro (1988a, 1988b) have found that when this practice is non-deceptive, that is, when consumers are able to distinguish the fakes from the originals, it can have welfare-enhancing outcomes if the added utility to consumers who decide to purchase the counterfeited good does not exceed the externalities imposed upon the trademark owners. Also in this case, the consumption of a sign, even if counterfeited, generates additional utility to consumers. What is more, the described effects can be enhanced in the presence of demand network externalities, as has been shown by authors in complementary fields (Grilo et al., 2001).

Although the overall evaluation of the social welfare effects remains unsatisfactory, the above-mentioned contributions still have the undisputed merit of pointing out an important change in the role of trademark: the sign has become, at least in part, an economic entity in its own right, producing specific utility, characterized by a specific willingness to pay, and which to a certain extent exploits the tangible dimensions of products to take part in exchanges.

The observation appears to be confirmed by international law, with the court decisions testifying to the gradual separation of signs from specific products. Some authors speak ironically of a 'divorce' of trademarks from the goods they are supposed to represent, entrained by the interpretation as a specific property right over a semiotic entity that takes part in exchanges in various ways (Lemley, 1999). This has naturally been accompanied by an increasingly broad interpretation of trademark scope – as evidenced by the concept of dilution discussed in Section 3.3 – and which marks a growing appropriation of the semiotic or semantic universe.

The end result is the transformation of trademark into a commodity (Beebe, 2004). The sign and its meaning, by their nature intangible, are exchanged in conjunction with other goods, not only to remedy information asymmetries but also to satisfy various needs of individuals within the psychological and social spheres. This is accompanied by the emergence of a 'sign value' that sometimes corresponds to the final price paid for the trademark – or rather to the differential with respect to an unbranded product – but can in reality have much wider implications that are not fully reflected by the monetary value. Individuals consume particular goods or signs to display status, to communicate their adherence to (or distance from) a social group, and to perform other complex social functions.[15]

This is the insight which Veblen (1899), in his celebrated book *The Theory of Leisure Class*, described with the term 'vicarious consumption': that is, that consumption of a good can sometimes include production of a message (a meaning) that is not strictly tied to the function of the good. Trademark, as a sign and hence a bearer of meaning, amplifies this dimension and can be shown to operate on two levels: one being the ordinary sphere of tangible economic values, and the other the more intangible spheres of communication, meaning and relationships between individuals. This argument, often put forward as a criticism of the neoclassical tradition by the heterodox approach and by the other social sciences (see Baudrillard, 1972; Babe, 1995), has also stimulated some original contributions in the mainstream economic tradition that seek to better understand consumer behaviour (Bagwell and Bernheim, 1996; Corneo and Jeanne, 1997). The initial results are intriguing; however, much remains to be done, and the challenge to researchers is open.

6. Conclusions

The purpose of this paper has been to summarize the extant theory as it relates to the economics of trademark, and to give some suggestions for further research referring to distinct streams of literature. The proposed line of study inevitably passes through the relationship – as yet not fully understood – between economics and signs.

The appearance of trademark as a sign used in exchanges can be traced to the increased separation between the points of production and sale, and so between the makers and buyers of a good. This process generates a market failure caused by the information asymmetry to consumers, who are no longer able to determine the provenance or quality of the products that they purchase. The result is the classic economics of information problem described by Akerlof (1970), in which the market is impoverished in terms of both transactions and quality. Trademark is the sign introduced to remedy the market failure; it facilitates purchase decisions by indicating the provenance of the goods, so that consumers can attribute to the offering specific quality attributes deriving from their own, or others', past experience. Trademark holders, on their part, have an incentive to invest in quality because they will be able to reap the benefits in terms of reputation. In other words, trademark law becomes an economic device which, opportunely designed, can produce incentives for maximizing market efficiency. This role must of course be recognized, as a vast body of literature has done, with many important economic results.

However from a broader perspective, trademark appears to do more than simply correct a market failure in the production of information: it has additional dynamic effects which, though largely overlooked, unequivocally contribute to the overall efficiency balance. Examples are the promotion of barriers to entry, market power and rent-seeking activities in general that bear little relation to information-conveying mechanisms or the attainment of efficiency, as well as the creation of a market of signs where very strong protection tends to be assured, even though the welfare effects are as yet poorly understood.

The economic analysis should increasingly pay attention to these issues when studying the efficiency implications of trademark.

Acknowledgements

The author is grateful to the MIUR-PRIN working groups on intellectual property rights for the helpful suggestion and two anonymous referees. The research is part of PRIN2005 research. The usual disclaimer applies.

Notes

1. This definition is widely accepted. See, for example, the dictionary section of MSN Encarta (http://encarta.msn.com/dictionary˙1861735074/sign.html) which defines a sign as a 'thing representing something else' and then as 'something that indicates or expresses the existence of something else not immediately apparent'.
2. The reference is based on the acrostic of the Greek word for fish 'ichtys' made up of the Greek initials of the phrase 'Jesus Christ, God's Son, Saviour' (Anonymous, 1985). In the remainder of this document this type of situation shall be described, using the language of trademark, with the term 'secondary meaning'.
3. 'A brand is a trademark, or combination of trademarks, which through promotion and use has acquired significance over and above its functional role of distinguishing the goods or services concerned' (Blakett, 1998, p. 8). Branding is a practice that uses the information and attraction leverage created by the brand – the so-called 'brand equity' – to capture consumers (see Aaker, 1991, 1996).
4. Some scholars have however noted that in certain situations trademark can be instrumentally used to reduce the amount of information available, and so to pursue rent-seeking strategies (Dogan and Lemley, 2004). These practices constitute the 'dark side' of trademark and will be discussed below.
5. The contribution of Png and Reitman (1994), along similar lines, points out the role of brand as an implicit guarantee of superior quality. See also Tadelis (1999).
6. On copyright and incentives see for example Towse (2006) and on the music market, Liebowitz and Watt (2006).
7. 'Lack of distinctiveness would make the mark incapable of identifying the good and recalling to a consumer the information (generated by previous experience with the good by him or other consumers)'. In such a case protecting the trademark would no longer answer the institutional objectives (Landes and Posner, 2003, p. 187).
8. The results of Grossman and Shapiro (1988a, 1988b), partly along the same lines, also show that under specific conditions, in the case of trade between different nations, the overall effect of trademark infringement may also be welfare enhancing.
9. Many regulations incorporate anti-dilution clauses. In Europe, anti-dilution regulations have been enacted by member states as an implementation of Directive

89/104/CE. In the US the Federal Trademark Act of 1946, universally known as the Lanham Act, has been amended to include a specific anti-dilution measure from the Federal Trademark Dilution Act in 1995.

10. The cost to the consumer can be expressed using the formula $\pi = P + H(T, Y, W)$, where π is the gross price paid by the consumer, P is the net price, and H is the information cost incurred by the consumer, which decreases as the strength of the brand (T) and the availability of signs (W) increases, but is more ambiguously related to other factors (Y) such as the number of competing signs/firms, the available technology for producing information, the cost of the buyer's time, etc. The firm can mark up the price of the good by an amount equal to the reduction in the information costs to consumers brought about via trademark.

11. 'Salience' is defined as the positive feeling which a consumer associates with a particular trademark or brand.

12. The economic theory has extensively dealt with differentiation strategies, producing a substantial body of literature. For a thorough introduction see Tirole (1988) and Shy (1995).

13. This argument applies in general to all intellectual property rights (Nicita *et al.*, 2005).

14. An example of brand extension is the production of iPod on the part of Apple. An example of brand stretching is the production of soft drinks by Virgin, an airline operator (and before that, a recording label).

15. An interesting reflection is put forward by Beebe (2004, p. 624): 'In asserting that trademarks do no more than facilitate search and encourage quality, the [Law and Economics approach] has long declined to acknowledge what is obvious: that firms produce trademarks as status goods, that consumers consume trademarks to signal status, and that courts routinely invest trademarks with legal protection in an effort to preserve this status-signalling function [...] Entire areas of trademark doctrine cannot be understood except as systems of rules designed to facilitate the commodification [...] of social distinction.'

References

Aaker, D. A. (1991) *Managing Brand Equity*. New York: Free Press.

Aaker, D. A. (1996) Measuring brand equity across products and markets. *California Management Review* 38: 102–120.

Akerlof, G. A. (1970) The market for lemons: quality uncertainty and the market mechanism. *Quarterly Journal of Economics* 84: 488–500.

Alchian, A. and Allen, W. (1977) *Exchange and Production*. Belmont, CA: Wadsworth Publishing.

Alford, W. P. (1995) *To Steal a Book is an Elegant Offense. Intellectual Property Law in Chinese Civilization*. Stanford: Stanford University Press.

Anderson, R. D. (1998) The interface between competition policy and intellectual property in the context of the international trading system. *Journal of International Economic Law* 1: 655–678.

Anonymous (1985) *Harper's Bible Dictionary*. San Francisco: Harper and Row.

Babe, R. E. (1995) *Communication and the Transformation of Economics*. Boulder, CO and Oxford: Westview Press.

Bagwell, L. and Bernheim, B. D. (1996) Veblen effects in a theory of conspicuous consumption. *American Economic Review* 86: 349–373.

Baroncelli, E., Fink, C. and Javorcik, B. S. (2005) The global distribution of trademarks: some stylised facts. *World Economy* 28: 765–781.

Baudrillard, J. (1972) *Pour une Critique de l'Economie Politique du Signe*. Paris: Gallimard (Eng. Trans: *For a Critique of the Political Economy of the Sign*).

Beebe, B. (2004) The semiotics of trademark law. *UCLA Law Review* 51: 621–704.

Beebe, B. (2005) Search and persuasion in trademark law. *Michigan Law Review* 103: 2020–2072.

Blackett, T. (1998) *Trademarks*. London: Macmillan.

Cabral, L. M. B. (2000) Stretching firm and brand reputation. *Rand Journal of Economics* 31: 658–673.

Carter, S. L. (1990) The trouble with trademark. *Yale Law Journal* 99: 759–800.

Choi, J. P. (1998) Brand extension and informational leverage. *Review of Economic Studies* 65: 655–669.

Corneo, G. and Jeanne, O. (1997) Conspicuous consumption, snobbism and conformism. *Journal of Public Economics* 66: 55–71.

De Alessi, L. and Staaf, R. J. (1994) What does reputation really assure? The relationship of trademarks to expectations and legal remedies. *Economic Inquiry* 32: 477–485.

Dixit, A. (1979) A model of duopoly suggesting a theory of entry barriers. *Bell Journal of Economics* 10: 20–32.

Dnes, A. W. (1996) The economic analysis of franchise contracts. *Journal of Institutional and Theoretical Economics* 152: 297–324.

Dogan, S. L. and Lemley, M. (2004) Trademarks and consumer search costs on the internet. Stanford Law School Working Paper, 294. Available at http://ssrn.com/abstract=560725.

Economides, N. (1988) The economics of trademarks. *Trademark Reporter* 78: 523–539.

Economides, N. (1998) Trademarks. In P. Newman (ed.), *The New Palgrave Dictionary of Economics and the Law* (pp. 601–603). London: Macmillan.

Ehrenberg, A. and Barnard, N. (1997) Differentiation or salience. *Journal of Advertising Research* 37: 7–14.

Grilo, I., Shy, O. and Thisse, J. F. (2001) Price competition when consumer behavior is characterized by conformity of vanity. *Journal of Public Economics* 80: 385–408.

Grossman, G. M. and Shapiro, C. (1988a) Counterfeit-product trade. *American Economic Review* 78: 59–75.

Grossman, G. M. and Shapiro, C. (1988b) Foreign counterfeiting of status goods. *Quarterly Journal of Economics* 103: 79–100.

Hart, O. (1995) *Firms, Contracts, and Financial Structure*. Oxford: Oxford University Press.

Jarrell, G. and Peltzman, S. (1985) The impact of product recalls on the wealth of sellers. *Journal of Political Economy* 93: 512–536.

Keller, K. L. (1993) Conceptualizing, measuring and managing customer-base brand equity. *Journal of Marketing* 57: 1–22.

Klemperer, P. (1995) Competition when consumers have switching costs: an overview with applications to industrial organization, macroeconomics and international trade. *Review of Economics Studies* 62: 515–539.

Kong, Y. and Seldon, J. R. (2004) Pseudo-generic products and barriers to entry in pharmaceutical markets. *Review of Industrial Organization* 25: 71–86.

Landes, W. M. and Posner, R. A. (1987) Trademark law: an economic perspective. *Journal of Law and Economics* 30: 265–309.

Landes, W. M. and Posner, R. A. (2003) *The Economic Structure of Intellectual Property Law*. Cambridge, MA: Harvard University Press.

Lemley, M. A. (1999) The modern Lanham Act and the death of common sense. *Yale Law Journal* 108: 1687–1715.

Liebowitz, S. J. and Watt, R. (2006) How to best ensure remuneration for creators in the market for music? Copyright and its alternatives. *Journal of Economic Surveys* 20: 513–545.

Lott, J. R. Jr. (1988) Brand names, ignorance and quality guaranteeing. *Applied Economics* 20: 165–176.

Luini, L. and Mangani, A.(2002) Brand extensions: i contributi della letteratura di industrial organization. *Rivista internazionale di scienze sociali* 110: 367–380 (Eng. Trans.: 'Brand Extensions: Contributions from the Industrial Organization Literature).

Lunney, G. S. Jr. (1999) Trademark monopolies. *Emory Law Journal* 48: 367–487.

Mathewson, G. F. and Winter, R. A. (1985) The economics of franchise contracts. *Journal of Law and Economics* 28: 503–526.

Menell, P. (1999) Intellectual property: general theories. In B. Bouckaert and G. De Geest (eds), *Encyclopedia of Law and Economics* (pp. 129–188). Cheltenham, UK and Northampton, USA: Edward Elgar.

Morton, F. M. (1999) Barriers to entry, brand advertising and generic entry in the US pharmaceutical industry. *International Journal of Industrial Organization* 18: 1085–1104.

Nicita, A., Ramello, G. B. and Scherer, F. M. (2005) Intellectual property rights and the organization of industries: new perspectives in law and economics. *International Journal of Economics of Business* 12: 289–296.

Pashigian, B. P. and Bowen, B. (1994) The rising cost of time of females, the growth of national brands, and the supply of retail services. *Economic Inquiry* 32: 33–65.

Pepall, L. M. and Richards, D. J. (2002) The simple economics of brand stretching. *Journal of Business* 75: 535–552.

Png, I. P. L. and Reitman, D. (1995) Why are some products branded and others not? *Journal of Law and Economics* 38: 207–224.

Ramello, G. B. (2005) Intellectual property and the markets of ideas. *Review of Network Economics* 4: 68–87.

Rangaswamy, A., Burke, R. R. and Oliva, T. A. (1993) Brand equity and the extendibility of brand names. *International Journal of Research in Marketing* 10: 61–75.

Riley, J. G. (1990) Signalling. In J. Eatwell, M. Milgate and P. Newman (eds), *Allocation, Information and Markets* (pp. 287–294). London: New Palgrave.

Rogers, E. S. (1910) Some historical matters concerning trade marks. *Michigan Law Review* 9: 29–39.

Schmalensee, R. (1978) Entry deterrence in the ready-to-eat breakfast cereal industry. *Bell Journal of Economics* 9: 305–327.

Schmalensee, R. (1982) Product differentiation advantages of pioneering brands. *American Economic Review* 72: 349–365.

Schetchter, F. I. (1925) *The Historical Foundations of the Law Relating to Trade-Marks*. New York: Columbia University Press.

Schetchter, F. I. (1927) The rational basis of trademark protection. *Harvard Law Review* 40: 813–833.

Shapiro, C. (1982) Consumer information, product quality, and seller reputation. *Bell Journal of Economics* 13: 20–35.

Shavell, S. (1987) *Economic Analysis of Accident Law*. Cambridge, MA: Harvard University Press.

Shy, O. (1995) *Industrial Organization*. Cambridge, MA: MIT Press.

Singh, N. and Vives, X. (1984) Price and quantity competition in a differentiated duopoly. *Rand Journal of Economics* 15: 546–554.

Tadelis, S. (1999) What's in a name ? Reputation as a tradable asset. *American Economic Review* 89: 548–563.

Tirole, J. (1988) *The Theory of Industrial Organization*. Cambridge, MA: MIT Press.

Towse, R. (2006) Copyright and artists: a view from cultural economics. *Journal of Economic Surveys* 20: 567–585.

Treece, J. M. (1968) Trademark licensing and vertical restraints in franchising arrangements. *University of Pennsylvania Law Review* 116: 435–467.
Veblen, T. (1899) *The Theory of Leisure Class. An Economic Study Of Institutions.* London: Macmillan.
Yoo, B. and Donthu, N. (1999) Developing and validating a multidimensional consumer-based brand equity scale. *Journal of Business Research* 52: 1–14.
Wilkins, M. (1992) The neglected intangible asset: the influence of the trade mark on the rise of the modern corporation. *Business History* 34: 66–95.
Williamson, O. (1985) *The Economics Institutions of Capitalism.* New York: Free Press.

5

COPYRIGHT AND ARTISTS: A VIEW FROM CULTURAL ECONOMICS

Ruth Towse

1. Introduction

In this paper, I survey work that relates copyright and cultural economics and I shall show that cultural economics offers another view to the 'standard' economics of copyright. The literature is not large but it throws an interesting light on the economic role of copyright in relation to artists (using that term in a broad way to mean creators and performers in all the various art forms).

Cultural economics[1] is the application of economics to the arts, heritage and the cultural industries and one of the subjects that it deals with is the supply of works of art, music, literature, etc. Copyright is supposed to influence the supply of artistic work in a positive way by providing an incentive through statutory protection but it may also raise the cost of creating new works and so reduce their supply; it also influences the demand for works of art, in part by raising prices; this is considered undesirable for goods like the arts, which are held to offer public good benefits (see Throsby, 2001).[2] It has also been argued that copyright's effects are asymmetric and that it benefits the distributor rather than the content creator. As cultural policy is concerned with stimulating creativity and with the provision of and access to the arts and culture, it follows that copyright law is important for cultural policy, as well as for cultural economics. These matters are all grist for the cultural economists' mill and they have a particular contribution to make to the study of the economics of copyright.

Cultural economics can also contribute to the discussion about alternatives to copyright law as a stimulus to creating works of art. One area of cultural economics, the study of artists' labour markets, specifically tries to understand artistic motivation and the likely impact of copyright on the supply of creative work. Moreover, the case for government intervention in the arts and heritage made by cultural economists has resonance for the economic rationale of copyright. As we shall see, copyright sceptics have often advocated a policy of giving grants and awards to artists as an alternative to copyright as the incentive to create works of art.

Most of the standard economic literature on copyright (as reviewed, e.g. by Liebowitz and Watt in this issue) ignores a number of aspects that have considerable significance for cultural production in general and for artists in particular. Specifically, there is little mention in that literature of moral rights, although artists set great store by them and they may also have economic effects;

no distinction is made between copyright for authors and neighbouring rights for performers; the distributional effects of copyright are barely referred to and the question of how much artists earn from copyright is ignored. Moreover, most writers assume that the interests of creators and performers are in perfect harmony with those of publishers, sound recording makers, broadcasters and all the other businesses that process and distribute their work as if there were no contractual problems between them over property rights. Caves (2000) has shown that there are economic explanations for the problems of contracting between artists and 'humdrum' enterprises dealing with the commercial side of the arts and culture. There are therefore good reasons to view copyright through the lens of cultural economics.

2. Comparing Cultural Subsidies and Copyright Law as Government Policy

Subsidies or grants to artists are one of the ways to stimulate creativity that have been proposed as an alternative to copyright law. Both are seen as overcoming market failure in cultural production. They were seriously considered by Macaulay in the 1840s (see Hadfield, 1992), by Plant (1934) and again by Hurt and Schuchman (1966); Macaulay grudgingly found copyright law to be preferable; the other authors opted for subsidies or a system of grants, prizes and awards.[3] Subsidy to the arts is one of the topics that have been thoroughly investigated by cultural economics, and much has been written on its benefits and costs. Accordingly, that research forms a basis from which to compare these government policies for the cultural sector.

In the 'high' arts, it is common to find state subsidy, and in some sectors and in some countries, there is also direct state provision. Subsidies typically take the form of direct grants of monetary aid to arts and cultural organizations (theatre and opera companies, orchestras, museums, etc.). In many European countries, museums and heritage buildings are mostly owned and operated by the state.[4] Subsidies also extend beyond the high arts to broadcasting, film, the press and even pop music as countries seek to maintain their language and national cultural identity. Public finance contributes a very high proportion of total income for the 'high arts' cultural organizations – in the Netherlands, for example, around 85% comes from government grants. Despite these high outlays, however, only a small proportion is typically spent on grants to individual artists, as government bodies tend to prefer to channel funds through cultural organizations, on the one hand, because transaction costs are high and, on the other, because there are moral hazard problems of supporting individuals.

The advantage of a reward system that directly targets the artist is that it can discriminate quality and the type of art that is perceived to be under-produced. By contrast, copyright is indiscriminate with respect to these features – any work within the scope of copyright attracts its protection and the threshold for originality is pretty low. It is worth noting that one of Plant's very perceptive (and frequently ignored) objections to copyright was that it encourages *over*-production of literary works (by contrast to the usual argument of under-production) and that it enables lower quality work to survive on the market because of the protection of the copyright monopoly than would otherwise be possible: too many artists and not good enough art. That is also the conclusion, however, of Abbing's (2002) review of the Dutch subsidy scheme of a minimum income for visual artists. The snags of public subsidies are that there is a danger of some concept of official state art developing if grants are administered by civil servants or cronyism if the job is delegated to artists themselves. This may also be a problem for prizes and other such awards (Wijnberg, 1994).

In some countries there are long-term grants or stipends to artists as incentives to creativity: in Finland stipends of up to 15 years' duration are awarded by a board of senior 'peer' artists to a select few creative artists, usually writers, visual artists and composers, and in the Netherlands visual artists receive grants under a general government funding scheme. Heikinnen (1995) and Rengers and Ploeg (2001) have studied these schemes and concluded that they display a 'winner-takes-all' character, that is, artists who are anyway successful on the open market tend to receive these awards. Thus, such grants are unlikely to provide an incentive to supply more or better quality work and may be mostly economic rent. Indeed, they may even be a disincentive owing to moral hazard (the composer Sibelius is often cited as an example; he is said to have composed less after receiving a lifetime stipend from the state). The possibility of a backward-bending supply curve always has to be considered as a response to higher rewards from whatever source.

The public finance of these two alternative systems is interesting to contrast. As Macaulay famously pointed out in 1841: 'Copyright is a tax on readers for the purposes of a bounty for writers.'[5] With copyright, it is the consumer who finances the incentive to create works of art (in the broadest sense), whereas with subsidies, taxpayers, who may well not be 'readers', do so. Cultural economists have shown that, at least for 'high arts', which absorb the lion's share of cultural subsidies, subsidy out of general taxation is regressive since arts consumers, who are only a small proportion of the population, generally have above-average incomes. While that is not the case for popular music or television programmes, it is something that should be taken into consideration in comparing the copyright law and subsidies as an incentive to create works of art. There are other differences: the subsidy or grant is an *ex ante* reward, while prizes and copyright are *ex post*. It may be that these have different incentive effects: the artist may have to satisfy certain criteria to obtain the grant, which could influence the work she plans to produce, and the success of that work (however it is evaluated) may influence her chances of a subsequent award. With copyright, the work gets automatic protection whatever the quality and there is no incentive to produce high quality work.[6] Subsidy, though, usually involves some evaluation of quality. Another point is that there is a significant difference in the timing of the outcomes: a copyright work involves a considerable inter-generational transfer before it is available in the public domain, depending upon the duration of the copyright term (if an artist creates a work aged 25 and lives to 75, the work is in copyright for 120 years with a term of 70 years *post mortem autoris*). Of course, most copyright works do not survive on the market for the duration and that raises the costs of access. Without copyright, a subsidized work would be in the public domain from its publication. This discussion is reminiscent of that about the public finance of cultural heritage – how much should we spend on it now for future generations, who will be wealthier and have different tastes? Finally, the copyright system relies heavily upon the market to make works available, thus leaving the choice of which works and which artists to promote in the hands of the commercial enterprises in the cultural industries. These industries are dominated by oligopolistic international corporations that are run in share-holders' interests, not those of the cultural policy of any given country. The Disney Corporation's interests do not necessarily coincide with those of Dutch television audiences! That brings into the discussion the public choice aspects of copyright, which take us too far from the one in hand but they should not be ignored.

In most developed countries, copyright and subsidies to the arts, along with prizes and other such awards, co-exist and are usually complementary. The popular arts rely more on copyright as an incentive while subsidies are used as well to stimulate creativity in the 'high' arts. It might be considered whether some version of works for hire should not be used for works of art that have been financed by taxpayers with the copyright belonging to the government or put in the public domain; such arrangements could be made by contracts between the funding body and the artist. Another variation could be a loan fund for artists established along the lines of a student loan system and artists required to pay a percentage of any royalties into it to pay off the loan (Towse, 2001a). These are details, however; the main point here is to show that there are contrasts and connections between copyright as an incentive system and subsidy to the arts, systems which have been considered in the literature as alternatives.

3. Variations on a Theme: Moral Rights, *Droit de Suite* and Performers' Rights

In this section, aspects of copyright law not usually dealt with in surveys by economists are considered: moral rights, *droit de suite* and performers' rights.

3.1 *Moral Rights*[7]

The economic analysis of copyright, being strongly influenced by American authors, is almost exclusively concerned with what are called 'economic' rights, as contrasted to the 'moral' right. The European tradition of authors' rights (*droit d'auteur*) stresses what have come to be called in English moral rights (*droit moral*) – rights of attribution, integrity, disclosure and withdrawal. In the European Union, the moral right is inalienable and unwaivable. With the globalization of the cultural industries and increasing standardization of copyright worldwide, the distinction between the civil law countries' emphasis on moral rights and copyright in the common law tradition is eroding. As part of this trend, a form of moral rights has been incorporated in both UK and US law, in the former as part of the 1988 Copyright Act and in the latter in the 1990 Visual Arts Rights Act (VARA).[8]

The moral right may also have been ignored because it was thought to have no economic value and to exist for equity reasons without efficiency implications.

The literature in cultural economics on moral rights shows this is not the case. Rushton (1998) argues that there is pecuniary benefit from the moral right and therefore they must be regarded as having efficiency effects: the moral right has an incentive effect for artistic production because it encourages artistic recognition of status and professionalism. It can also have significant hold-up power and so be used in bargaining situations. Hansmann and Santilli (1997) consider both equity and efficiency arguments for artists' moral rights. As an example, they present an economic perspective on the right of integrity; knowing who the artist is, and therefore the stock of works on which her reputation is based, is important market information. Landes (2001) and Landes and Posner (2003), though, are dismissive of this argument in the light of VARA. It would be interesting to see an economic analysis of moral rights in a country, such as France, where the rights are stronger and fully established and the moral rights may not be waived as they can be in the USA.

It seems likely that there are relatively high transaction costs in connection with moral rights, for while it is a fairly simple matter to identify the creator of a work of visual art, such as a painting or sculpture, it will be more difficult or even impossible to do so in other areas of the cultural industries, such as multimedia and sound recording. This is also an issue with performers' rights, where costly arrangements have to be made to identify their contribution to works. The World Intellectual Property Organisation (WIPO), the UN agency responsible for IP treaties, in 1996 negotiated the WIPO Performers and Phonograms Treaty (WPPT), which required the recognition of performers' moral rights for the first time (this treaty has now been translated into national law by most European countries, in the USA through the Digital Millennium Copyright Act, and by a considerable number of other countries). This is discussed in relation to performers' rights in Section 3.3 below.

3.2 Droit de Suite or Artists' Resale Right

Although not part of the copyright proper, *droit de suite* (known in English as the artist's resale right) is linked closely to it. It is an *ad valorem* levy on the resale of paintings over a certain price in public sales which has existed for many years in most European countries[9] and in the state of California; more often than not, it is not exercised by artists, as predicted when it was introduced (Rottenberg, 1975). In Europe, it is an inalienable and unwaivable right designed, with the best will in the world, to assist artists in obtaining their share of any increase in the price of their work once it has passed out of their hands, but is generally believed by economists to reduce prices for the work of young artists and thus have unintended adverse incentive effects. As with other incomes of artists, it seems that *droit de suite* royalties, where they are collected, for example in France, are a significant source of income for the top artists but pay little to, or even harm, young artists by depressing prices (Perloff, 1998; Ginsburgh, forthcoming). Moreover, *droit de suite* is likely to act as a disincentive to dealers etc. to promote artists' work (Perloff, 1998). The effect of *droit de suite* on the art market should be testable empirically. Although there is now a considerable literature of econometric work on art as an investment, almost no one has tested the impact of *droit de suite* on art prices.

However, Solow (1998) introduces a new approach that challenges the negative view of *droit de suite*. He analyzes its dynamic external effect on an artist's work over her lifetime. By having a claim on resale prices of past works, the artist has an interest in the future value of her early work, creating an incentive to maintain her reputation. Thus resale prices are 'endogenized'. The question of complementarity and substitutability between early and late works of a still-producing artist is an interesting one in other areas too, such as in sound recordings and literature where the value of back catalogue can be enhanced by present activities, such as going on tour, being interviewed by the media and so on. Cheung (1986) is relevant to this question; he has argued that unless both parties, licensor and licensee (e.g. author and publisher), share revenues, the licensee will obtain market information on the value of the invention, which is not signalled directly to the licensor (and authors have the incentive to overstate the value of their work and publishers to understate it).

An alternative to *droit de suite* that has been suggested is to give artists an exhibition payment right, a share of the entrance charge to public exhibitions of their work (Santagata, 1995). An interesting question that could be analyzed in this context is the different values of the bundle of rights that are sold with a painting or the work of art; although the buyer acquires the painting, the copyright remains with the artist, who then has reproduction and other secondary use rights. An objection to a scheme for exhibition payments, however, is that it would have high costs of tracing artists; any royalty scheme necessitates keeping in touch with copyright owners and that is also the case to a lesser extent for *droit de suite*. A similar proposal for a display right is discussed in Hansmann and Santilli (2001).

3.3 *Performers' Rights*[10]

Performers did not become vulnerable to having their performances copied until the advent of home-taping and later CD burning and downloading. However, in the first half of the 20th century, they suffered considerable loss of work owing to the substitution of records and radio play for live performance. Performers do not have copyright proper but property rights related to copyright or neighbouring rights. The conventional justification given in law books and the like is that copyright and authors' rights are the reward and stimulus for creativity but performers do not create works, they just 'execute' the performance of existing works and that does not merit the grant of the exclusive right as for the author. I have argued (Towse, forthcoming) that this does not make economic sense, as explained below. There has been no other economic analysis of performers' rights of which I am aware.

The recognition of the case for performers' rights began with the onset of commercial sound recording and early on performers acquired some rights; to give the example of the UK, in 1925 performers acquired the right to control the fixation and use of their performances (mainly in sound recordings). The full establishment of performers' rights really began with the 1961 Rome Convention on neighbouring rights, which forms the basis of national laws and also forms the basis for the WPPT. In 1992, the so-called EC Rental Directive[11] was drawn up, which basically enforced the Rome Convention for all European Union countries. Musical performers[12] acquired the right to control the recording of live performances, fully assignable property rights and individual rights to equitable remuneration for public performances of sound recordings, for which protection lasts 50 years from the date of fixation. Rights to remuneration are essentially compensation for compulsory licences that override the general copyright principle that the author/creator has the exclusive right to control exploitation of his or her work (Gallagher, 2002). In the case of sound recordings, what this means in practice is that once a performer has contracted with a record label to make a sound recording, she has no further control over its exploitation (e.g. by public performance) but she receives payment for these uses. (The same applies in this case to composers as well.)[13]

The apparent intention of the Rental Directive was to correct the weaker bargaining position of non-featured performers, and that was done by laying down the requirement that equitable remuneration could only be administered by a collecting society set up for that purpose. This is one of perhaps many examples where the law has been used in the attempt to 'correct' a perceived market failure for equity rather than efficiency reasons.[14] Non-featured performers were targeted in this way because they do not have a royalty contract with, in the case of the music industry, a record label, and are typically paid a standard fee, for example, for a studio recording.

As mentioned earlier, the WIPO Performances and Phonograms Treaty (WPPT) has made important changes to performers' rights introducing a new exclusive right in favour of performers, who make their works available on-line to the public (known as the 'making available right'). It also mandates the prohibition of the circumvention of copyright protection (TPMs – technological protection measures) and of tampering with rights management information (DRM – digital rights management). Thus, with the WPPT, performers now have an individual exclusive right (though not a full copyright) more or less equivalent to that of authors. The USA has not signed the Rome Convention and performers there have rights only in digital works.

Turning to the economics of performers' rights, we note that as the economic aim of copyright law is to offer an incentive to create works of art, literature, music and so on, we may reasonably assume that this aim applies to the creation of performances by performers. Performers are identified in UK copyright law as persons who have rights in their performances. A performance is formed by talent, years of training and investment in human capital and involves considerable risk of how it will be received by audiences. A performance is a work in the sense of copyright law and so the same economic logic should apply to it as it does to the work of an author. However, the difference is that the performance, while a work in its own right, cannot be separated from the work being performed. The received view is that when performers perform a work created by an author – say an existing song already written by a composer – their performance is already 'propertized' by copyright law so there is no need to intervene further by granting other property rights on the same work: the performer is only able to produce her performance on licence from the composer. Thus the law favours the creator over the performer. I dispute this rationale, however, because it fails to take into account how value is added to the author's work by the performer. When a singer makes a song famous, thus adding value to the song due to her talent, the singer should be awarded the value added but, instead, the benefit accrues to the composer, who cannot have anticipated (in most cases) that the singer would perform the work. The composer therefore 'free-rides' on the singer's performance. Coasean logic would suggest that well-known singers should commission songs from a lesser known composer and therefore own the song and, indeed, that did happen historically (Towse, forthcoming).

Until the introduction of legislation following the WPPT, non-featured performers, such as backing singers and instrumentalists, received only collective remuneration but now they also have individual exclusive rights. It is frequently argued that these performers have already been paid for their work and therefore a royalty on top of that would just be paying them twice for the same thing. However, even if the performer were already on salary with an orchestra or chorus, economic efficiency requires that their pay reflect the revenues received by the organization employing them; if they receive payment through other means, for example, royalties, then economists would expect that the 'spot' pay for work (fees or salary) would be reduced to take into account the future royalty or remuneration payment. That principle raises an issue that has only been touched on (Towse, 2001a) – 'Who pays' for extended rights for performers (or any other claimant, in fact)? And when a new claimant is introduced, where is the money to come from – higher consumer prices, less for authors or lower profits for (in the case of music) sound recording makers?

One argument against royalties for non-featured performers is that the transaction costs of tracing, contracting and maintaining contact with many performers would be high for the sound recording maker; however, a composers' collecting society incurs similar costs. Apparently, this objection to performers' rights is now deemed to be outdated by the possibility of DRM as the WPPT has caused individual exclusive rights to be introduced. It remains to be seen how effectively 'ordinary' non-star performers are able to exercise these rights. So far, DRM is not standardized and it is not clear who will bear the associated costs. There is scope for a great deal more work on the economics of performers' rights, both analytical and empirical, the more so as the European Commission is currently pursuing collecting societies for anticompetitive behaviour.

4. Distributional Aspects of Copyright for Artists

Economists' concentration on the efficiency aspects of copyright has meant that its distributional effects have received little attention. Several topics are considered under this heading: analysis of contracting between 'art and commerce', the economic analysis of copyright collectives and empirical studies of artists' earnings from royalties and other copyright remuneration.

4.1 *Contracting Between 'Art and Commerce'*

Caves (2000) analyzes the economic organization of creative industries by applying the insights of contract theory to deals between artists and the firm in the cultural industry over the control of rights. He shows that the firm always has the incentive to acquire control over the creator's copyrights when it has to incur an outlay on sunk costs, the typical situation, say, with an advance to an author or the costs of publication or marketing. It does so in part to avoid hold-up problems, which may arise in the creative industries because of the author's or artist's particular concern over her reputation and care for artistic content, and in part because of the inherent radical uncertainty (Caves' 'nobody knows') surrounding the fruition and reception of creative work. A royalty contract is a typical incentive contract that forces the creator or performer to share with the publisher in the success or failure of the final product and the associated risk. Caves' focus is on industrial organization in the creative industries rather than on the distribution of the share of rewards for the artist, although, along the way, he demonstrates very well the weak bargaining position in which most artists find themselves. Alonso and Watt (2003) provide a formal model of the contract for sharing revenues, showing that the barrier to an efficient contract lies in the differing attitudes to risk on the part of the parties involved – the creator likely being more risk averse than the publishing firm that markets the product.

Artists are typically at a disadvantage in relation to firms in the cultural industries for several reasons: as individuals, artists have poor access to the capital market and therefore need to contract with a firm to get their work distributed, whereas the firm, often a multinational giant corporation in an oligopolized industry, has easy access to capital. With little capital reserves, artists have to sell their work within a short time of its creation; thus their time preference rate is much shorter than a firm's; and artists have a relatively small portfolio of work and cannot pool risks, unlike a large firm with a huge portfolio of copyrighted work, which it can exploit when market conditions are favourable. Another source of asymmetry is in relation to market information; artists have considerably less experience of market conditions than do firms. Moreover, individual artists cannot afford the legal costs of defending their rights in court, whereas firms can.

Transaction costs of contracting often lead to standardization of contracts as a means of reducing the costs. Standard contracts, of course, are not tailored to the specific work of its creator and therefore do not provide an individual incentive. Towse (1999) observes that different combinations of the incentive to produce high quality work, willingness to share risk and transaction costs that are to be found in different types of contracts and payment methods. The incentive to do high quality work depends on whether the payment is a flat-rate single-spot payment or a royalty on sales. The former offers little incentive to improve quality and therefore is more likely to result in, or be more commonly associated with, routine work and a standard contract. However, with a flat-rate fee the artist bears no risk. Under the royalty system, the contract ties author and publisher in a longer term relationship and the artist shares risk with entrepreneur. That gives the artist the motive to do good quality work now and in the future since it provides a feedback for the present work to increase the sales of earlier work. A pure royalty deal has a stronger incentive than if an advance on the royalty is paid because it is a combination of spot and future payments.[15] The outcome turns on the response of the artist not only to the amount and type of the payment but also to her attitude to risk-taking and ability to sustain risk.

4.2 *Economic Analysis of Copyright Collectives*

The above, of course, assumes that contracting is possible between the artist and the user of her work; that is the case in the primary market for copyright works – the author contracts with the publisher, the song writer and the performer with the record company and so on. That is not feasible with secondary users of their work, such as photocopying of books and public performance of sound recordings. The same type of contracting problems is faced by copyright-collecting societies, which act collectively on behalf of authors and performers with secondary users. The need to economize on transaction costs of contracting and monitoring usage leads to 'blanket licensing' of the whole repertoire of the society (Hollander, 1984; Besen *et al.*, 1992; Watt, 2000; Liebowitz, 2005). This minimizes transaction costs but has the disadvantage from the economic point of view that the individual creator's contribution to the demand for the licence is not distinguished. Transaction costs are further reduced by the natural monopoly of collecting societies, which often specialize in administering one or a closely related bundle of rights. Kretschmer (2003), however, finds fault with the economic explanation of transaction cost minimization and argues instead that collective rights management is a form of unionization or 'solidarity'. In a paper whose title says it all, 'Copyright Societies Do Not Administer Individual Property Rights: the Incoherence of Institutional Traditions in Germany and the UK' (Kretschmer, 2003), he argues that the joint membership of publishers with authors or performers in collecting societies reduces their ability to concentrate on the interests of the creator members because the economically stronger publishers dominate the societies.

The first work on the economics of copyright collectives was by Peacock and Weir (1975) on the UK Performing Rights Society (PRS). The PRS was formed in 1914 as a private co-operative society to administer musical copyrights and it is a monopoly because it requires the exclusive assignment of copyrights in order to license use. For the distribution of income to members, it holds a large database of information about its members and their works, as well as lists of music users and work-by-work use and it is this database that makes it a natural monopoly. There are economies of scale in royalty administration and duplication of this information would increase costs. The PRS had several concerns at the time of Peacock's research: one was the low earnings of many of their composer members and the unequal distribution of distributed income; a second was the increasing use of home taping devices; and the third was the fact that their biggest single customer was the BBC (British Broadcasting Corporation) with its monopoly on music broadcasts of live concerts and recorded music. Peacock and Weir therefore undertook a three-pronged research into composers' earnings (from all sources, not just from royalties), ways of compensating copyright holders for private home-taping (for which they recommended the introduction of a 'blank tape' levy) and analysis of the de facto bilateral monopoly between the PRS and the BBC (Peacock, 1993). This analysis has proved to be prototypical of the problems facing collecting societies.

This was pioneering work and it established the basic economic analysis of copyright collectives as natural monopolies operating blanket licensing and dealing with other monopolies in the form of trade associations that collectively negotiate licence fees for their members, thus reducing the transaction costs for the composer and for the user. Other work on the economics of collecting societies is by Hollander (1984), Besen *et al.* (1992), MacQueen and Peacock (1995), Watt (2000), Einhorn (2002), Liebowitz (2005) and Snow and Watt (2005). These authors have all investigated a range of efficiency questions about the optimal size of the membership, the effect of competition on the natural monopoly, blanket licensing, setting the tariff and, lately, the effect of digital delivery on the collective administration of copyrights. Watt (2000) points out, in addition to these questions, that collecting societies' practice of distributing the revenues from blanket licensing on an individual basis according to use increases the costs of administration that the blanket licence saves. Snow and Watt (2005) add another dimension by arguing that collecting societies could pool risks and thus reduce the risk bearing of their members.

4.3 *Empirical Studies of Artists' Earnings from Royalties and Other Copyright Remuneration*

The points discussed above are efficiency questions and they ignore both equity matters and the actual distribution of revenues to individual artists. For that, we have to look at empirical evidence on the distribution of earnings of collecting society members. It is important to stress that such data do not show what artists earn from all their copyright works, just what they earn from one right or a limited number of rights that the collecting society exercises on their behalf. Towse (1999) found evidence of the value of remuneration for the public performance of sound recordings resulting from performers' rights that were newly introduced in the UK following the EU Rental Directive and compared the figures for those of similar Swedish and Danish societies, which had been in existence for some 20 years (the figures and distributions were all similar). Kretschmer (2005) uses figures submitted by the PRS in its evidence to the Monopolies and Mergers Commission enquiry into its operation and in addition provides data for the German performing rights society GEMA and the Künstlersozialkasse (social insurance fund for artists) on the distribution of remuneration. Matsumoto (2002) presents detailed figures on performers' remuneration earnings for sound recordings in Japan. These figures all follow what has come to be seen as a familiar pattern in artists' labour markets – the so-called winner-takes-all phenomenon, whereby by the top earners, the few superstar singers, bands, authors, film directors and suchlike who dominate the markets in the cultural industries, also earn the highest royalties. The available evidence (and there is very little of it made public) shows that the top few receive highly disproportionate shares of the total revenues, while many members (sometimes 50% or so) earn less than the minimum that is distributed.

Another issue that has not been deeply investigated is the distribution of the costs of administering the copyright system. While there has been some interest on the part of regulatory bodies (and now by the European Competition authorities) in the often-considerable charges made by collecting societies for the services of administering their members' rights, these are not the only costs of administration. Maintaining databases of the use of copyright material is costly and there is a strong incentive to push the costs onto others. As mentioned above in relation to performers, it is not yet clear who will pay the costs of DRM administration or how much it will cost. In some countries, collecting societies are state or quasi-official bodies and the state bears some of the costs. The state usually bears the cost of protection and also for conflict resolution through a copyright board or tribunal.

To sum up on this section, then: there is more than a strong suspicion to be found in these economic studies that the main benefits of copyright are enjoyed by the 'humdrum' side of the cultural industries rather than the creators and, while it may well be the case that collecting societies have considerable revenues, the distributions of royalties to artists other than the top few stars show how relatively little they get through the copyright system.

5. Artists' Labour Markets and Artists' Motivation

The economics of artists' labour markets is a well-researched area of cultural economics. It has established some by now stylized facts about the economic life of the artist through empirical evidence in a number of countries. These are as follows: artists' median annual earnings are below the national average, given their age and level of education; there is a highly skewed distribution of income within artistic professions, with many earning very little, while the few superstars have very high earnings; most artists have frequent and prolonged periods of unemployment and experience high search costs as they frequently change jobs; most artists are multiple-job-holders because they earn insufficient income from their chosen arts occupation and so must do other sorts of work to make ends meet; and most artists work on standard contracts and at standard fees. Even so, there is an excess supply of artistic services at all levels of payment, something that is exacerbated by subsidy to training and grants to artists. It is believed by most cultural economists that this excess supply is the main reason not only for low earnings but also for their weak bargaining position leading to poor contracts, frequent spells of unemployment and no set career structure (Towse, 2001a).

These disadvantages raise questions about the motivation of artists, whether they are rational maximizers and if so what is it they seek? Research has shown that artists' labour supply is responsive to the (imputed) wage rate: the higher the rate of payment for arts work, the more hours artists spend on art work. There is also positive cross elasticity – when they earn more from *non-arts* work, they devote more time to *arts* work (Throsby, 1997, 2001). Abbing (2002) argues that when artists obtain an increase in earnings, whether from arts work, non-arts work or a grant, they reinvest it in equipment, etc. in order to improve their production of art, rather than raise their material standard of living. Other writers have pointed to the risky nature of work in the arts and, given the absence of information on the artist's chances of success, the only way to find out one's chances are to 'have a go' (Mac-Donald, 1988). Caves (2000) sees this as applicable to all markets in the cultural sector, dubbing it the 'nobody knows' characteristic of the creative industries.

Bruno Frey, in his book *Not Just for the Money* (Frey, 1997), has developed an economic analysis of intrinsic and extrinsic motivation, applying the study of artistic motivation developed in social psychology. Creative artists are said to have 'intrinsic' motivation, inner drive, which is motivated by intrinsic reward – inner satisfaction, fame, recognition, etc. Extrinsic motivation and reward refers to the 'normal' assumption in economics that financial reward is a motivation to effort. The particular contribution of Frey is his 'crowding out' theory – that an inappropriate type of reward could have the opposite of the desired effect. In particular, intrinsic motivation may be crowded out by extrinsic reward.[16] Moreover, financial payment (extrinsic reward) could even inhibit intrinsically motivated people by stifling their inner drive. This led Frey to distinguish two kinds of creativity, institutional and personal. Arts organizations of necessity have to be institutionally motivated to be creative by extrinsic reward in the form of financial grants; personal creativity, however, is only motivated by intrinsic reward (Frey, 2000). Frey believes that cultural policy, with its reliance on financial payments, may all too easily crowd out true artistic creation. In Towse (2001b), I argue that the combination of the economic and moral rights in copyright/authors' rights satisfies Frey's requirement for intrinsic as well as extrinsic reward for creativity. Over and above its role as establishing property rights so that authors can obtain their economic reward, copyright intrinsically rewards creativity through moral rights. It is therefore an instrument of cultural policy that may be more significant to artists than the extrinsic financial incentive of a subsidy.

As a final observation on this topic, it should be said that the dearth of empirical studies on artists' response to copyright and their motivation to supply works of art in general is a real criticism not only of cultural economics but of all those international and national bodies as well that so strongly advocate copyright as a stimulus to creativity. We have to stop simply assuming that stronger copyright means higher earnings for artists and that this therefore leads to greater and better creative output. It is not an easy task to test these relationships – indeed, cultural economists who have worked in this area know how difficult it is to research artists' labour markets – but lack of information on the subject does not strengthen the case for copyright; it weakens it.

6. New Technologies and New Arts

The effect of digitalization on the music industry has by now been well researched by economists and well documented by Liebowitz and Watt in this volume.

Digitalization has its effects on other of the cultural industries too, especially broadcasting, the press and journalism, publishing and film production (although the full effect of movie downloading has yet to impact on the industry). Media economists, whom one could call close cousins of cultural economists, have a significant research programme in this area, particularly looking at the impact of the Internet on these industries and the new business models it calls for (Küng, 2004; Picard, 2004). However, there is little that specifically deals with copyright. In cultural economics, there has been some interest in the effect of digitalization on artists' work and on new types of art and the implications this has for copyright. Farchy and Rochelandet (2002) discuss the protection of copyright holders with private copying using digital technologies, Einhorn (2002) discusses the effect of digitalization on licensing musical copyrights in different platforms and Liebowitz (2005) deals with different ways of collecting licence fees with music downloads. Farchy (2003) deals with a question that has been on many people's lips – does digitalization enable the artist (creator or performer) to break loose from the intermediaries (the 'publishers') in the cultural industries and go it alone using the Internet for publicity and marketing? So far, there is little evidence of this and Farchy suggests that it is unlikely to develop to any great extent. This is another topic that calls for detailed empirical research.

Lastly, a topic that has begun to be analyzed is the copyright implications of new art forms, specifically, borrowed images and appropriation art (Landes, 2002) and musical sampling (Thèberge, 2004). Rushton (2001) discusses the economic aspect of artists' rights and moral rights in similar contexts. Not unrelated is the question of copyright and the digitalization of museum images (Aalberts and Beunen, 2002) and archives; here the concern is about the power of digital rights management to cut off works in the public domain or for 'fair use' reasons (for a general discussion, see Schneider and Henten, 2005). These are very specialized subjects, however, even within cultural economics.

7. Conclusion

The purpose of this survey paper has been to show that economists have been concerned with a wider aspect of copyright than with just economic rights. Moreover, economists working specifically in the field of culture tend to look at the economics of copyright from a rather different standpoint than the general welfare economics or property rights approach adopted by economists and law and economists. In this paper, I have put the focus on the artist and selected the issues for review on that basis. I do not think that all of the people whose work is cited here would regard themselves as cultural economists but I hope they would acknowledge that it adds up to a distinct body of work. Cultural economics' main distinction is that it applies economics to the production and consumption of the arts and culture, areas in which copyright supposedly has a strong influence. The insights of cultural economics about cultural policy seem to throw some additional light on the more general questions about the economic and cultural role of copyright in a world that increasingly emphasizes creativity and the creative industries as the source of economic growth in the post-industrial world.[17]

'Do artists need copyright?' is a question that many people have asked since its introduction in England in 1710. What this survey shows is that the answer is a complex one. There has been some interesting work in economic history on creation without copyright and on artists' earnings, especially in the case of composers (Scherer, 2001; Tschmuck, 2002) and it is obvious that a great deal of the canon of great Western art (and no doubt of Eastern art too) was created without the intervention of copyright or state subsidy.

There is good reason to believe that copyright is asymmetric in its effects and favours the industry side of the creative industries rather than the creators and performers whose work they exploit. If we are to believe that copyright, or more precisely authors' and performers' rights, are fundamental to cultural production, we need far more evidence than at present exists to demonstrate the case. Moreover, it may be that artistic motivation and the incentive to produce works of art are not just due to financial rewards and economic rights but also to moral rights. Economists may have to venture out of their usual eeries to investigate these things. If they do not, they should be far more careful in following the line that what is good for Sony is good for the world of art.

Acknowledgements

I am grateful to Michael Rushton and Richard Watt for reading and commenting on this paper.

Notes

1. For a comprehensive survey of cultural economics, see Blaug (2001). For a general introduction and short chapters on many of the topics mentioned below, see Towse (2003). Towse (2005) traces the development of cultural economics over the last 35 years.
2. The economic arguments for copyright are not rehearsed here – see Liebowitz and Watt in this volume or for a fuller treatment, Landes and Posner (2003).
3. Shavell and van Ypserle's (2003) suggestion for a reward system for innovation does not discuss its application to copyright.
4. In some European countries, there has recently been a programme of deétatization, that is, turning the management over to self-managing non-profit organizations.
5. Cited in Hadfield (1992, pp. 29–31).
6. That is not true of *droit de suite*, the artists' resale right, which does give the incentive to maintain quality and reputation (see Section 3.2).
7. This section draws on Towse (2001a).
8. Boylan (2005) makes it clear that the US version differs considerably from its European origins.
9. The right did not exist in the UK, Ireland or the Netherlands until the recent EU Directive that harmonized its provision throughout Europe.
10. This section draws on Towse (2006).

11. The European Council Directive 'on rental and lending rights and on certain rights related to copyright in the field of intellectual property' (EC Directive, 1992).

12. Audio visual performers, such as film actors, were not included in this legislation. There is now talk of their acquiring copyright protection.

13. Rushton (2003) discusses criticisms of compulsory licensing in the arts.

14. However, in so doing, it risked creating a situation in which the increased transaction costs to users threaten to swamp any benefits (see Towse, 2001a). Burrows (1994) has argued that all copyright is based on equity arguments alone.

15. In practice in the cultural industries there are many different ways of rewarding artists that include prizes, wages, wages plus a bonus and profit-sharing deals besides spot fees and royalties (see Towse, 2004).

16. The 'classic' case is that of blood donorship, where voluntary donation is displaced or 'crowded out' if financial payment is made. Not only that – there is also a moral hazard problem because people who sell blood (i.e. they are extrinsincally motivated) are likely to be less healthy that those who are intrinsically motivated to donate.

17. A topic that has not been discussed in this article is the attempt to measure the effect of copyright in these industries. For a recent review of this topic, see the articles in the Symposium on the Empirical Measurement of the Contribution of Copyright to National Economies, *Review of Economics of Copyright Issues* volume 1, number 1, June 2004.

References

Aalberts, B. and Beunen, A. (2002) Exploiting museum images. In R. Towse (ed.), *Copyright in the Cultural Industries* (pp. 178–194). Cheltenham: Edward Elgar Publishing.

Abbing, H. (2002) *Why Are Artists Poor? The Exceptional Economy of the Arts*. Amsterdam: Amsterdam University Press.

Alonso, J. and Watt, R. (2003) Efficient distribution of copyright income. In W. Gordon and R. Watt (eds.), *The Economics of Copyright* (pp. 81–103). Cheltenham: Edward Elgar Publishing.

Besen, S., Kirkby, S. and Salop, S. (1992) An economic analysis of copyright collectives. *Virginia Law Review* 78: 383–441.

Blaug, M. (2001) Where are we now in cultural economics? *Journal of Economic Surveys* 15(2): 123–143.

Boylan, P. N. (2005) Reconciling artist's moral rights with economic principles and the problem of parody: Some modest proposals. *Journal of Law and Communications* 1(1) Spring 2005 (no page numbers).

Burrows, P. (1994) Justice, efficiency and copyright in cultural goods. In A. Peacock and I. Rizzo (eds.), *Cultural Economics and Cultural Policies* (pp. 99–110). Dordrecht: Kluwer.

Caves, R. (2000) *Creative Industries: Contracts Between Art and Commerce*. Cambridge, MA and London: Harvard University Press.

Cheung, S. (1986) Property rights and invention. In J. Palmer (ed.), *The Economics of Patents and Copyrights* (pp. 5–18). Greenwich, CN, and London: Research in Law and Economics Series 8. JAI Press.

EC Directive (1992) *On Rental Right and Lending Right and on Certain Rights Related to Copyright in the Field of Intellectual Property*. 92/100/EEC. Luxembourg.

Einhorn, M. (2002) Music licensing in the digital age. In R. Towse (ed.), *Copyright in the Cultural Industries* (pp. 165–177). Cheltenham: Edward Elgar Publishing.

Farchy, J. (2003) Internet: culture. In R. Towse (ed.), *A Handbook of Cultural Economics* (pp. 276–280). Cheltenham: Edward Elgar Publishing.

Farchy, J. and Rochelandet, F. (2002) Copyright protection, appropriability and new cultural behaviour. In R. Towse (ed.), *Copyright in the Cultural Industries* (pp. 178–194). Cheltenham: Edward Elgar Publishing.

Frey, B. (1997) *Not Just for the Money*. Cheltenham: Edward Elgar Publishing.

Frey, B. (2000) *Arts and Economics, Analysis and Cultural Policy*. Berlin, Heidelberg, New York: Springer.

Gallagher, T. (2002) Copyright compulsory licensing and incentives. In R. Towse (ed.), *Copyright in the Cultural Industries* (pp. 85–98). Cheltenham: Edward Elgar Publishing.

Ginsburgh, V. (forthcoming) The economic consequences of *droit de suite* in the European Union. www.ecare.ulb.ac.be/ecare/people/members/ginsburgh/papers/134.droit%20de%20suite.pdf.

Hadfield, G. (1992) The economics of copyright: an historical perspective. *Copyright Law Symposium* 38: 1–46. Reprinted in R. Towse (ed.), (1997) *Cultural Economics: The Arts, the Heritage and the Media Industries I*, pp. 129–174.

Hansmann, H. and Santilli, M. (1997) Authors' and artists' moral rights. *Journal of Legal Studies*, 95–143.

Hansmann, H. and Santilli, M. (2001) Royalties for artists versus royalties for authors and composers. *Journal of Cultural Economics* 25(4): 259–281.

Heikinnen, M. (1995) Evaluating the effects of direct support on the economic situation of artists. *Journal of Cultural Economics* 19(3): 261–272.

Hollander, A. (1984) Market structure and performance in intellectual property. *International Journal of Industrial Organisation* 2: 199–216.

Hurt, R. and Schuchman, R. (1966) The economic rationale of copyright. *American Economic Review* 56: 421–432.

Kretschmer, M. (2003) Copyright societies do not administer individual property rights: the incoherence of institutional traditions in Germany and the UK. In R. Towse (ed.), *Copyright in the Creative Industries* (pp. 140–164).

Kretschmer, M. (2005) Artists' earnings and copyright: a review of British and German music industry data in the context of digital technologies. In www.firstmonday.org/issue10_1/kretschmer.

Küng, L. (2004) What makes media firms tick? Exploring the underlying drivers for firm performance. In R. Picard (ed.), *Strategic Responses to Media Market Changes*. Jönköping: Jönköping International Business School.

Landes, W. (2001) What has the Visual Artist's Rights Act of 1990 accomplished? *Journal of Cultural Economics* 24(4): 283–306.

Landes, W. (2002) Copyright, borrowed images and appropriation art: an economic approach. In R. Towse (ed.), *Copyright in the Cultural Industries* (pp. 9–31). Cheltenham: Edward Elgar Publishing.

Landes, W. and Posner, R. (2003) *The Economic Structure of Intellectual Property Law*. Cambridge, MA: The Belknap Press of Harvard University Press.

Liebowitz, S. (2005) MP3s and copyright collectives: A curse worse than the disease? In L. N. Takeyama, W. J. Gordon and R. Towse (eds.), *Developments in the Economics of Copyright: Research and Analysis* (pp. 37–59). Cheltenham, UK and Northampton, MA: Edward Elgar.

MacDonald, G. (1988) The economics of rising stars. *American Economic Review* 78: 155–166.

MacQueen, H. and Peacock, A. (1995) Implementing performing rights. *Journal of Cultural Economics* 19(2): 157–175.

Matsumoto, S. (2002) Performers in the digital era: empirical evidence from Japan. In R. Towse (ed.), *Copyright in the Cultural Industries* (pp. 196–209). Cheltenham: Edward Elgar Publishing.

Peacock, A. (1993) *Paying the Piper: Culture, Music and Money.* Edinburgh: Edinburgh University Press.

Peacock, A. and Weir, R. (1975) *The Composer in the Marketplace.* London: Faber.

Perloff, J. (1998) Droit de Suite. In *New Palgrave Dictionary of Law and Economics,* pp. 645–648. London: Macmillan.

Picard, R. (2004) (ed.) *Strategic Responses to Media Market Changes.* Jönköping: Jönköping International Business School.

Plant, A. (1934) The economic aspects of copyright in books. *Economica,* May, 1: 167–195.

Rengers, M. and Ploeg, E. (2001) Private or public? *Journal of Cultural Economics* 25(1): 1–20.

Rottenberg, S. (1975) The remuneration of artists. Reprinted in R. Towse (ed.), (1997) *Cultural Economics: The Arts, the Heritage and the Media Industries, I*, pp. 590–594.

Rushton, M. (1998) The moral rights of artists: droit moral or droit pecunaire? *Journal of Cultural Economics* 22(1): 1–13.

Rushton, M. (2001) The law and economics of artists' inalienable rights. *Journal of Cultural Economics* 25(4): 243–257.

Rushton, M. (2003) Artists' rights. In R. Towse (ed.), *A Handbook of Cultural Economics* (pp. 76–80). Cheltenham: Edward Elgar Publishing.

Santagata, W. (1995) Institutional anomalies in the contemporary art market. *Journal of Cultural Economics* 19(2): 187–197.

Scherer, F. M. (2001) The evolution of free-lance music composition, 1650–1900. *Journal of Cultural Economics* 25(4): 307–319.

Schneider, M. and Henten, A. (2005) In 'DRMS, TCP and the EUCD: technology and law'. *Telematics and Informatics* 22(1–2): 25–39.

Snow, A. and Watt, R. (2005) Risk sharing and the distribution of copyright collective income. In L. N. Takeyama, W. J. Gordon and R. Towse (eds.), *Developments in the Economics of Copyright: Research and Analysis* (pp. 23–36). Cheltenham, UK and Northampton, MA: Edward Elgar.

Solow, J. (1998) Economic analysis of *droit de suite. Journal of Cultural Economics* 22(3): 209–226.

Théberge, P. (2004) Technology, creative practice and copyright. In S. Frith and L. Marshall (eds.), *Music and Copyright,* 2nd edition (pp. 139–156). University of Edinburgh Press.

Throsby, D. (1997) Artists as workers. Reprinted in R. Towse (ed.), *Cultural Economics* (pp. 261–268). Aldershot: Edward Elgar.

Throsby, D. (2001) *Economics and Culture.* Cambridge, UK and New York: Cambridge University Press.

Towse, R. (1999) Copyright, incentives and performers' earnings. *Kyklos* 52(3): 369–390.

Towse, R. (2001a) *Creativity, Incentive and Reward.* Cheltenham, UK: Edward Elgar Publishing.

Towse, R. (2001b) Partly for the money: rewards and incentives to artists. *Kyklos* 54(2/3): 473–490.

Towse, R. (ed.) (2003) *A Handbook of Cultural Economics.* Cheltenham, UK and Northampton, MA: Edward Elgar Publishing.

Towse, R. (2004) Copyright and cultural policy for the creative industries. In O. Granstrand (ed.), *Economics, Law and Intellectual Property* (pp. 419–438). Boston/Dordrecht/London: Kluwer Academic Publishers.

Towse, R. (2005) Alan Peacock and cultural economics. *The Economic Journal* 115: F262–F276.

Towse, R. (2006) The singer or the song? Developments in performers' rights from the perspective of a cultural economist. Mimeo.

Tschmuck, P. (2002) Creativity without a copyright: music production in Vienna. In R. Towse (ed.), *Copyright in the Cultural Industries* (pp. 210–220). Cheltenham, UK: Edward Elgar Publishing.

Watt, R. (2000) *Copyright and Economic Theory: Friends or Foes?* Cheltenham, UK: Edward Elgar Publishing.

Wijnberg, N. (2003) Awards. In R. Towse (ed.), *A Handbook of Cultural Economics* (pp. 81–84). Cheltenham, UK: Edward Elgar Publishing.

6

INDIGENOUS KNOWLEDGE AND INTELLECTUAL PROPERTY: A SUSTAINABILITY AGENDA

Dora Marinova and Margaret Raven

1. Introduction

The protection of intellectual property is one of the pillars of capitalism and the market economy. Intellectual property, as a utilitarian and instrumentalist construct, guarantees private ownership over creations of the human mind while encouraging inventiveness and innovation (Carlaw *et al.*, 2006, in this issue present a historical analysis of this). A main argument in favour of establishing clear intellectual property rights is that once they are implemented, no other market interventions are needed as the market automatically assigns rewards (Batabyal and Beladi, 2001, p. 107). Human knowledge and creativity, however, span beyond the time and geographical boundaries of the Western industrial society and its globalizing market economy. There have been significant concerns, for example, as to whether patents guarantee financial benefits to the already rich and powerful parts of the world inhibiting economic progress in the less-developed areas or disadvantaged sections of society (Harry, 2001). An underlying tension associated with the use of patents, in sharing and distributing benefits, is whether they are an appropriate tool for recognizing the total value (economic, environmental, social, cultural and spiritual) of information or knowledge.

Patent protection has been extensively used in particular to guarantee returns on research and development investments in the medical and pharmaceutical industries (Brockhoff *et al.*, 1999; Kingston, 2001) making them among the most profitable worldwide (Organisation for Economic Cooperation and Development [OECD], 2001). These industries have been able to reap enormous benefits from drugs and medications, which are potentially life saving for populations affected by HIV/AIDS and other infectious diseases in Africa, Asia, South America or the poor in the West. On the other hand, these same industries have been accused of exploiting traditional knowledge about plants to produce new drugs without giving recognition or any economic benefits to the people who have developed and carried this information throughout the centuries (see, e.g. Posey and Dutfield, 1996).

Much of the debate surrounding indigenous knowledge and intellectual property rights takes place in the context of access and benefit sharing (ABS) of genetic and biological resources established through the Convention on Biological Resources. In one framework, ABS combines conservation of biological diversity and issues of equity and property rights, 'which are usually dealt with in separate disciplines and debated in distinct political institutions' (Siebenhüner *et al.*, 2005, p. 440). Although not explicitly stated, the discourse of ABS is an attempt to give value to genetic and biological resources, and indigenous knowledge in ways that are consistent with the requirements of sustainability. It is in this context that issues surrounding the adequacy of current intellectual property systems and laws in protecting indigenous knowledge are questioned.

The concept of 'sustainability' has been associated with a wide range of human activities related to the use of resources, including natural, human and financial, implying long-term continuity and ability to carry on with these activities indefinitely. Since the mid-1970s, however, the term became laden with value judgements about justice in the distribution and use of resources. This was started by the World Council of Churches during its 1975 Assembly in Nairobi (Cobb, 1992), followed by the publication of Our Common Future (or the Brundtland Report) by the World Commission on Environment and Development (WCED) in 1987, the 1992 United Nations' Earth Summit in Rio de Janeiro (which adopted Agenda 21) and continued through the adoption of the Millennium Development Goals by the United Nations' General Assembly in 2000 and the 2002 World Summit in Johannesburg. As early as in 1992, Pezzey (1992) published dozens of definitions of the term, including the most widely cited Brundtland definition: 'Sustainable development is development that meets the needs of the present without compromising the ability of future generations to meet their own needs' (WCED, 1987, p. 43). Several years later Jacobs (1999) accepted that the concept would remain contested and politically fluid because of the different stances taken in relation to what can be considered 'fair'. The Western Australian State Sustainability Strategy states: 'sustainability is defined as meeting the needs of current and future generations through an integration of environmental protection, social advancement, and economic prosperity' (Newman and Rowe, 2003, p. 24), and this is the definition adopted in the analysis to follow. The Strategy's website (http://www.sustainability.dpc.wa.gov.au/docs/CaseStudies.htm) also includes 53 case studies which cover examples of activities that aim at bringing this State closer to sustainability. Anand and Sen (2000) claim that sustainability is analogous to the concept of usufruct rights (i.e. the right to use another's property without changing its substance) extended beyond the economic realm to cover social and environmental aspects of human activities. This latter explanation is also of particular interest as it provides valuable insights into the use of indigenous knowledge.

The paper argues that the current intellectual property system and its underlying assumptions are limited in scope in their application to indigenous knowledge. First, indigenous knowledge has developed independently and outside the notion of private ownership – it is holistic and community-owned, which is at odds with the spirit and provisions of the patent legislation; and second, other forms of management, governance and rights regimes, for protecting indigenous intellectual property, exist that guarantee similar and sustainable returns to the people who own this knowledge.

The structure of the remaining of the paper is as follows. First, it examines the notion of indigenous knowledge and its intrinsic characteristics. Then, it analyzes how the two main provisions of patenting, namely, recognition of authorship and protection of economic benefits have (not) been applied in the case of indigenous knowledge. This leads to a discussion of a possible alternative way of protection of intellectual property based around the approach of the Western Australian company Mt Romance. Finally, the paper concludes with policy recommendations within a sustainability framework.

2. Indigenous Knowledge

Indigenous peoples are broadly defined as 'peoples in independent countries who are regarded as indigenous on account of their descent from the populations which inhabited the country, or a geographical region to which the country belongs, at the time of conquest or colonization or the establishment of present state boundaries and who, irrespective of their legal status, retain some or all of their social, economic, cultural and political institutions' (Caslon Analytics, 2005).

Two aspects of the above definition deserve particular attention. First, the term 'indigenous people' is used in the context of colonization where colonial history 'has left a predominant national culture and autochthonous cultures that coexist and compete for limited resources, especially land' (Brush and Stabinsky, 1996, p. 5). Hence, it is used mainly in the context of imposed Western presence on the land under the modern nation states, and consequently is inappropriate for places such as Africa or Asia 'where a single hybrid or creole culture is not dominant' (Brush and Stabinsky, 1996, p. 5). Second, the last part of this definition stresses the retention of social institutions within indigenous societies, which often means that the new institutions on the lands of indigenous peoples cannot serve the same purpose. In the case of the patent system, this legal institution imposed by the West is not only in conflict with the traditional values within indigenous societies, it can also reflect a conception and practice that are colonialist, racist and usurpatory (Coordinating Body for the Indigenous Organisations of the Amazon Basin [COICA], 1995). An extreme example of this is the US patent issued in 1995 when the genetic material of an indigenous person from Papua New Guinea was claimed as part of the US Human Genome Diversity project (http://www.cptech.org/ip/dna.txt, accessed 21 December 2005). A major aspect of the legacy of colonial domination is the expropriation of resources without due compensation or attribution (Brush and Stabinsky, 1996).

Specifically in Australia, the term 'indigenous' is used to link the politico-religious, social, environmental and economic challenges faced by Aboriginal and Torres Strait Islander peoples to indigenous peoples around the world. Against the national governance structures (see, e.g., Meyers and Malcolm, 2002; Nettheim *et al.*, 2002), it is an attempt to create an international agenda through the connection to international institutions such as the World Trade Organization (WTO), World Intellectual Property Organization (WIPO) and the UN Convention on Biological

Diversity (CBD). Other terms also used to describe indigenousness are 'native' and 'traditional'.

Indigenous knowledge is often referred to as traditional knowledge and 'encompasses the content or substance of traditional know-how, innovations, information, practices, skills and learning of traditional knowledge systems such as traditional agricultural, environmental or medicinal knowledge' (World Intellectual Property Organization [WIPO], 2005, p. 4). It can also be expressed in folklore, such as songs, chants, dances, narratives, motifs and designs. According to a WIPO–UNEP report (Gupta, 2002, p. 11), some indigenous knowledge 'may be kept confidential to the originator(s) and their descendants and may be accessed only with restrictions, some may be disseminated locally, but may nonetheless, be restricted in scope or in terms of accessibility, and some of this knowledge may be shared widely within the community and with outsiders'. Because of the wide definition of indigenous knowledge, which is an attempt to define cultural forms and processes, the protection of intangible property extends throughout the intellectual property framework and encompasses copyright law, plant breeders' rights, patent law, geographic indicators and trademark law.

The focus of the analysis to follow, and specifically the case study, is on ABS knowledge and materials related to plants; therefore, this paper concerns itself mainly with patents. Brush and Stabinsky (1996) distinguish between: (1) crop germplasm and farmer knowledge of domesticated plants which have developed during the millennia in connection to human selection; and (2) natural products derived from wild plants and knowledge about the plants and products. Utility patents are increasingly being used in the USA, the world's largest and technologically most advanced market (Marinova, 2000), to protect intellectual knowledge related to crop plants, particularly biotechnologically and genetically manipulated. Another booming area of patenting is the myriads of plant-based compounds, substances, composures, mixtures and so on. There is not, however, a mechanism to protect the wild plants per se (Brush and Stabinsky, 1996) leaving indigenous knowledge associated with these plants open to the good (or bad) will of individuals, organizations and the community. Moreover, a major aspect of the traditional in indigenous knowledge is the communal and intergenerational ownership which contradicts the notion of exclusive individual use espoused by patent laws and encouraged by the entrepreneurial West.

Before continuing, a distinction needs to be made between 'indigenous knowledge' and 'indigenous intellectual property'. There is a tendency in the discourse of protection of indigenous knowledge to refer to indigenous knowledge as indigenous intellectual property. The conceptualization of indigenous knowledge as indigenous intellectual property has both benefits and costs for indigenous and non-indigenous communities, individuals and organizations. The use of the term 'indigenous knowledge' or 'indigenous intellectual property', or any other term, is ultimately the choice of the owners of this knowledge according to indigenous customary law and wider social–political–economic–environmental agendas. However, it seems necessary to outline some of the costs and benefits associated with the choice between the terms.

Referring to indigenous knowledge as indigenous intellectual property creates benefits by situating the debate about protection of indigenous rights to knowledge firmly within the realm of intellectual property (IP) and the measures that this discourse offers. As intellectual property, indigenous knowledge is also seen as a legitimate form of IP that can be more readily conceptualized as a form of capital, which legal, economic and market-based mechanisms are more capable of handling. It also situates indigenous knowledge in a place that provides mechanisms for creating market-based values. Such an approach may provide the necessary scope for the development of systems that adequately and accurately value indigenous knowledge in innovation and development projects; and thus provide the equity (understood as fairness, balance and opportunity) necessary for some indigenous communities and individuals to create wealth. Economic and legal recognition of the value of indigenous knowledge in the creation of wealth, through innovation, may be all that is necessary for some indigenous communities and individuals to break the cycles of poverty institutionalized through colonialism.

Costs associated with the use of the term 'indigenous intellectual property' is that it defines indigenous knowledge in terms of the 'utility' perceived through market-based approaches. It is limited in scope for recognizing utility, which is not economic or does not have a market, such as social, cultural or spiritual.

It is possible to capitalize indigenous knowledge but in many instances, this capitalization does not fit into the WIPO definition needed in order to fulfil the requirements of patent law as defined through WIPO. Indigenous knowledge is often defined as holistic and impossible to fragmentize to fit the requirements for novelty, practicality, originality and non-obviousness under the patent law. In the case of Aboriginal knowledge, Blakeney (1999) writes that it is intimately connected to Dreamings, ceremonies, sacred sites and objects. In its wholeness, it is inseparable from spiritual values, beliefs and the notion of country. Maintaining indigenous knowledge requires maintaining the social and physical environment that has created it (WIPO, 2005), which the current intellectual property framework has been unable to achieve.

Even if it were possible to fragmentize and capitalize indigenous knowledge, would it be desirable? The notion of 'holistic' does seem to provide some kind of basic understanding of the collective systems of ownership and governance of indigenous knowledge; however, some indigenous knowledge is also individually 'owned' or for which individuals have special totemic connections, and thus have more knowledge of and responsibility for. This increases the complexity of the issues even further and far beyond the scope of the patent law.

3. Sustainability Framework

The best way to approach issues related to indigenous knowledge is from a holistic long-term perspective that also allows for diversity and differences in values. First, the patent law fails to achieve this because it recognizes only economic or commercial value and does not cover non-market purely spiritual, cultural, environmental, social or political values; and second, because the protection offered is only for a limited period of time, for example, 17 years – the duration of the issued patent under the US 20-year patent term (the remaining 3 years are on average the period of patent pending before approval); which is quite short from the point of view of protecting indigenous knowledge. In other words, an approach is needed that can provide a systematic all-encompassing framework that crosses the boundaries of institutions, regulations, research disciplines and tradition.

The sustainability concept is a valuable conceptual framework in this respect as it acknowledges the integrated importance of social, environmental and economic issues as well as the importance of relationships and partnerships to achieve this. Sustainability is not outside of economic theorizing; however, it gives value to genetic and biological resources (as already pointed out in the introduction in relation to ABS), and indigenous knowledge for what it represents, for how it is constructed and conserved.

Indigenous sustainability, in particular, as a new movement in the field of sustainability (Kinnane, 2002), is concerned with addressing the disadvantages experienced by indigenous people in all aspects of society. Under a sustainability framework, there is also a role for customary law in recognizing value and giving value to indigenous knowledge. A new intellectual property protection should allow for maintaining the social, political, cultural and physical environment where indigenous knowledge is created. According to McGrath *et al.* (2005), 'indigenous people, whose spiritual practices connect with country and have the potential to provide a foundational ethic for sustainability generally have much to offer the Eurocentric rationalists who have separated themselves from ecological cycles between the earth, air and water and are thus disconnected from the spiritual self'. This 'offering' comes with certain obligations established through customary law that are also recognized through Western legal regimes. Example of the latter is fiduciary, the legal term used to describe the relationships between a person who occupies a particular position of trust, power or responsibility with respect to the rights, property or interests of another trustee or the community (Wikipedia, 2005). Such relationships of trust are essential in partnerships, which are an important mechanism for achieving a more sustainable development and way of living.

The 'one size fits all' models for protecting intellectual property do not work within the sustainability concept. On the contrary, sustainability requires respect for local knowledge and practices, and argues for diversity to be allowed to flourish. Although the Western legal system recognizes *sui generis* rights as 'a legal classification that exists independently of other categorizations because of its uniqueness or due to the specific creation of an entitlement or obligation' (Wikipedia, 2005), there is a need for alternatives that cater synergistically for economic, social and environmental considerations and reflect the values of sustainability.

Alternative approaches to indigenous knowledge and indigenous sustainability ought to allow among others for caring for country, for preservation of languages programmes, for improved health and living standards, for political representation and participation. In other words, they need to support a people–culture–country continuum, and not treat indigenous knowledge as something that sits in isolation from reality.

However, before we discuss such alternatives, let us examine in more detail the functions of patent laws in relation to indigenous knowledge.

4. The Current Patent Law Approach

The issue of a patent (as a subset of the protection of intellectual property) confers the patentee 'the right to exclude others from making, using, offering for sale, or selling the invention throughout the United States or importing the invention into the United States' (United States Patent and Trademark Office [US PTO], 2005) or any other territory covered by the patent law. Although the exact role of a patent is the 'right to exclude', in reality patents have a twofold role: first, they recognize ingenuity; and second, they allow for a monopoly over economic benefits. These two functions are potentially equally applicable to indigenous knowledge, that is, it results from ingenuity and creativity, and should generate economic benefits; however, the current system for intellectual property protection has failed to deliver on both accounts. The use of patents in achieving ABS in biodiversity conservation, in particular, was addressed by some authors in a recent special edition of the journal *Ecological Economics* (see Siebenhüner *et al.*, 2005). Some further analysis and discussion are presented below.

4.1 *Recognition*

There is a lot of controversy in relation to how traditional knowledge has been exploited by multinational companies. Zerda-Sarmiento and Forero-Pineda (2002, p. 103) talk about biopiracy – the non-consensual extraction of traditional knowledge, biological resources and/or proprietary rights, converting them into one's own 'inventions' and not sharing the benefits. Blakeney (1999) draws attention to the use of native plants and the traditional medical knowledge of indigenous peoples in identifying biological resources for commercial exploitation, including establishment of genetic banks. Khor (2003) claims that patenting is leading to an even greater concentration in a few global corporations of control over the world's food crops such as maize, potato, soybean and wheat, giving them enormous unsustainable economic power.

Indigenous knowledge has barely received official recognition in registered patents (or inventions). Some even argue that it can hardly contribute to technological advance (Granstand, 2004, p. 505). A keyword search with 'indigenous knowledge' of patent texts (claims, abstracts, titles and descriptions) at the world's largest patenting institution, namely the US Patent and Trademark Office (US PTO) generates 0 hits between 1976 and 2004. This is not surprising. Given the prominence on the application of the public domain to indigenous knowledge, as something that has been disclosed and available in the public domain for longer than

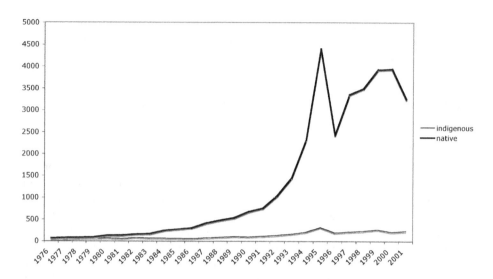

Figure 1. US Patents Related to Indigenous Topics and Native Species.
Notes: 1. The patent numbers are by date of patent application (as distinct from date of patent issue).
2. The data were extracted from the US PTO on-line database http://patft.uspto. gov/netahtml/search-adv.htm on 10 September 2005.

1 year, without been patented during this time, cannot be patented. Consequently, the patent system cannot provide any recognition to the owners of indigenous knowledge for their creativity or ingenuity. If used, indigenous knowledge has been hidden or developed further under 'scientific' terms making it unrecognizable and alienated from the place where it originated.

For example, keyword searches for patent descriptions incorporating words such as 'indigenous' or 'Aboriginal' generate some, be it a very small number of hits – a total of 3,508 or 0.1% of all patents registered at the US PTO during 1976–2004 (see also Figures 1 and 2). A further search on the use of native species in the wording of patent attributes results in a total of 36,584 or 1.2% of all patents during the same period. Although the information provided in patent documents does not allow to estimate how much of the knowledge about these native species (plants, insects or animals) was newly discovered in scientific labs and how much was the contribution of native knowledge (held by or derived from indigenous people), there is a clear logical connection between the two. Case studies of particular patents related to the use of native species such as, for example, the neem tree, the turmeric herb (discussed below) or the medicinal kirar, habul, ber, almatash and dhok bushes in India, show that the scientific and technical interest of inventors was backed up by publicly available indigenous knowledge.

It is also quite interesting that the late 1980s and the 1990s was the time when the world witnessed the greatest expansion in the scope of intellectual property rights (Maskus, 2000). This is also demonstrated in the number of successful US

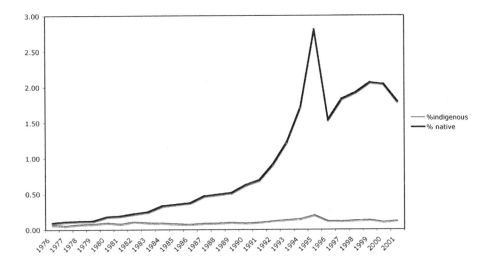

Figure 2. Shares (%) of US Patents Related to Indigenous Topics and Native Species.
Notes: 1. The patent numbers are by date of patent application (as distinct from date of patent issue).
2. The data were extracted from the US PTO on-line database http://patft.uspto.gov/netahtml/search-adv.htm on 10 September 2005.

patent applications related to native species (see Figure 1). Starting from very low numbers in the 1970s, the number of these patents surged in the 1980s to reach an all time high peak in mid 1990s. Another very important observation is that the rise was not only in absolute numbers, it was also equally pronounced in the relative shares of patents related to native species compared to all patents issued in the USA (see Figure 2). The year 1995 was a big peak with 4,407 successful patent applications lodged which translated to a high 2.8% of all US patents. The consequent relative drop in 1996 and relatively lower levels since are most likely due to the 1995 'draining' of the pool of technical knowledge. However, later on, the patents issued on the base of 1999 and 2000 applications, 3,929 (or 2.06%) and 3,944 (or 2.04%) respectively, were an all over high for two consecutive years confirming that the interest in native species continued strongly.

Let us take, for example, the neem tree. Its properties are mentioned in Indian texts written more than 2,000 years ago (Schuler, 2004). The US PTO has issued 255 patents (including to Australian inventors and companies) since 1976 for insect repellents, disinfectants, fungicides, gels and treatments of wrinkles, control of crawling insects, treatment of asthma and wood preservatives, to mention a few, based on the properties of the neem tree. Although 37 of these patents have been lodged by individual Indian inventors (with 32 assigned to Indian companies and organizations), the commercial benefits to the Indian farmers who have used extracts from the neem seeds for generations are only secondary, driven by the increased demand for (and consequently price of) neem seeds.

Similarly, the anti-oxidant, anti-inflammatory, anti-bacterial, anti-fungal proper-ties and other health benefits of the yellow spice turmeric used extensively in traditional Indian cooking have been known for centuries. The number of US patents issued on the basis of the scientifically and technologically proven properties of turmeric since 1976 is 580, and only two of them are to Indian inventors. The patents cover medical uses, such as treatment and prevention of skin disorders, osteoarthritis, rheumatoid arthritis and improved joint function; cooking products, such as coloured and flavoured frozen French fries, frozen dessert novelties and food additives; and other products, such as paints, disposable cloth wash, carpet yarn treatment to increase repellence. Again, there is only some economic benefit for Indian farmers derived from the increased demand for the large-leaved herb.

It is clear from the above examples that the patent system is not geared towards recognizing the indigenous peoples' knowledge held collectively within the community. While the USA has been providing patent protection to individual inventors for more than two centuries (namely, since 1790), it was only in the 1990s when the UN Commission on Human Rights' major study on the protection of indigenous intellectual property opened for the first time the debate about the use and recognition of indigenous knowledge. This coincided with the time of sharp increase in the number of patents based on native species, which provided no recognition for indigenous knowledge.

4.2 *Economic Benefits*

As patents provide exclusive use of the registered inventions, economic benefits are the major drive behind patenting (see e.g. Freeman, 1982 or Rosegger, 1996). These are collected through a myriad of different mechanisms and arrangements, including profits from a temporary guaranteed market monopoly, royalty payments through licensing, income from patent sales or royalties from patent infringements. Patent pooling arrangements are also common; for example in 1998, Sony, Pioneer and Philips made a three licensors agreement for DVD ROM and DVD-Video formats (Clark *et al.*, 2000). Economic benefits from patents can be very difficult to track down and separate from other business activities, and generalized data are difficult to obtain.

The importance of economic benefits from protected intellectual property is particularly voiced within today's globalized world where countries such as China, Taiwan, Indonesia, Brazil or the former Eastern Europe, are often accused of breaching patent and copyright laws. The WTO estimates that if developing countries were to pay their intellectual property royalties, this would generate about US$60 billion per year going towards the coffers of the developed world (Finger, 2002). The infringement of patent laws is considered unethical; however, the grounds for this are purely economic. It is interesting to note that a lot of this ethical/economic criticism comes from the USA, which according to Plasencia (1999) was 'a major intellectual property pirate' (p. 288) for half of its existence. This was also the time when it developed its economic prowess.

The aim of the WTO's Agreement on Trade-Related Aspects of Intellectual Property Rights (TRIPS) negotiated during the 1986–1994 Uruguay Round was to narrow the gaps between laws that govern intellectual property in various parts of the world, aligning them with the Western model, which is believed to encourage technical innovation and economic development. The TRIPS Agreement obliges member countries to enforce revenue collection mechanisms for the use of protected intellectual property. According to Finger (2002, pp. 13–14), 'More simply, it has the effect of creating claims by intellectual property owners against intellectual property users. As developing countries are more often users than vendors of intellectual property, the impact is a significant economic obligation on developing countries – users owe royalties, copyright fees, etc. on the use of knowledge not previously protected in their countries by patents, copyrights, etc.' The 2001 Doha Round under the WTO negotiations was characterized with the willingness to assist developing countries and generously allow for special and differential treatment. Interestingly enough however, there are still no agreement or negotiations as to using indigenous knowledge about plants, animals, other living species, organic and non-organic materials that would allow for the enforcement of the reversed revenue collection mechanisms, as the examples of the neem tree and turmeric show. The behaviour of individuals, companies and countries that expropriate such economic benefits can be seen as rent-seeking if indigenous knowledge is assumed to constitute a public good, or even worse, as free-riders, if indigenous knowledge is seen as indigenous property. Rent-seeking behaviour can also be associated with trademarks (see the paper by Ramello (2006) in this issue) or places of origin, but the need for a change is even greater when the rent-seeking or free-riding is done on the backs of the most unprivileged and disadvantaged parts of humanity.

Following Finger (2004), the issue about indigenous knowledge, however, is how to help these (poor) people benefit commercially using modern methods from their traditional wisdom. In collaboration with another partner and in combination with scientific knowledge and methods, it may be possible for indigenous peoples to use patents to secure some rights over their knowledge, while gaining economic benefits. In this instance, market-driven economic benefits can be derived by those individuals and communities that have the capacity, ability and desire to both divulge their knowledge and to negotiate with other partners to create market-based economic values. Indigenous knowledge then becomes background intellectual property, and through this process enters into the public domain, a route not without political, ethical and moral implications. However, through the formation of 'new' intellectual property, indigenous peoples can, albeit for a limited time, gain some recognition of their rights to knowledge, while creating opportunities for market-based value of their knowledge, and thus economic stability.

The majority of examples provided by Finger and Schuler (2004) demonstrate how indigenous people can successfully fight against the exploitation of their knowledge in newly issued patents and 'fit' within the existing intellectual property system in order to gain economic outcomes. Although this may be one way of adjusting, it implies superiority of the current institutional and social arrangements with little respect for traditional cultures. It also does not address concerns about reconciling economic rewards and moral obligations (the papers by Towse (2006) and Verspagen (2006) in this issue talk, respectively, about similar disparities in the areas of copyright and creative artists, and patents and publicly funded university research). Most important, it does not serve the tradition of community ownership and responsibility for nature that exists in most indigenous cultures.

5. Alternative Approaches

Are there any alternatives to the widely accepted and fast globalizing intellectual protection laws? Is there a way of dealing with intellectual property that could provide recognition and economic rewards outside the WIPO and WTO laws? The paper by Liebowitz and Watt (2006) in this issue poses similar questions in the case of digital technologies and copyright in music. However, the proposed alternatives there are aimed again to generate only economic benefits in a well-defined market-based world; while the area of indigenous knowledge is much more complex. Any alternatives need to be holistic in order to provide economic as well as social and environmental benefits.

There seems to be a subconscious belief that ABS as part of the Convention on Biological Diversity may be a useful way for conservation of indigenous knowledge. It may be a better mechanism with positive intentions, but there are at least two considerations which demonstrate its challenges in relation to indigenous knowledge: (1) 'protection' seems to be the only concept used when reference is made to indigenous knowledge; and (2) particularly in the context of Australia, given the wide distribution of some plant species (e.g. Acacia aneura), the same knowledge may be spatially distributed across a large geographical area making its protection even more complex. Nevertheless, it encourages the usage of best practices and case studies as to how this access to genetic resources and benefit sharing can be done.

Below are several case studies that help demonstrate such alternative approaches.

5.1 *The Mt Romance Case Study*

Early in 2005, *The Guardian* wrote:

> You've probably given some thought to what your face cream is doing to your skin – but do you ever think about where the ingredients come from? Over-harvesting of rare plants, use of non-sustainable petrochemicals (mineral oil, petroleum), destruction of rainforests and ecosystems, patenting of native plants, and the pilfering of indigenous people's knowledge of flora and fauna without financial recompense are all things our bathroom cabinet conceal. (Hancock, 2005, p. 43)

What followed after that was a report on the groundbreaking indigenous plant accreditation protocol of the Songman Circle of Wisdom in partnership with the

USA-based multinational cosmetics company Aveda Corporation and the exporter of Australian sandalwood oil Mt Romance. This world's first event of global importance was launched in November 2004 at Murdoch University in Perth, Western Australia. According to this protocol, both Aveda and Mt Romance donate $50,000 each to the Kutkabubba Aboriginal community for sourcing their products from Australia using the land and knowledge of the indigenous people. The money is then used by the community with no strings attached. The partnership under the accreditation protocol provides a new approach to protecting indigenous knowledge, which is vastly different from the patenting law. Although as at 15 September 2005, there were 1,371 sandalwood patents issued by the US PTO between 1976 and 2005, none of them relates to the indigenous knowledge or usage by Aveda, Mt Romance or the Kutkabubba community. The indigenous accreditation is a voluntary undertaking under a sustainability framework that allows for a holistic approach to indigenous knowledge. In a way, it is similar to environmental management systems accreditation under ISO 14001 (see e.g. Marinova and Altham, 2002), which represents a voluntary recognition of the importance for business operations of sustaining the natural environment. Sustaining indigenous communities where indigenous knowledge is created is equally important and can be achieved by working in partnerships.

The way Dr. Richard Walley, the Songman Circle of Wisdom's Convenor, describes the accreditation is

> When we go into these partnerships, we don't go with weakness saying, 'Please, Mr Aveda' or 'Please, Mr Consumer – help us', . . . We go in saying, 'We are a strong group of people who've got a philosophy. We know this culture, we know this land, we can help you – not you help us. We can help you. (Hancock, 2005, p. 43)

An important component of the partnership are the changing attitudes of the business community. The driver in this case was Mt Romance, a company which almost went into liquidation in 1997 following the meltdown of the Asian import market where it was originally sourcing its products (Morgan, 2004). Having to sell off the family farm and experiencing the difficulties of finding creditors, the company founders Steve and Karen Birbeck created a small range of emu oil cosmetics to be sold at local markets and also turned to industrial tourism. Looking for long-term sustainability for his business, Steve discovered the pure Australian sandalwood oil as a niche market but approached it with respect and responsibility to the culture and land of the indigenous people (Austrade, 2005):

> I discovered the tangible link tribal people had with the indigenous plants and perfumes when I lived with Aboriginals for 10 years in the Western Desert. . . . Mt Romance has drawn on input from these important elders in the discovery and commercial development of the natural ingredients sourced from Western Australia.

Although Mt Romance recently was sold to the Melbourne-based company Holistic Products, the indigenous accreditation protocol remains.

The third partner in the partnership, Aveda, is also renowned for its good environmental image and sustainable business practices. The company is committed to building sustainable business partnerships with indigenous people worldwide in the sourcing of its plant-derived ingredients. According to the company's president Dominique Conseil (Aveda, 2005):

> At Aveda, we believe in beauty with a purpose . . . Our ingredients must be not only high-quality, but high-integrity. We are dedicated to changing the way the world does business.

The relationship established between Mt Romance, Aveda and Kutkabubba Aboriginal community, through the protocol and through ongoing negotiations, raises a number of challenges; not necessarily unique to itself. For instance, how does one interpret the $50,000? In another reading, it could be seen as a welfare handout. From a perspective heavily invested in international standards, critique could be levelled at seeming to lack an adequate framework for access and benefit sharing. These agreements may be helpful in initially side-stepping challenges associated with rewarding and recognizing existing intellectual property, and giving it a financial value. However, how is this value determined, and what percentage of this value should go to indigenous communities? Another issue includes the rewarding of any new intellectual property.

The most important point in this case study, however, is that a new value system is required for a change towards sustainability where the integration of economics, environment, culture, spirituality and society can occur simultaneously and in a balanced way. The pursuit of economic-only benefits as the underlying motivation behind the patenting law not only creates disparities and unsurmountable tensions but also destroys the foundations of life on Earth.

5.2 *Other Examples*

Although first by its nature, the formal partnership between Mt Romance, Aveda and the Kutkabubba community is not unique by its intention. It is an implementation of ethical values and ideas that have been endorsed by other companies with high moral standards and respect for indigenous knowledge.

Another example is Shaman Pharmaceuticals – a small San Francisco-based pharmaceutical company established in 1989 with the intention to use the medical knowledge of the shamans (indigenous healers) to develop medical drugs and treatments and adequately financially compensate them for this. Its focus was particularly on tropical rainforests (Bierer *et al.*, 1996), and by 2000, it employed 14 people and contributed 15% of its costs to community projects in Peru, Papua New Guinea, Brazil, Ecuador and Indonesia. Shaman Pharmaceuticals, however, went into bankruptcy in 2001 giving up to the fierce competition from the larger players and high risks in the pharmaceutical field. Some commentators (Clapp and Crook, 2002) claim that nevertheless this was a positive story as the company has been much more successful than major firms such as Merck & Company or Searle & Company in screening plant extracts for medically useful compounds due to the use of indigenous knowledge. Its demise is attributed more to its management and its inability to simultaneously maintain the triple bottom line than to the failure of the company's vision.

The Desert Knowledge Protocol currently being developed in Australia is another innovative approach to indigenous knowledge. It is coordinated by Desert Knowledge Australia (http://www.desertknowledge.com.au/), which is a networking institution established in 2000 as a consortium of desert Australian industry, Aboriginal organizations, government and non-government parties that aims at creating sustainable opportunities in desert Australia though gathering, sharing, developing and marketing the indigenous knowledge of desert people. A major player in Desert Knowledge Australia is the Desert Knowledge Cooperative Research Centre established in 2003, which is a joint venture with 15 partners and 13 associate partners for research related to the desert. It hosts several research projects that explore issues related to the development of Aboriginal community protocols and a research code of ethics in consultation with central Australian Aboriginal communities. It is expected these that protocols, including contracts and agreements, will provide recognition, protection and utilization of indigenous knowledge that encourage innovations and sustainable practices for Aboriginal communities. Although the Protocol is still being developed, building partnerships is the main strategy adopted by Desert Knowledge towards achieving sustainability in the desert lands of Australia.

The usufruct rights of indigenous people in Brazil, for example, are protected by the country's Federal Constitution and such a legal environment is potentially much more encouraging to partnerships similar to the ones demonstrated in the above case studies. Western countries, including Australia, are yet to provide this.

6. Conclusion

The inadequacy of the current intellectual property laws is well documented. Shiva (2000) describes the patenting of indigenous knowledge as double theft – first, big companies acquire ownership over something that does not belong to them; and second, the established patent rights prevent indigenous people from exploiting the economic opportunities linked to this indigenous knowledge.

There is very little in the current patent laws that could have prevented Mt Romance (and consequently Aveda) as well as Shaman Pharmaceuticals or any research organization to use the same approach and reap economic benefits comparable to the world richest pharmaceutical or for that matter any 'top ranking' businesses. What has made the change is the sustainability value system existing in these organizations, which has driven the search for an alternative approach. Economic recognition of the indigenous contribution is an important aspect of the sustainability triad that can help synergistically social and environmental sustainability.

The (paternalistic) encouragement of indigenous people to learn and use the 'advantages' of the current patenting systems is not an appropriate policy. There should be policies in place to insure that alternative approaches, such as indigenous partnerships with commercial companies, are applied to prevent the theft and exploitation of indigenous intellectual property as well as deliver sustainable benefits to its traditional owners. Siebenhüner *et al.* (2005), for example, state that the proper implementation of the Convention on Biological Diversity requires new intellectual property rights and new regimes that challenge the existing legal doctrines because of the complex interactions with pre-existing cultural frameworks. Conserving the diversity of cultural knowledge of indigenous peoples is even harder as the only way to keep it alive is to keep it in use (Brush and Stabinsky, 1996) and to maintain in a sustainable way the environment that creates it.

Acknowledgements

The first author acknowledges the financial support of the Australian Research Council; and both authors are grateful to all indigenous peoples around the world for their wisdom and care for the planet Earth.

References

Anand, S. and Sen, A. (2000) Human development and economic sustainability. *World Development* 28(12): 2029–2049.
Austrade (2005) Export makes scents for Mount Romance. *Trademark.* Australian Government, www.austrade.gov.au/corporate/layout/0,,0_S1-1_1z1c-2_-3_PWB110520482-4_-5_-6_-7_,00.html, accessed 15 September 2005.
Aveda (2005) Taking care of business: a dialogue on environmentally balanced economics. aveda.aveda.com/about/press/wharton˙conference.asp, accessed 15 September 2005.
Batabyal, A. A. and Beladi, H. (2001) *The Economics of International Trade and the Environment.* Boca Raton, FL: CRC Press.
Bierer, D. E., Carlson, T. J. and King, S. R. (1996) Shaman Pharmaceuticals: integrating indigenous knowledge, tropical medicinal plants, medicine, modern science and reciprocity into a novel drug discovery approach. Network Science. http://www.netsci.org/Science/Special/feature11.html, accessed 20 December 2005.
Blakeney, M. (1999) Intellectual property in the dreamtime – protecting the cultural creativity of indigenous peoples, WP 11/99. *OIPRC Electronic Journal of Intellectual Property Rights*, www.oiprc.ox.ac.uk/EJWP1199.html, accessed 12 September 2005.
Brockhoff, K. K., Ernst, H. and Hundhausen, E. (1999) Gains and pains from licensing – patent-portfolios as strategic weapons in the cardiac rhythm management industry. *Technovation* 19: 605–614.
Brush, S. B. and Stabinsky, D. (eds.) (1996) Valuing Local Knowledge: Indigenous People and Intellectual Property Rights. Washington, DC: Centre for Resource Economics, Island Press.
Carlaw, K., Oxley, L., Walker, P., Thorns, D. and Nuth, M. (2006) Beyond the hype. Intellectual property and the knowledge society/knowledge economy. *Journal of Economic Surveys* 20: 633–690.
Caslon Analytics (2005) Intellectual property guide. www.caslon.com.au/ipguide13.htm, accessed 12 September 2005.
Clapp, R. A. and Crook, C. (2002) Drowning in the magic well: Shaman Pharmaceuticals and the elusive value of traditional knowledge. *Journal of Environment & Development* 11(1): 79–102.

Clark, J., Piccolo, J., Stanton, B. and Tyson, K. (2000) Patent pools: a solution to the problem of access in biotechnology patents? Alexandria: United States Patent and Trademark Office.

Cobb, J. B. (1992) *Sustainability: Economics, Ecology, and Justice*. Maryknoll, NY: Orbis.

Coordinating Body for the Indigenous Organisations of the Amazon Basin (COICA) (1994) Statement of the regional meeting on intellectual property rights and biodiversity, also in D. A. Posey and G. Dutfield (eds), *Beyond Intellectual Property: Toward Traditional Resource Rights for Indiquenous Peoples and Local Communities*. Ottawa, Canada: IRDC Books. Appendix 9.

Freeman, C. (1982) *The Economics of Industrial Innovation*, 2nd edition. London: Frances Pinter.

Finger, J. M. (2002) The Doha agenda and development; A view from the Uruguay round. Manila: Asian Development Bank. www.adb.org/Economics/pdf/doha/Finger_paper.pdf, accessed 15 September 2005.

Finger, J. M. (2004) Introduction and overview. In J. M. Finger and P. Schuler (eds), *Poor People's Knowledge: Promoting Intellectual Property in Developing Countries* (pp. 1–36). Washington, DC: World Bank and Oxford University Press.

Finger, J. M. and Schuler, P. (eds) (2004) *Poor People's Knowledge: Promoting Intellectual Property in Developing Countries*. Washington, DC: World Bank and Oxford University Press.

Granstand, O. (ed.) (2004) *Economics, Law and Intellectual Property: Seeking Strategies for Research and Teaching in a Developing World*. Dordrecht, The Netherlands: Kluwer Academic Publishers.

Gupta, A. K. (2002) *WIPO-UNEP Study on the Role of Intellectual Property Rights in the Sharing of Benefits Arising from the Use of Biological Resources and Associated Traditional Knowledge*. Ahmedabad, India: WIPO/UNEP.

Hancock, L. (2005) Beating beauty's ugly side: on the ethics of cosmetics. *The Guardian*. (UK) 8 January, 43.

Harry, D. (2001) Biopiracy and globalisation: indigenous peoples face a new wave of colonialism. *Splice* 7(2&3): www.ipcb.org/publications/other_art/globalization.html, accessed 20 December 2005.

Jacobs, M. (1999) Sustainable development as a contested concept. In A. P. Dobson (ed.), *Fairness and Futurity* (pp. 21–45). Oxford: Oxford University Press.

Khor, M. (2003) IPRs, biodiversity, and the theft of indigenous knowledge. *Interdisciplinary Science Reviews* 28(1): 7–10.

Kingston, W. (2001) Innovation needs patent reform. *Research Policy* 30: 403–423.

Kinnane, S. (2002) Recurring visions of Australindia. In A. Gaynor, M. Trinca and A. Haebich (eds), *Country: Visions of Land and People in Western Australia* (pp. 21–31). Perth, WA: Museum of Western Australia and the Centre for Studies in Western Australian History, University of Western Australia.

Liebowitz, S. J. and Watt, R. (2006) How to best ensure remuneration for creators in the market for music? Copyright and its alternatives. *Journal of Economic Surveys* 20: 513–545.

Marinova, D. (2000) Eastern European patenting activities in the USA. *Technovation* 21(9): 571–584.

Marinova, D. and Altham, W. (2002) Environmental management systems and adoption of new technology. In A. Jamison and H. Rohracher (eds), *Technology Studies and Sustainable Development* (pp. 199–220). München: Profil.

Maskus, K. E. (2000) *Intellectual Property Rights in the Global Economy*. Washington, DC: Institute for International Economics.

McGrath, N., Marinova, D. and Flatau, P. (2005) Institutionalising a participatory culture for indigenous sustainability in Western Australia. In D. Gardiner and K. Scott (eds), *Proceedings of the International Conference on Engaging Communities*. Brisbane, Australia: Queensland Department of Main

Roads. http://www.engagingcommunities2005.org/abstracts/Marinova-Dora-final.pdf, accessed 8 July 2006.

Meyers, G. D. and Malcolm, R. (2002) Native title rights and the protection of indigenous cultural knowledge. *Intellectual Property Forum* 50: 12–25.

Morgan, G. (2004) Masters of reinvention, entrepreneur of the year. 2004 Annual Review Magazine. Ernst & Young. www.ey.com/global/download.nsf/Ireland_EOY_E/thought-leadership-reinvention/$file/EOY_Masters_Of_Reinvention.pdf, accessed 22 December 2005.

Nettheim, G., Meyers, G. D. and Craig, D. (2002) *Indigenous Peoples and Governance Structures: A Comparative Analysis of Land and Resource Management Rights.* Canberra: Aboriginal Studies Press.

Newman, P. and Rowe, M. (2003) *Hope for the Future: A Vision for Quality of Life in Western Australia* (The State Sustainability Strategy). Perth: Western Australian Government.

Organisation for Economic Cooperation and Development (OECD) (2001) International trade by technology intensity, STI Scoreboard 2001. www1.oecd.org/publications/e-book/92-2001-04-1-2987/PDF/D71.pdf, accessed 3 September 2005.

Pezzey, J. (1992) Sustainable Development Concepts: An Economic Analysis, World Bank Environment Paper No. 2. Washington, DC: World Bank.

Plasencia, M. M. (ed.) (1999) *Privacy and the Constitution.* New York: Garland Publishing.

Posey, D. A. and Dutfield, G. (1996) *Beyond Intellectual Property: Toward Traditional Resource Rights for Indigenous Peoples and Local Communities.* Ottawa, Canada: IDRC Books.

Ramello, G. B. (2006) What's in a sign? Trademark law and the economic theory. *Journal of Economic Surveys* 20: 547–565.

Rosegger, G. (1996) *The Economics of Production & Innovation: An Industrial Perspective,* 3rd edition. Oxford, UK: Butterworth-Heinemann.

Schuler, P. (2004) Biopiracy and commercialisation of ethnobotanical knowledge. In J. M. Finger and P. Schuler (eds.), *Poor People's Knowledge: Promoting Intellectual Property in Developing Countries* (pp. 159–182). Washington, DC: World Bank and Oxford University Press.

Shiva, V. (2000) Poverty and globalisation. BBC Reith Lectures 2000. http://news.bbc.co.uk/hi/english/static/events/reith_2000/lecture5.stm, accessed 16 September 2005.

Siebenhüner, B., Dedeurwaerdete, T. and Brousseau, E. (2005) Introduction and overview to the special issue on biodiversity conservation, access and benefit-sharing and traditional knowledge. *Ecological Economics* 53: 439–444.

Towse, R. (2006) Copyright and artists: a view from cultural economics. *Journal of Economic Surveys* 20: 567–585.

United States Patent and Trademark Office (US PTO) (2005) General Information Concerning Patents. www.uspto.gov/web/offices/pac/doc/general/index.html#patent, accessed 21 December 2005.

Verspagen, B. (2006) University research, intellectual property rights and European innovation systems. *Journal of Economic Surveys* 20: 607–632.

Wikipedia (2005) The free encyclopaedia. http://en.wikipedia.org/wiki/, accessed 21 December 2005.

World Commission on Environment and Development (WCED) (1987) *Our Common Future.* Oxford, New York: Oxford University Press.

World Intellectual Property Organization (WIPO) (2005) Intellectual Property and Traditional Knowledge, Booklet 2. New York: WIPO.

Zerda-Sarmiento, A. and Forero-Pineda, C. (2002) Intellectual property rights over ethnic communities' knowledge. *International Social Science Journal* 54(171): 99–114.

7

UNIVERSITY RESEARCH, INTELLECTUAL PROPERTY RIGHTS AND EUROPEAN INNOVATION SYSTEMS

Bart Verspagen

1. Introduction – University Patenting in the USA and Europe

While innovation was long seen as a 'linear' process in which 'basic' knowledge from academia automatically flows to the business sector in order to be applied in innovation, the emergence of the concept of 'innovation systems' (e.g. Freeman, 1986; Lundvall, 1992; Nelson, 1993) has put more emphasis on the circumstances in which knowledge can actually flow between researchers from the public and private sector. In the innovation systems perspective, interaction is important because the development of technology and innovation is a learning process, in which technology transfer is greatly facilitated by direct contact between researchers.

Interaction between researchers working in private firms and those working in publicly financed institutions such as universities is seen as particularly important because it may provide unique competitive advantages (e.g. associated with specific competencies of high-quality universities). The European Commission (2003) lists this as one of the six priorities for European universities in the immediate future, and concludes that 'it is vital that knowledge flows from universities into business and society. The two main mechanisms through which the knowledge and expertise possessed and developed by universities can flow directly to industry are the licensing of university intellectual property, and spin-off and start-up companies' (European Commission, 2003, p. 7).

This quotation points to one of the prominent debates in the literature, i.e. the role of intellectual property rights in the process of public–private knowledge transfer. In the USA, there is a longstanding policy debate on the potentially beneficial impact on public–private knowledge transfer of universities taking out patents on their research results (see Mowery and Sampat, 2001, for an overview starting in the 1930s). With the introduction in 1980 of the so-called Bayh-Dole Act, which gave US universities the right to patent discoveries resulting from federally funded research, this debate was decided in favour of those supporting active patenting by universities. The subsequent rise in university patenting observed in the USA, and the success stories of some university discoveries that yielded high-income streams from licensing, have induced European policy makers to also consider Bayh-Dole-like legislation (OECD, 2003). This argument is made against a background of, often anecdotal, empirical evidence that European universities are not very active in patenting.

This paper intends to give an overview of the debates surrounding the introduction of the Bayh-Dole Act in the USA, and the possible adoption of similar legislation in Europe. The aim of the paper is not to provide the final answer to the question whether Europe needs legislation similar to the Bayh-Dole Act. Rather, the ambition is to provide an overview of the academic literature in economics that deals with university patenting, and to draw policy lessons from this. In this way, it is hoped that the general directions that the discussion on university patenting in Europe should take will become clear. The survey will focus on two main issues. First, which arguments can be given in favour of university patenting to facilitate public–private knowledge interaction, and what empirical evidence exists to support (or not) these arguments? Second, how do these arguments fit into the specific European context? This second issue is important because, as will be shown below, the European situation is different in many respects from the US context.

The paper is structured as follows. Sections 2, 3 and 4 give an overview of the (economic) theory behind university patenting. Section 2 starts with a broad discussion of the economic characteristics of a patent system, and the specific considerations that play a role with regard to university patenting. This section concludes by summarizing the common arguments in favour of an active role of universities in patenting. Section 3 summarizes a less commonly found argument about university patenting. This section deals with the role of intellectual property rights in public–private research joint ventures (RJVs), and summarizes a model by Aghion and Tirole that argues that market failure may exist in these RJVs. Section 4 discusses the potential negative impacts of university patenting.

Section 5 broadly compares the US and European institutional contexts in relation to the debate on university patenting. This section will highlight a number of crucial differences between Europe and the USA, and will summarize some of the variety of legislation that exists in Europe. This section also reassesses the empirical evidence on patenting by European universities using a novel data source, and concludes that statistics based on official patent databases run a serious risk of underestimating university patenting in Europe. Section 6 summarizes the empirical debate after the introduction of Bayh-Dole, and asks what the impact of this legislation on university research in the USA has been. Section 7 summarizes the paper and discusses the implications for the European innovation system.

2. A Tale of Two Paradoxes: Patents, Universities and Technology Transfer

The nature of knowledge as an economic good reminds us of the biblical story in which Jesus uses 5 loaves of bread and 2 fishes to feed a crowd of several thousands of people (John 6). When Jesus breaks the bread, it is not used up, and he can keep on distributing it until the whole crowd is fed. At that point, food is still left in abundance. Such wonders do not normally happen in economic production. When a consumer buys a loaf of bread at a bakery and consumes it, the baker will have to devote new resources to supply a different consumer with a similar loaf of bread.

In other words, the normal state of affairs is that an economic good has a *rivalrous* nature: it cannot be consumed more than once.

Knowledge is completely different in this respect. Once a piece of knowledge has been developed, it can be used ('consumed') by a multitude of parties, without the use by one party hindering the use by other parties. This characteristic of knowledge is obviously the main principle on which any educational system must necessarily be based. It is also a potential source of welfare increases. Knowledge is an important factor of production, and leads to both greater varieties of consumption goods and increased productivity in producing them. The fact that this production factor is, in principle, non-rivalrous, leads to strong economies of scale. Using knowledge throughout the global economic system can in principle be realized at relatively little extra cost in addition to the costs induced by the original developer of the knowledge.

However, unlike in the case of Jesus at the Sea of Galilee, the nature of knowledge as a public resource also poses problems in terms of non-excludability. This becomes obvious when one considers the faith of a firm that develops a piece of knowledge by investing in R&D, and that is subsequently forced to put this knowledge into the public domain. This may, for example, happen if the knowledge is embodied in a product that can be reverse-engineered, and no patent or other form of intellectual property rights system exists. Competitors may use the knowledge embodied in the product at little or no cost, and hence put on the market a similar product as the original one, but at a lower price (they do not have to earn back R&D investments). If the originally innovating firm cannot exclude such competitors from using its knowledge in this way, it will be forced to leave the market. For a rationally behaving firm, such a prospect will, of course, be discouraging, and the R&D project leading to the new product will not be undertaken. In other words, the non-excludable nature of knowledge provides an incentive problem when profit-motivated firms are the main driver of technological change (see the contribution by Carlaw *et al.* in this issue for a broader discussion).

Several institutions have been used to solve this incentive problem. David (1993) distinguishes three broad forms of such institutions, and ranks them under three Ps: Property Rights (of which Patents are perhaps the most prominent form[1]), Patronage and Procurement. Property rights or Patents will be the main topic of the analysis here, and hence will be discussed in more detail below. Patronage refers to a mechanism in which governments take financial responsibility for the development of new knowledge, by means of instituting a publicly financed system of research that is aimed at generating and diffusing new knowledge. Obviously, modern universities and other public and semi-public research organizations are the main example of such a system. In such a way, the incentive problem is solved in the same way in which markets for other so-called public goods (e.g. national defense or a tornado siren) are organized: the government institutes the productive system for the public good and finances it from tax income.

Procurement refers to a situation in which the development of a specific piece of knowledge is the topic of a contractual agreement between the producer of the knowledge and a party that is particularly interested in the knowledge, and hence is willing to act as a financer and procurer in the contract. Such an arrangement is often used, for example, in the defense industry, where a ministry of defense may procure new weapon systems. We will discuss the mechanism of procurement in combination with property rights issues in the next section, and will continue here to focus on the patent system.

Patents are the main form of intellectual property rights employed for the production of new knowledge, although copyrights and trademarks may also play a role (see e.g. David, 1993, for a broad discussion of various form of intellectual property rights). A patent is a legal monopoly for the use of a specific piece of knowledge, to be awarded to the firm, person or organization that first develops the knowledge and is willing to apply it in a commercial way. All advanced economies in the world have instituted a patent system in some form, although there are still major differences in the exact rules under which inventions may be patented in the various systems.[2]

The patent system embodies a major paradox. On the one hand, it is aimed at stimulating the development of new knowledge, as a result of the recognition that knowledge is a primary source of increased welfare and economic growth, but that a free enterprise system without intellectual property rights may generate too little incentives for the development of such new knowledge. But on the other hand, the legal monopoly that a patent constitutes is in essence a restriction on the free flow of knowledge, while such a free flow is in fact the actual source of the welfare enhancing effect of knowledge. When knowledge is restricted from flowing to users, it becomes much like any other (rivalrous) economic good.

The patent system recognizes the trade-off between providing incentives and enabling the flow of knowledge. Thus, a major element of any patent system is that all patented knowledge must be made public (in the actual patent document), that not all knowledge related to the patent becomes the property of the patent holder, and that there is a maximum time length of the patent (after which the patented knowledge becomes public property).

The maximum time length of a patent (around 20 years in most patent systems) provides the most obvious restriction of rights for the patent holder, in favour of other users of the knowledge. But the publication of patented knowledge is also intended to provide a basis for further development of the area in which the patent is awarded, and thus potentially benefits others than the patent holder. Other researchers than those employed by the patent holder (including, for example, R&D workers at a competing firm) may thus use the knowledge described in the patent to develop new knowledge. In other words, patented knowledge may take the form of 'idea-creating' knowledge spillovers.

The restriction of patentable knowledge to only a part of the newly developed knowledge is the subject of patent design. Both *ex ante* written patent law and jurisprudence put important restrictions on patentable knowledge. For example, in the field of genetic research, European patent law (in the making) specifies that only a specific application of genetic code may be patented. This implies that a firm cannot simply patent a piece of genetic code as such, but must always write up a specific application using the genetic code (e.g. a therapy based on the genetic information). Applications that are not immediately discovered (i.e. are unknown at the time of patenting) do not fall under the patent, and are thus freely available for future research and commercial development. In the US patent system, on the other hand, patents on genetic code are much broader, and may include a wide range of yet undiscovered applications. Such a broad patent obviously provides a higher reward (and thus incentive) for the patent holder, but also limits the benefits to society at large.

In summary, the patent system embodies a major paradox related to the trade-off between providing incentives and enabling a free flow of knowledge throughout the economy. The design of the patent system must strike a balance between the two sides of the trade-off. Striking such a balance is obviously a delicate issue, for which, arguably, general principles are of limited value because of the highly differentiated nature of patentable innovations and inventions. While in some cases (e.g. the AIDS crisis in Africa) public interest may call for weak patents, other cases may call for broader protection of the patent holder.

A second paradox emerges when we consider more closely the issue of patenting by universities. As already argued, the university system is the prime example of a system of patronage, i.e. an alternative system to the patent system. The reason why such a system of patronage may co-exist with a patent system is that some forms of research, in particular basic research without immediate applicability, is not directly addressed by the patenting system. For example, Nelson (1959) and Arrow (1962) argue that private firms motivated by profit may severely under-invest in basic research, and hence an important role is reserved for universities and other public research organizations.[3] Along this line of argument, the innovation system consists of different types of actors, each of which have a particular role and derive incentives in different ways.

From such a point of view, the issue of university patenting is paradoxical because it implies that universities fall under two incentive systems that are normally seen as alternatives to each other (patronage and property rights). Why would it be necessary to provide an incentive, in the form of a patent, for research that has been financed by public money, and to which no individual person, firm or organization can hold any rights that restrict the free flow of knowledge through the economy? As argued by Mowery *et al.* (2001, p. 103):

> When a good is non-rivalrous in use...[p]olicies impeding access to a scientific discovery by any party that can make use of it impose costs on that party and on the economy as a whole. Where private investors are the primary source of financial support for scientific research, as is the case with industrial R&D, granting a patent on the results of such work may be necessary in order to induce private R&D investment. But the economic theory of scientific research...argues that patenting the results of publicly financed research is unnecessary to induce the research investment and that any restrictions on use associated with patents reduce the social returns to this public investment.

Despite this economic logic, the already mentioned Bayh-Dole Act was passed in the USA in 1980 (Eisenberg, 1996, provides an overview of the debates surrounding the introduction of the Bayh-Dole Act). This law provides universities in the USA with the right to own patents on research that was sponsored from federal sources such as the National Research Foundation (NSF). What was the economic logic behind the introduction of this Act?

The main argument in favour of university patents is that these patents will facilitate technology transfer from universities to private firms. When university research generates knowledge that may be applied in commercial products or processes, private firms may be interested in this knowledge. But when it comes to making additional investments in order to transform the university-generated knowledge into a commercial application, the same incentive problem that was sketched above may pose itself. A firm that endeavours to undertake the additional R&D that is necessary to develop the commercial application will only consider this a useful undertaking when it has a prospect of deterring imitation by competitors.

The logic supporting the Bayh-Dole Act says that this is only warranted if the firm that develops the applied knowledge to turn the basic knowledge developed by the university into a commercial application has an exclusive right to do so. Otherwise competitors may move in and use the freely available university knowledge to develop a competing application, and this prospect is enough to discourage private investment following up university research. The only way in which the firm that develops the university knowledge may obtain exclusivity, is when the university patents its discovery, and grants an exclusive license to the firm.

Note that this argument rests on two implicit assumptions. The first is that the additional costs necessary to develop the university discovery into a commercial innovation are non-trivial. If these costs would be (very) low, simple competitive pressures might drive all firms in the industry in which the discovery can be applied to adopt it. This would be a matter of survival, and ultimately be to the benefit of the buyers (consumers) in the market. In other words, in such a case, the traditional competitive process would do its work and yield an optimal market outcome. Only in case development costs are non-trivial is the working of the competitive process ruled out because of an incentive problem (Mowery *et al.*, 2001, p. 103).

The second implicit assumption is that the additional R&D work that is necessary to develop the university discovery cannot be patented separately, or alternatively, that there are many technical ways to develop the discovery and that a single firm cannot patent all of these. If this would not be the case, i.e. when the firm that develops the applied knowledge following up on the university discovery can apply for a patent on this knowledge, granting a patent to the applied part of the innovation only could solve the incentive problem.

These conditions may be warranted in many practical situations, which would indeed be an argument in favour of an active university patent policy on the grounds that it facilitates technology transfer to the private sector, and hence enhances welfare by means of stimulating technological progress. But surprisingly little case research exists to support the broad applicability of the argument that university patents facilitate knowledge transfer from the public to the private sector (Mowery *et al.*, 2001; Geuna and Nesta, 2006; see also Section 6 below).

Additional arguments in favour of university patents may also be raised. Two issues that played a role in the early discussion in the 1930s in the USA, but did not re-enter the debate surrounding Bayh-Dole in the 1970s (Mowery and Sampat, 2001, pp. 384–385) are the potential 'pirating' of university discoveries, and the quality control of the application of university research. The latter of these points argues that if a university holds a patent to a discovery, it may control who develops the discovery further, and hence exclude applications with inferior quality, or unethical applications. The issue of patent 'piracy' argues that without a university patent to a discovery, opportunistic firms may move in to patent the knowledge developed originally by a university, and hence appropriate publicly financed research and limit its free applicability. Note that both these arguments imply that the university patent is licensed-out (at least potentially) in a non-exclusive way, something that runs against the above-used logic of technology transfer.

A final argument in favour of university patents is that the possibility of university patenting raises awareness of commercially useful research results in universities themselves. In the pre-Bayh-Dole era, so it is argued, many useful discoveries remained within the clutches of the ivory tower of the university, simply because the researchers who discovered them had no interest in commercial issues. Post-Bayh-Dole, almost all US universities have technology transfer offices (TTOs), who actively stimulate (and in many case oblige) researchers to disclose their useful discoveries so that they may be patented.

This argument is often used in combination with the financial benefits that may arise from licensing-out patented discoveries. As will be illustrated in Section 6, licensing income of some discoveries at US universities is considerable. Being aware of useful knowledge by its employees thus becomes of potentially large financial value for universities. In this way, the issue of university patenting is also connected to the issue of financing of university budgets, and hence the political dimension of the issue is broadened to include aspects of government finance. While governments may consider any form of private financing of public tasks as a welcome relief to the expenditure side of their budget, the budgetary aspects of this are secondary to the main issue of this paper: the innovation system and the role of universities in it. Hence we will only address this aspect of university patenting when it becomes relevant to the way in which universities perform their role in the innovation system.

3. Research Joint Ventures between Universities and Firms: A Case of Market Failure?

Surprisingly, the Bayh-Dole debate has not focused much on the issue of research joint ventures (RJVs) between universities and private firms. The arguments given in favour of university patenting in the previous section all seem to assume implicitly a 'linear model' in which universities perform basic research that is an input into the more applied or experimental research that firms undertake to arrive at commercial products or services. But such a linear view has long since come under criticism (e.g. Kline and Rosenberg, 1986), and hence it may be more appropriate to consider the issue of university patenting in a context in which private firms and universities work together in a research project from the very start. This is where the theory of public–private RJVs becomes of interest.

Aghion and Tirole (1994) have suggested that the role of intellectual property rights in such public–private RJVs is crucial. They argue that in the case of joint research projects between universities and private firms, the assignment of property rights (patents) to the firm instead of the university may lead to market failure, i.e. the innovation resulting from the collaboration has a lower value than could have been the case if the university had owned the patent. Obviously, this is an additional argument in favour of Bayh-Dole-like legislation.

In the Aghion and Tirole model, a university undertakes a research project for a private firm. Both parties need to invest in the project, and the relationship between both investments and the probability of success (i.e. an innovation) is given by a concave function. Due to the uncertainty, the actual content of the innovation is non-negotiable *ex ante*. Therefore, the contract drawn up for the research project is incomplete: it specifies only the attribution of the property right (who owns the patent, the university or the firm?), the license fee that the university obtains in case the patent is assigned to the firm, and the amount of investment of the firm. As an assumption, only one of the two parties involved may own the patent resulting from the project. The model assumes profit/utility maximization by both parties.

In this setting, the payoffs of the invention to the two parties are related to ownership. If the firm owns the invention, the university does not share in the profits from the invention. Instead, it is paid a pre-bargained fee that covers its research efforts. On the other hand, if the university owns the invention, both parties share the payoff by means of a licensing fee levied by the university. The university and the firm bargain *ex ante* over ownership of the expected invention, taking into account these (expected) benefits. Then, the answer to the question of who will own the patent depends on two factors: the relative marginal impacts of the research efforts of both parties, and the *ex ante* bargaining power of both parties. We discuss both factors in turn.

The relative marginal impacts of the research of the two parties are important because the university only has an incentive to make the maximum effort in case it owns the patent. Due to the incompleteness of the research contract, the firm does not have the means to control whether or not the university makes the maximum effort. Thus, if the university does not own the invention, its best strategy is to 'shirk', i.e. provide a minimal research effort. Such a shirking university is obviously a problem for the firm, because it will lead to a less valuable invention. If the relative marginal impact of the university's research effort is large, this becomes a serious problem, and the firm is therefore likely to leave ownership to the university.

In the formal model, Aghion and Tirole compare the payoffs to the firm under both modes of ownership. If the firm owns the patent, it gets the full amount of payoffs (net of the lump sum payment to the university). If the university owns the invention, the firm gets only part of the total payoff. Thus, the firm compares a shared payoff under maximum effort by the university to the full payoff with a 'shirking' university. Obviously, the higher the marginal impact of the university effort, the more likely it is that the first of these situations will lead to a higher payoff for the firm. Thus, the higher the marginal impact of the university effort, the higher the willingness of the firm to leave ownership of the invention to the university.

Bargaining power for the university also influences the assignment of the patent. For example, if the university has specific knowledge that makes it a research monopolist, the firm may have to choose between no project at all (and hence no payoffs) and sharing payoffs with the university. As long as the shared payoffs are positive, the firm will then still undertake the research project and leave the patent to the university (which would be socially optimal).

A case of market failure may emerge when the university does not have strong bargaining power and the relative marginal impacts of the two parties are such that the firm is unwilling to leave the patent to the university. To see how this emerges, let us call the value of the innovation under firm ownership of the patent (i.e. minimum effort by the university) V^0. Now assume that the extra effort that the university would be willing to make in exchange for ownership leads to an increase in the invention value equal to $\Delta > 0$. Obviously, as long as $\Delta > 0$, the social value of the innovation goes up with a transfer of the patent to the university. But, because in this case the firm only gets a share of the invention value, its private payoff may be lower. Assume the firm gets a share σ (Aghion and Tirole assume $\sigma = \frac{1}{2}$). Then, $\sigma(V^0 + \Delta) < V^0$, or $\Delta < V^0 (1 - \sigma)/\sigma$ would be sufficient to withhold the firm from making the socially efficient decision to leave the patent to the university.

The extra effort of the university need not always lead to a larger value of the invention ($\Delta > 0$) because the effort of the firm is endogenous. Then, the optimal firm effort may go down as a result of increased university effort. In such a case, market failure does not take place, and the allocation of the patent to the firm is optimal.

Note that market failure only results if the university is cash-constrained, which is an assumption of the model, and the firm has a large degree of bargaining power. If the university would not be cash-constrained, it would be able to pay the firm the difference $V^0 - \sigma(V^0 + \Delta)$ and still have positive payoffs itself. Because the firm is not assumed to be cash-constrained, market failure is not a possibility in case the university owns the patent (e.g. when it has high *ex ante* bargaining power).

Whether the strong assumption on payoff maximizing and cash-constrained universities is realistic, can be debated. As long as the firm behaves in a strictly profit-maximizing way, market failure due to a lack of university ownership of patents is a possibility. Arguably, in the framework of the Aghion and Tirole model, universities not being interested in monetary payoffs only reinforce the possibility of market failure.

Market failure due to a lack of bargaining power on the side of universities may be solved by legislation that provides the university with this bargaining power. In this case, a law that specifies that the property rights of research in which universities (or publicly financed research institutes) are involved automatically lies with the university (or research institute) would rule out the possibility of market failure. Arguably, this is a stronger case than the Bayh-Dole Act in the USA, or the legislation that exists on university patenting in European countries.

4. Potential Negative Effects of University Patenting

The literature also points to potentially negative effects of increased university patenting (see e.g. Geuna and Nesta, 2006; Mowery and Sampat, 2001 for broad discussions of potential negative impacts). These disadvantages of increased university patenting can be categorized under three broad topics.

The first set of disadvantages is related to the impact that patenting has on the 'culture of open science'. This refers to the fact that, contrary to much research that goes on in firms, scientific research usually works in an atmosphere of openness and sharing of knowledge, data, and research results. It is exactly this open nature of the scientific process that is responsible for much of its success: the development of new knowledge flourishes because researchers build upon each other's results, cross-fertilize each other's perspectives by means of discussion of (early) research results, share data sources, etc. (Dasgupta and David, 1994).

Patents may turn this open culture into a more closed one for two reasons. First, when patents and their potential financial rewards are an important research aim, researchers may feel tempted to operate in a competitive mode, rather than the cooperative mode that characterizes the open culture of science. Second, an important aspect of patenting is the fact that any knowledge that is patented cannot be published in any form before the application of the patent, implying that a university researcher who is interested in patenting a discovery, must keep all information related to the research project internal. Thus, when universities become more interested in patents as an output of their research, there is a danger that in the long run, the open nature of the scientific process is threatened, and hence scientific progress is hampered.

A second disadvantage of patenting lies in the potential blockade that patents may form for future research. This is especially relevant in areas where progress is to a large extent cumulative, i.e. where new results build upon old research in a strong way. A contemporary case is in the life sciences, where, for example, tools for genetic sequencing are of utmost importance for any research being undertaken in the area. Where these tools are patented, access to them will be restricted, and this will have a negative impact on scientific progress.

This is an issue that has implications beyond just university research and university patents (as is evident from discussions surrounding patents in genetic research that are owned by firms), but is especially relevant for our discussion when we realize that many university discoveries appear in basic research. Such 'basic' discoveries are more likely to have an impact on a whole range of subsequent 'applied' research topics, and thus have a strong potential for blocking such future research.

The third and final set of disadvantages is related to the strategic behaviour of universities. When patents are an increasingly important output for universities, there may be an incentive to do research in those areas where patents are easily obtained. It has been argued (e.g. Henderson *et al.*, 1998; see also the discussion in Section 6 below) that especially applied research offers opportunities for 'quick patenting', and that universities would thus have an incentive to move away from basic research with long-run impacts (in favour of applied research with short-run impact). In other words, patenting may cause universities to behave more like firms, and hence, from an innovation systems perspective, important synergies between universities and firms would disappear.

Some of these disadvantages have been addressed in patent law and the discussion around it. With regard to the issue of research tools, many patent systems allow the use of patented knowledge in research (as opposed to commercial applications; the so-called 'research exception'), which implies that future research cannot be blocked by a patent. However, this is an exception that is in many cases weak, because the patent holder may challenge it in court (Geuna and Nesta, 2006).

A recent proposal to amend (European) patent law is to allow a 'grace period' for university researchers between the application for the patent and publication of the research (see e.g. OECD, 2003). This means that in effect, university researchers may publish and speak about their invention in scientific circles without losing the right to patent the discovery afterwards. It may thus be possible to 'solve' some of the disadvantages to university patenting by specific parts of patent law, but this remains in many respects a solution that is inferior to the starting point of 'open science'.

5. The Institutional Context of University Patenting in the USA and Europe

Mowery and Sampat (2001) describe how in the USA in the 1970s and 1980s, many different trends came together in the field of university–industry relations. They situate the start of these developments in the 1930s, when a first debate about university patenting emerged in the USA. During this period, US universities were mainly financed from state resources, and the state governments that decided on these resources pushed strongly for research that had an impact on local business. Hence the same questions that surrounded the introduction of the Bayh-Dole act in 1980 were debated in the 1930s.

This led many of the top universities in the USA to adopt a university-wide patent policy in the 1930s, and to stimulate faculty to apply for patents on their discoveries. Many of these universities decided to leave the issue of the commercial management of these patents to independent third parties, which were often foundations with an explicit aim of fostering the useful and economy-wide application of university research. One of these 'patent managing' institutions was the Research Corporation, who managed patents of, e.g., the University of Wisconsin, Columbia University, MIT and Princeton (Mowery and Sampat, 2001, Table 1, p. 790).

After the Second World War, the involvement of federal financial resources in university research grew considerably. Especially the biomedical sciences attracted a lot of federal funding, mainly through the National Institute of Health. Molecular biology emerged as a field in which university research had many direct applications in medicine, and in which universities could earn significant income from licensing out their patented discoveries. More and more universities also decided to take the commercial management of their patent portfolio in their own hands, and hence institutions such as the Research Corporation became less important.

An important aspect of this process was that the federal funding of research posed important questions with regard to ownership of the rights to the research results. Funding bodies such as the NIH and NSF could legally claim rights because they (co-)financed the research, and universities could equally do so because they financed part of the research themselves, and because they employed the researchers and owned the labs in which the research was done. US law did not provide an immediate and clear answer as to who held the rights to patent federally funded research. Hence the funding bodies and the universities usually engaged in complicated negotiations over these rights. First, these negotiations were taking place on a case-by-case basis, but later on so-called Institutional Patent Agreements (IPAs) were introduced by the larger funding agencies (National Science Foundation, NSF and the Department of Health, Education and Welfare, HEW).

The Bayh-Dole Act was introduced in order to streamline the multiple arrangements in this field. Bayh-Dole entitled universities to patent all discoveries that resulted from federally funded research (so-called 'blanket permission'). The Act was thus a great simplification of the intellectual property rights situation at universities. But as Mowery and Sampat (2001) argue, the Bayh-Dole Act was not the starting point of increased university patenting in the USA. The Act was a result of the desire of American universities to patent their inventions, and their efforts to do so. It facilitated the administrative procedures around university patenting, but was not the prime cause of the increase in university patents. Scientific developments in the field of biomedical research (in particular molecular biology) and the increasing role of federally funded research in this area had induced universities to patent more of their discoveries already long before the introduction of the Bayh-Dole Act.

The US specific issue of federal research funding does not arise to such a strong extent in the European context. Although the European Commission, which is the closest thing in Europe to a 'federal government', finances a considerable amount of scientific research at universities through its Framework Programmes, issues of intellectual property rights do not arise in this context because the European Commission does not claim rights on the outcome of the research that it finances.[4]

On the other hand, in some European countries, individual inventors, although they are employed by universities or public research institutes, are entitled to privately own the patents that emerge from their research in the service of the university (or public research institute) (OECD, 2003). In Europe, this is currently the case for Finland, Iceland, Italy and Sweden. In all these countries, as a result of legal arrangements, it is common for university-employed inventors to privately hold patents resulting from their work (OECD, 2003, Table 1.2, p. 26). In Switzerland, private holding of patents by university inventors is legally possible, but less common (*ibid.*). In all other European countries included in the OECD (2003) study (Austria, Belgium, Denmark, France, Germany, Ireland, Netherlands, Norway, Poland, Spain, UK), universities generally have a right to own patents on the research that they conduct (*ibid.*). In Germany, a change of legislation implemented in 2001 gave ownership of patents to the university, while before it had belonged to university employees. Italy, on the other hand, changed the law in the other direction in 2001: whereas universities held ownership before, now employees generally own patents.

Private ownership of patents by university inventors, as found in some European countries, raises specific questions with regard to the efficiency of technology transfer. As is argued in OECD (2003, p. 23), a situation in which individual researchers hold the right to their inventions may well be sub-optimal, because individuals are generally less well placed to exploit these rights than large institutions such as universities are. But exactly for this reason, university inventors may turn to firms to actually apply for the patent. In this way, because of the fact that individual inventors are first entitled to own patents from their research, such patents may relatively easily be transferred (whether formally in the patent document itself, or through some other means) to private firms, who are accustomed to dealing with patent applications.

This fits the discussion on RJVs in Section 3 above (Aghion and Tirole model) very well. When individual researchers own patents, university bargaining power in public–private RJVs is very low, and the risk of market failure as a result of a 'wrong' assignment of property rights becomes larger. Viewed from this perspective, the legal situation with regard to ownership of university patents in Finland, Iceland, Italy and Sweden is inefficient.

Apart from the legal possibility for universities to patent the results from their (publicly funded) research, the general awareness of universities of application-worthy research has been argued to be an issue in the European context. It was noted that in the USA, an increased interest of universities in patenting preceded the introduction of the Bayh-Dole Act, corresponding to an increased awareness of the opportunities for application of basic research in commercial innovations. Because this is seen by some influential researchers (Mowery and Sampat, 2001) as an important driving force behind public–private research interaction in the USA, it is interesting to investigate the European situation in some detail.

Unfortunately, the empirical basis for comparing awareness to commercial opportunities among university researchers in different countries is very weak. The evidence is either anecdotal, or based on indirect indicators. The lack of patenting by European universities has been used as an indicator of the lack of general commercial awareness, for example by Michael Porter (2001, p. 37), in his 'Innovation Lecture' delivered at the Ministry of Economic Affairs in the Netherlands: '[u]niversities in the Netherlands have traditionally been much less commercially oriented than in the U.S., where commercial activities are more highly regarded. In the Netherlands, universities have little contact with companies, and filing patents and seeking to license technology to the private sector is not part of the culture'. Porter further presented empirical evidence that Dutch universities are not very active in patenting: on a list ranking Dutch firms and organizations with regard to the number of US patents they obtained during 1996–2000, the first university (Leiden) ranked 45th, with only 13 patents. The largest US university, the University of California, obtained 1558 US patents during the same period.[5]

But there are indications (e.g. Geuna and Nesta, 2006) that the (European) statistics on university involvement in patenting are biased. The reason for this is that in many cases, university researchers are involved in the research that leads to a patent, but the university (their employer) does not appear as an applicant on the patent.[6] This may, for example, be the case when the university researcher has a private consulting contract with a firm (which may be facilitated by legislation that gives individual researchers title to the patent resulting from their research), or when the university is involved in an RJV with a firm, and it has been (contractually) agreed that the firm will hold the intellectual property rights.

Geuna and Nesta (2006) cite evidence from Italy, Finland and Belgium that the number of university patents (in a broad sense) is severely underestimated when only patents with universities as applicants are counted.[7] Similar evidence emerged in a case study of the French Université Louis Pasteur (ULP, Strasbourg).[8] Comparative evidence for six European countries exists in the form of the 'Patval' survey (Giuri *et al.*, 2005), which was conducted among inventors of European patents filed from the Netherlands. The survey was aimed at granted patents only (non-granted applications were excluded), with a priority date in the period 1992–1997.

Using the 'Patval' data, one may distinguish two 'types' of university patents. The most narrow type is a patent that has a university as (one of) the applicant(s). These are the patents that would appear on Porter's list that was referred to above. The second type of university patents are those that do not have a university applicant, but do have at least one inventor that was employed by a university. These patents (broadly) correspond to the case of the Aghion and Tirole RJV model, with the university leaving ownership of the project outcomes to the firm. Additionally, the Patval survey allows distinguishing patents in which university knowledge played an important role as an input. We define the latter as those patents in which the inventor ranked university knowledge as 'important' or 'very important' for the patent.

Figure 1 displays the share of these three types of patents in the total sample of patents in the Patval survey, for the Netherlands (NL), United Kingdom (UK), Spain (ES), Germany (DE), France (FR) and Italy (IT), as well as the (weighted) average for these six countries (Total). Note that the categories are additive, i.e. a patent can never fall into more than one category, and will be categorized in the 'first' category that it fits in (i.e. first as university-owned patents, then as patents with a university inventor, and finally as patents in which university knowledge is important).

In terms of the total of the three categories, the countries differ substantially, with the Netherlands leading with a percentage that is about twice as large as the country with the lowest value, Italy. In all the countries, the fraction of patents in which universities are involved actively (i.e. the first two categories) is small compared to the third category. This may indeed point to low commercial awareness of university researchers, but unfortunately, no reference material exists to make a comparison with, for example, the USA.

The figure also confirms the impression (Geuna and Nesta, 2006) that statistics with regard to university ownership of patents underestimate university involvement. In all countries, patents in which university inventors are involved but which are not owned by the university, form a substantial (compared to university ownership) category. Only in Spain is the fraction of university-owned patents larger than the fraction of non-owned, but university-inventor-involved patents. In Germany, France and Italy, university-owned patents are a very minor fraction of the total $(<0.8\%)$[9], but the fraction of non-owned, university-inventor-involved patents is larger than 2.5% in all three cases.

Thus, the Patval data point out that at least in Europe (we have no comparable data for the USA), universities are more often involved in patenting as a result of some kind of cooperative work with the private sector (indicated by non-university ownership of the patent), than by patenting results from their independent research. This suggests that the type of market failure that has been pointed out by Aghion and Tirole in the context of public–private RJVs may be an important phenomenon, although this has been largely overlooked until now in the discussion on university patents.

In conclusion, the institutional context in the USA and Europe with regard to patenting of university inventions is quite different. Issues with regard to federal sponsoring of research do not arise as strongly in Europe as in the USA. On the other hand, Europe may have its 'own' issue in university patenting in the form of

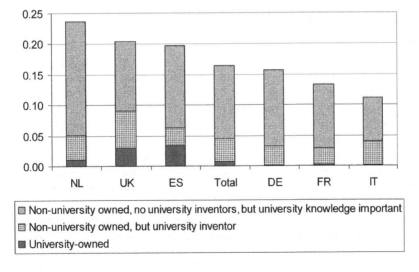

Figure 1. University Patents in Europe, 1992–1997, as Percentage of all Patents; Various Definitions of University Patents.

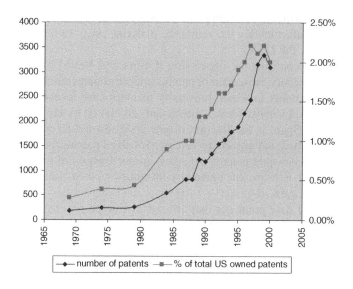

Figure 2. Patenting by US Universities, Total Number of University Patents and
University Patents as a Percentage of all Domestic US Patents.
Source: USPTO and Mowery *et al.*, 2001.

potential market failure in public–private RJVs. This implies that arguments from
the US debate may not be readily transferable to the European discussion.

6. The Effects of Bayh-Dole – an Empirical Assessment

Although patenting by US universities was already on the rise before the Bayh-
Dole Act (1980), the data show an acceleration after 1980, both in terms of the
total number of university patents and university patents as a percentage of total
domestic US patents. This is evident from Figure 2, which summarizes the trends
in US university patenting over the period 1969–2000. Towards the end of the
period, university patenting comprises around 2% of total patenting in the USA.
Comparing this percentage to the data in Figure 1, European university patenting
as a percentage of all patents does not seem to be much below the US numbers,
if the non-university owned patents with university inventors are included in the
definition of university patents (but we have no data on this phenomenon for the
USA).

The topic of US universities patenting after the Bayh-Dole Act has attracted
relatively much recent empirical research. Two results stand out in the descriptive
statistics: the large share of a limited number of technology fields in total university
patenting, and the fact that a small share of patents is responsible for a large share
of the total licensing income (and a large share of patents yields only very low
licensing income).

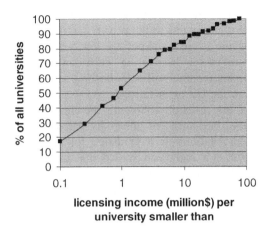

Figure 3. The (Cumulative) Distribution of Licensing Income over US Universities, 2002.

Source: AUTM, 2002.

Henderson *et al.* (1998) find that at the end of the 1980s, drugs and medicines is the largest field in which US universities patent (around 35% of all university patents). Chemicals (20–25%), electronics (20–25%) and mechanical technologies (10–15%) are the next largest fields. Compared to the total sample of patents, this implies a strong over-representation of medical technology, and an under-representation of mechanical technology. Relatively little work has been done on the explanation of this finding, but it seems likely that the major explanatory factor is the fact that medical technology is a field in which the science base is very strong, as a result of recent scientific advances in, among others, molecular biology.

The second finding that stands out from the descriptive statistics on US university patenting is the fact that the majority of patents generates only comparatively little licensing income, while there is a small number of patents that are responsible for the bulk of licensing income. Figure 3 displays the distribution of licensing income in 2002 over 150 US universities. The figure shows that roughly half of all universities has licensing income below 1 million US$ (per year). Only about 10% of universities has licensing income above 10 million US$.

The same skewed distribution is found at the level of individual patents. Mowery *et al.* (2001) present data for Columbia University, Stanford University and the University of California. Their most recent data are for 1995, and in this year, the top 5 patents in terms of licensing income were responsible for 94%, 85% and 66% of gross total income (respectively for Columbia, Stanford and the University of California, Mowery *et al.*, Table 2, p. 107). All three of these universities are at the top of the list of big earners: their total gross licensing income in 1995 was 32 million, 36 million and 59 million (respectively, with the same order of universities), which implies that the top patents of these universities are indeed responsible for a very large share of total licensing income at US universities.

Together, these findings show that only a few universities can be expected to 'get rich' from selling their patents to the private sector. Without a medical school, the chances of hitting the license jackpot are low, and even in medical research, there are few opportunities for discovering 'cash-cow' patents. Overall, it cannot be expected that licensing income will soon become a major source of income for universities, whether in the US or in Europe.

A different part of the research following the introduction of the Bayh-Dole Act has focused on the 'basicness' of university patents. Henderson *et al.* (1998) proposed to use patent citations as a yardstick for the basicness of patents. In Trajtenberg *et al.* (1997), it had been shown that university patents have quite different citation profiles than corporate patents. Specifically, university patents seem to be cited more often, especially so by others than the original inventor, and university patents seem to be cited in more distinct technology fields than corporate patents.

Henderson *et al.* (1998) investigate the change in these citation measures over time, and conclude 'that the relative importance and generality of university patents has fallen at the same time as the sheer number of university patents has increased. This decrease appears to be largely the result of a very rapid increase in the number of 'low-quality' patents being granted to universities' (p. 126). This finding would seem to indicate that with the rise in university patenting following the introduction of the Bayh-Dole Act, universities have shifted their research more in the direction of low-impact, possibly more applied, research. In other words, university patents are becoming more and more like corporate patents, possibly as the result of a tendency to focus on research that is easier to patent.

However, in a series of papers, Mowery *et al.* (2002), Mowery and Ziedonis (2002) and Sampat *et al.* (2003) qualified the conclusions of Henderson *et al.* (1998). Mowery and Ziedonis (2002) investigate citation patterns of individual universities. They conclude that for two important cases, Stanford and the University of California, no significant changes in the 'basicness' of patents were observed after 1980. The fall in 'basicness' observed by Henderson and Trajtenberg is addressed to the effect of universities who started to patent after 1980. It is argued that these 'entrants' have lower patent 'quality'. Mowery *et al.* (2002) further find that the patent 'quality' of these entrants improved during the late 1980s and 1990s. Finally, Sampat *et al.* (2003) find that when a longer stream of citations is used, no significant decline in 'basicness' of university patents can be observed.

In summary, it can be concluded that the evidence with regard to a shift of university patents to more 'applied' research is mixed. The more recent evidence (based on the most advanced methods and most recent data) seems to suggest that such a shift did not happen, or at best was due to the fact that the universities that started to patent after Bayh-Dole produced more 'applied' patents than the universities who were already engaged in patenting before Bayh-Dole.

Although the statistical analysis of patenting data can reveal much about the impact of Bayh-Dole, the perhaps most crucial question, i.e. whether or not the increased level of university patenting has led to more efficient technology transfer from universities to the private sector, remains to an important extent outside the realm of patent data. This broad question has been addressed from multiple perspectives, ranging from case studies of individual discoveries or universities, to large-scale surveys among university researchers.

At the end of this spectrum covering the case studies, Colyvas *et al.* (2002) study 11 university discoveries, made at Stanford or Columbia. The cases are spread over a number of technology fields, and, most importantly, can be divided into the two categories 'useable without further development Yes/No'. This means that an important aspect of the invention that was stressed in Section 2 above is controlled for. It was argued there that patents do not seem to be necessary, and in fact may hinder knowledge diffusion, in cases where a university discovery can be used without much further development by the private sector. Seven of the case studies by Colyvas *et al.* (2002) required further development by the private sector (so-called 'embryonic inventions'); four did not (so-called 'off the shelf inventions').

In line with the discussion in Section 2, Colyvas *et al.* conclude 'that intellectual property rights are likely to be most important for embryonic inventions, and unimportant for inventions that are useful to industry 'off the shelf'. For the inventions...that were licensed nonexclusively, patents allowed the universities to collect revenues, but did nothing to facilitate technology transfer' (p. 67). This conclusion reiterates the point stressed in Section 2 that a general policy of strong patents for university research will not fit all research projects, and may hinder knowledge diffusion in some cases just as well as it may facilitate technology transfer in other cases.

A different research methodology has been used in studies by Cohen *et al.* (1998), Cohen *et al.* (2002) and Agrawal and Henderson (2002). These studies employ various data sources to assess the relative importance of various channels of technology transfer from universities to firms. Agrawal and Henderson (2002) focus on MIT, and collect publication and patent data, and conduct interviews with MIT faculty members. Their results show that MIT faculty sees patents as a relatively unimportant aspect of their research, and publications in high-ranking journals are the preferred research output type.

The interviews with MIT staff identify consulting activities as the most important source of knowledge transfer, followed by publications, the recruitment of graduates, and collaborative research. Patents and licenses rank low as important means of knowledge transfer (Agrawal and Henderson, 2002, Figure 5, p. 52). An analysis of collaborative publishing between MIT faculty and researchers employed in the private sector, and an analysis of citations of MIT papers and patents, reveals that there is only a small overlap between firms that cite papers or patents, and firms who collaborate on papers or patents. This implies that the firms for whom patents are an important form of knowledge transfer are quite different firms than those for whom publication is an important source. Thus, focusing on patents as the sole source of knowledge transfer will reveal a biased picture. Hence, Agrawal and Henderson (2002, p. 45) conclude 'that patenting may play a relatively small role in the transfer of knowledge out of the university'.

A much similar conclusion is reached in the papers by Cohen *et al.* (1998) and Cohen *et al.* (2002) that make use of the Carnegie Mellon Survey on Industrial R&D.

This survey is undertaken at the 'demand side' of public–private knowledge transfer, i.e. R&D managers in the private sector. The results of this survey underline that the impact of university research on business innovation is highly different between economic sectors, and that the ways in which this impact is realized again differ between sectors. As in the research by Agrawal and Henderson, patents emerge as a relatively unimportant source of knowledge transfer. Publications, meetings and conferences, informal interaction and consulting all rank as clearly more important mechanisms than patents. The results also show that large firms are more likely to use the results of public research in their own R&D projects.

A last type of analysis aimed at directly assessing the intensity of technology transfer from universities to private firms deals with the possibility of market failure in RJVs (as in the Aghion and Tirole model). This has been addressed by Crespi *et al.* (2006), who use the Patval data of Figure 1 above to assess whether university-owned patents resulting from university–firm RJVs are more often applied, or are more valuable, than privately owned patents resulting from these RJVs. They apply various matched sampling techniques, but always conclude that university-owned patents do not differ significantly from privately owned patents. Hence they conclude that there is no evidence for market failure in European public–private RJVs.

Summarizing, the studies that have addressed directly the question whether university patenting has fostered knowledge transfer from the public to the private sector tend to show that patenting is one of the potential sources of knowledge transfer, but other sources as probably more important.

7. Conclusions and Discussion

The European Commission has put increased emphasis on public–private research interaction in its strategic policy for Europe's role in the 'knowledge economy'. Observing what happened in the USA, the economic and technological leader of the world, suggests that university patenting may play an important role in this interaction process. The USA adopted legislation (the so-called Bayh-Dole Act) that allows universities to patent the results from federally funded research. At the introduction of the Bayh-Dole Act in 1980, it was believed that university patents would facilitate technology transfer to the private sector because firms interested in developing university discoveries into commercial innovations could now obtain the exclusive right to do so (by taking an exclusive license from the university).

Following suggestions in the policy debate, this paper asked the question whether it would be beneficial for the European innovation system if there were a 'European Bayh-Dole Act'. This question is rooted in the general (policy) awareness that public–private research interaction is relatively weak in Europe, and that university patents may stimulate this, by facilitating institutional arrangements for knowledge transfer as well as by increasing the awareness of European universities for the commercial potential of some of their research.

Intellectual property rights are a rather special and difficult policy field. The patent system, both in a broad sense (where issues of patent scope are important) and in the specific sense of university patenting, is a system that must strike a balance in a trade-off between granting rights (and thus incentives) to an inventor, and leaving enough scope for positive benefits (technology spillovers) to society at large. Obviously, stronger patents are not always better. Because it is not always easy to identify on which side of the optimal trade-off the current situation lies, it is difficult for policy makers to design an optimal policy. This holds *a fortiori* for the topic of university patents. The issue of whether university patents facilitate technology transfer is hard to investigate in a quantitative way, and it is again likely that the answer differs on a case-to-case basis. The potential disadvantages of university patents are equally difficult to quantify. We are thus left with the impression of a policy field in which 'muddling-through' is the way in which policy must proceed: any decisions are necessarily based on incomplete information, and will be hard to evaluate. This does not imply that no policies should be made, or that existing policies should not be changed. On the contrary, it implies that policy makers must be like entrepreneurs, ready to implement new ideas, willing to take the risk of failure, and able to admit when this has happened.

In line with this, the debate cannot easily be concluded at a theoretical level. Arguments against and in favour of increased university patenting both exist. On the 'positive' side of the scales is the potential beneficial impact on technology transfer. On the negative side, several arguments can be raised: the danger to the 'open culture of science', a potential incentive for universities to perform more applied (less 'basic') research (to become more like firms), and the potential of 'strategic' patents to block future progress in an area.

At the institutional level, it was noticed that the European innovation system is quite different from the US one. In the USA the specific issue of federal funding provided the context for the Bayh-Dole Act, and this issue is largely absent from the European context. On the other hand, in some of the European countries, individual university researchers are entitled to the patents emerging from their (university-funded) research, which leads to a lack of bargaining power of universities in these countries in negotiations over ownership of their inventions. More specifically, it was argued on the basis of empirical survey evidence that in Europe, research joint ventures (RJVs) between universities and private parties are relatively frequent. This is indicated by the fact that patents in which university researchers are listed as inventor, but in which the university is not the owner of the patent, are more common in Europe than patents in which the university is the owner.

In the case of such public–private RJVs, there is a risk of market failure, as indicated by the theoretical model introduced by Aghion and Tirole (1994). A lack of bargaining power of universities with regard to the ownership of patents may lead to lack of university commitment in joint projects with firms, and this may lead to less valuable innovations. Such market failure is asymmetric: it may exist if private parties own the patent from a public–private RJV, but not if the university owns the patent. Given the European context in which such public–private RJVs seem plentiful, this may amount to a strong argument in favour of legislation that facilitates universities to own patents from their research, but whether or not such market failure actually exists is an empirical matter (the little available evidence seems to point out that it does not).

More broadly, the empirical research again arrives at mixed results with regard to the potential of increased university patenting. On the one hand, there does not seem to be convincing evidence that universities change their research strategy, and hence one of the potential dangers of university patents does not seem to have happened in the post-Bayh-Dole era in the USA. But on the other hand, the evidence that patents actually facilitate knowledge transfer is mixed, and patents appear to be a relatively unimportant source of knowledge transfer. The effects of patents on the open culture of science is still an ill-researched area, although some evidence on 'data-withholding' exists (Campbell *et al.*, 2000).

We may thus conclude that the theoretical debate, and the empirical research that is related to it, does not give us a clear-cut conclusion. A prudent policy maker may conclude that as long as the benefits of increased university patents are not clearly demonstrated, a policy effort like Bayh-Dole is undesirable. But the data suggest that European universities are already more heavily engaged in patenting than was believed on the basis of official patent statistics. This implies that the discussion about European university patents may to an important extent be outmoded. More knowledge may be flowing from European universities to the private sector than policy makers are aware of. But it may also be the case that the negative effects of university patenting, such as a negative impact on the open culture of science, may already be a reality in the European university system.

More research on the links between university researchers and the private sector is necessary to further enlighten these issues. In this respect, two lines of research might prove particularly useful. First, the study of individual cases of successful and unsuccessful cases of technology transfer may highlight the factors that may play a role in this process. Case studies would be particularly helpful in this respect, and they might lead the way for subsequent surveys aimed at reaching more representative results.

Second, a closer study of the networks in which university researchers are embedded may enlighten the different mechanisms of technology transfer between the public and private sector. University researchers use firms as the subject of their study, they supervise undergraduate and graduate students who do practical work in firms, they do consultancy, they visit conferences and workshops at which businesses are also represented, etc. In short, the university researcher operates in a network, in which firms are another important type of player. More knowledge about the nature of these networks, and the role that university researchers play in them, would be valuable for the study of public–private knowledge transfer. Both quantitative data (at the micro-level), such as publications and citations, and more qualitative data on network relations may be helpful in painting a more complete picture of this network.

One issue remains, and this is the role of patents as a source of finance for universities. When universities patent their discoveries, and license them to firms, license income may become an important source of finance. In an era when governments budgets are squeezed, especially so in higher education, this may be a welcome prospect for both university officials and government policy makers (European Commission, 2003, p. 13). However, the available evidence shows that the payoffs are so hugely varying between inventions, that it can hardly be imagined that licensing income is a stable source of finance for universities. In the US context, half of all universities has less than 1 million US$ licensing income per year (which is a relatively small amount, even when compared to the budget of an average European university). Moreover, only a few patents are responsible for the majority share of licensing income, suggesting that this source of finance has important characteristics that are similar to a lottery.

Acknowledgements

The research leading to this paper has been sponsored by the European Commission, under the DIME Network of Excellence, FP6, and parts of this paper draw on an earlier paper commissioned by the Ministry of Finance in the Netherlands. Neither the European Commission nor the Ministry of Finance can be held responsible for the views expressed in the paper.

Notes

1. But property rights also include copyrights (see Towse, 2006; Liebowitz and Watt, 2006), and trademarks (see Ramello, 2006).
2. This is even the case among European countries. Although the existence of a European Patent Office (EPO) suggests that a single European patent may be obtained, the practical situation is that the EPO grants several national patents, and the applicant has to pay for each one of these. Current political discussions are about changing this situation and establishing a single European patent.
3. On the other hand, Pavitt (1993) asks the question 'what firms learn from basic research' and argues that there may be certain incentives for firms to invest in basic research.
4. The only country in the EU that has a federal structure, Germany, is discussed below.
5. One may argue that Porter's patent data are a bit selective. While Porter presents a ranking list of all Dutch firms/organizations, he only presents universities in the case of the USA. The USA list thus hides the rank of the universities. According to information of the US Patent and Trademark Office, in 2000 (the last year of Porter's period), the first university is found at rank 32 (vs. 45 for Leiden University in the case of the Netherlands, 1996–2000). Moreover, the first US university, the University of California, is in fact more a federation of universities, with campuses in all major cities in California. The next university on the US list, MIT, has less than half the patents of the University of California (605), and does not rank in the top 100 in 2000.
6. A patent lists both the applicants (prospected owners) of the patent, and the inventors. Inventors are usually not listed with their affiliations, and there is nothing that prevents inventors from not being employed by the applicants of the patent.
7. The cited studies are Balconi *et al.* (2004) for Italy, Saragossi and van Pottelsberghe (2003) for Belgium and Meyer (2002) for Finland.
8. Calculations made by Patrick Llerena (ULP) show that more than half of all patents from research undertaken by university researchers at ULP in the period 1970–2000 are owned by private parties. These data were presented officially to the French Ministry, but are not yet published.

9. Interestingly, only in Germany can this low fraction be explained by the legislation that gives private researchers the right to own patents. At the time to which the Patval survey refers, such legislation was effective in Germany, but not yet in Italy.

References

Aghion, P. and Tirole, J. (1994) The management of innovation. *Quarterly Journal of Economics* 109: 1185–1209.

Agrawal, A. and Henderson, R. (2002) Putting patents into context: exploring knowledge transfer from MIT. *Management Science* 48(1): 44–60.

Arrow, K. J. (1962) Economic welfare and the allocation of resources for invention. In R. R. Nelson (ed.), *The Rate and Direction of Inventive Activity: Economic and Social Factors*. New York: National Bureau of Economic Research.

Association of University Technology Managers (2002) AUTM Licensing survey 2002: AUTM.

Balconi, M., Breschi, S. and Lissoni, F. (2004) Networks of inventors and the role of academia: an exploration of Italian data. *Research Policy* 33(1): 127–146.

Campbell, E. G., Weissman, J. S., Causino, N. and Blumenthal, D. (2000) Data withholding in academic medicine: characteristics of faculty denied access to research results and biomaterials. *Research Policy* 29: 303–312.

Carlaw, K., Oxley, L., Walker, P., Thorns, D. C. and Nuth, M. Beyond the hype: Intellectual property and the knowledge economy/knowledge society. *Journal of Economic Surveys* 20: 633–690.

Cohen, W. M., Florida, R., Randazzese, L. and Walsh, J. (1998) Industry and the academy: uneasy partners in the cause of technological advance. In R. Noll (ed.), *Challenges to Research Universities* (pp. 171–191). Washington, DC: Brookings Institution Press.

Cohen, W. M., Nelson, R. R. and Walsh, J. P. (2002) Links and impacts: the influence of public research on industrial R&D. *Management Science* 48(1): 1–23.

Colyvas, J., Crow, M., Gelijns, A., Mazzoleni, R., Nelson, R. R., Rosenberg, N. and Sampat, B. N. (2002) How do university inventions get into practice? *Management Science* 48(1): 61–72.

Crespi, G., Geuna, A. and Verspagen, B. (2006) University IPRs and knowledge transfer. Is the IPR ownership model more efficient? Mimeo SPRU, University of Sussex and Ecis, Eindhoven University of Technology.

Dasgupta, P. and David, P. (1994) Towards a new economics of science. *Research Policy* 23: 487–521.

David, P. A. (1993) Intellectual property institutions and the Panda's Thumb: Patents, copyrights, and trade secrets in economic theory and history. In M. B. Wallerstein, M. E. Mogee and R. A. Schoen (eds.), *Global Dimensions of Intellectual Property Rights in Science and Technology* (pp. 19–61). Washington, DC: National Academy Press.

Eisenberg, R. (1996) Public research and private development: patents and technology transfer in government-sponsored research. *Virginia Law Review* 83: 1663–1727.

European Commission (2003) *The Role of Universities in the Europe of Knowledge*, Brussels, COM(2003) 58 final.

Freeman, C. (1986) *Technology Policy and Economic Performance: Lessons from Japan*. London: Pinter.

Geuna, A. and Nesta, L. J. J. (2006) University patenting and its effects on academic research: the emerging European evidence. *Research Policy* 35: 790–807.

Giuri, P., Mariani, M., Brusoni, S., Crespi, G., Francoz, D., Gambardella, A., Garcia-Fontes, W., Geuna, A., Gonzales, R., Harhoff, D., Hoisl, K., Lebas, C., Luzzi, A.,

Magazzini, L., Nesta, L., Nomaler, Ö., Palomeras, N., Patel, P., Romanelli, M. and Verspagen, B. (2005) *Everything you Always Wanted to Know about Inventors (but Never Asked): Evidence from the PatVal-EU Survey*. LEM Papers Series, 2005/20, Laboratory of Economics and Management (LEM), Sant'Anna School of Advanced Studies, Pisa, Italy.

Henderson, R., Jaffe, A. and Trajtenberg, M. (1998) Universities as a source of commercial technology: a detailed analysis of university patenting, 1965–1988. *Review of Economics and Statistics* 80: 119–127.

Kline, S. J. and Rosenberg, N. (1986) An overview of innovation. In R. Landau and N. Rosenberg (eds), *The Positive Sum Strategy: Harnessing Technology for Economic Growth* (pp. 275–304). Washington, DC: National Academic Press.

Liebowitz, S. J. and Watt, R. (2006) How to best ensure remuneration from creators in the market for music? Copyright and its alternatives. *Journal of Economic Surveys* 20: 513–545.

Lundvall, B.-A. (1992) *National Systems of Innovation. Towards a Theory of Innovation and Interactive Learning*. London: Pinter.

Meyer, M. (2002) Do patents reflect the inventive output of university research? Leuven/Helsinki: KU Leuven/Finnish Institute for Enterprise Management.

Mowery, D. C., Nelson, R. R., Sampat, B. N. and Ziedonis, A. A. (2001) The growth of patenting and licensing by US universities: an assessment of the effects of the Bayh-Dole Act of 1980. *Research Policy* 30: 99–119.

Mowery, D. C. and Sampat, B. N. (2001) University patents and patent policy debates in the USA, 1925–1980. *Industrial and Corporate Change* 10(3): 781–814.

Mowery, D. C., Sampat, D. N. and Ziedonis, A. A. (2002) Learning to patent: institutional experience, learning, and the characteristics of US university patents after the Bayh-Dole Act, 1981–1992. *Management Science* 48(1): 73–89.

Mowery, D. C. and Ziedonis, A. A. (2002) Academic patent quality and quantity before and after the Bayh-Dole act in the United States. *Research Policy* 31: 399–418.

Nelson, R. R. (1959) The simple economics of basic scientific research. *Journal of Political Economy* 67: 297–306.

Nelson, R. R. (1993) *National Innovation Systems. A Comparative Analysis*. Oxford: Oxford University Press.

OECD (ed.) (2003) *Turning Science into Business. Patenting and Licensing at Public Research Organizations*. Paris: OECD.

Pavitt, K. (1993) What do firms learn from basic research? In D. Foray and C. Freeman (eds), *Technology and the Wealth of Nations* (pp. 29–40). London and New York: Pinter Publishers.

Porter, M. (2001) Innovation and competitiveness: findings on the Netherlands. Den Haag: Ministry of Economic Affairs, the Netherlands.

Ramello, G. B. (2006) What's in a sign? Trademark law and economic theory. *Journal of Economic Surveys* 20: 547–565.

Sampat, B. N., Mowery, D. C. and Ziedonis, A. A. (2003) Changes in university patent quality after the Bayh-Dole Act: a re-examination. *International Journal of Industrial Organization* 21: 1371–1390.

Saragossi, S. and van Pottelsberghe de la Potterie, B. (2003) What patent data reveal about universities: the case of Belgium. *Journal of Technology Transfer* 18: 47–51.

Towse, R. (2006) Copyright and artists: a view from cultural economics. *Journal of Economic Surveys* 20: 567–585.

Trajtenberg, M., Henderson, R. and Jaffe, A. (1997) University versus corporate patents: a window on the basicness of invention. *Economics of Innovation and New Technology* 5: 19–50.

8

BEYOND THE HYPE: INTELLECTUAL PROPERTY AND THE KNOWLEDGE SOCIETY/KNOWLEDGE ECONOMY

Kenneth Carlaw, Les Oxley, Paul Walker, David Thorns
and Michael Nuth

1. Introduction

Much has been made about whether anything is 'new' about the 'New Economy' with the conclusion being that we now *are* a knowledge-based society. But in what sense, if at all, are we any more of a knowledge society now than we were in Neolithic times, the Renaissance, and the Industrial Revolution? What is the role of intellectual property (IP) and the intellectual commons in the process of innovation, growth and economic development? What role does technology and technological knowledge play both in the process of innovation and economic growth and in the protection of IP itself? To answer some of these questions requires a clear understanding of 'the nature of the beast', what we mean by the New Economy, how we measure the level and growth of innovations and how we test for association/causation between knowledge (both embodied in human capital and disembodied) and any consequences it might generate (both good and bad), and how we protect IP.

Foss (2002) argues that '[w]hatever we think of this journalistic concept [of the knowledge economy], it arguably does capture real tendencies and complementary changes'. What might these 'new' tendencies be?

> We define the knowledge economy as production and services based on knowledge-intensive activities that contribute to an accelerated pace of technical and scientific advance, as well as rapid obsolescence. The key component of a knowledge economy is a greater reliance on intellectual capabilities than on physical inputs or natural resources. (Powell and Snellman, 2004)

Here the 'modern' emphasis seems to be on 'knowledge' (yes) 'accelerated technical and scientific advance' (yes) and 'greater reliance on intellectual capabilities than physical inputs or natural resources' (yes). Is this all new? Marshall (1890) states that 'Knowledge is our most powerful engine of production'. MacLeod argues that '[t]he unreformed [pre-1852] patent system was at best ineffective, or at worst, a brake on invention and its dissemination' (MacLeod, 1988). Furthermore Ashton (1955) suggests that '[i]f Watt's Fire Engine Act had not extended the life of his steam engine patent we would have had a railway system earlier' and Boehm and Silbertson (1967) state that '[E]vidence placed before the 1851 Select Committee ... certainly throws doubt on a strong causal connection between our early patent system and the British industrial revolution'.

In other papers in this special issue a number of authors[1] will consider, in particular, the role of IP in the process of innovation creation/limitation and economic development. In this paper we will emphasize a *historically grounded* approach to consider what, if anything, is fundamentally 'new' about the knowledge economy/society and whether it constitutes a modern economic and social 'revolution'. The themes we will investigate mirror some of the issues raised above as potential indicators of a 'changed world' and include (1) *the role of entrepreneurship, technological knowledge creation and obsolescence*; (2) *intellectual capabilities and intellectual knowledge*; and (3) *the role of science and research and development*. In order to consider whether the modern world is 'fundamentally' different we will, through the lens of history, consider these issues with a view to then analyzing what the current literature on the knowledge economy/society really has to say.

In particular, in Section 2, we explore characteristics of the British Industrial Revolution of the 18th and 19th centuries and similar episodes in Europe, with a view to 'setting the historical scene' for subsequent comparisons with the 'modern eras' of the 'new' 'information' and 'knowledge' societies emerging in the latter half of the 20th and the beginning of the 21st centuries. Section 3 focuses on the role of the *entrepreneur* as risk taker and innovator in a world characterized by uncertainty, complementarities and elective affinities. The analysis is illustrated with references to a range of developments that led to and potentially 'caused' the Industrial Revolution. This section continues to 'set the scene' to allow us to consider whether the world is 'fundamentally different' now to then. In Section 4, four particular forms of IP and its protection are considered including patents, secrecy, 'first-to-the-market' and copyright, to identify their historical origins, historical developments and their potential roles in the two epochs contrasted here. Section 5 presents the case for the critical role of *science and research and development* in the European Industrial Revolutions to allow an historical comparison with current debates on the assumed primacy of such elements in 'New Economy' and the potentially changing role of IP that modern developments and ownership create. With this historical background in place, Section 6 undertakes a detailed analysis of what might now define a modern knowledge economy/society via extensive reference to what others have said on such matters. The evidence from this section is that 'quantifiable, non-circular' definitions are frustratingly absent; however, 'knowledge' and the resultant role of IP creation and protection are a key component in all the cited authors' discussions. Whether IP and knowledge are 'uniquely' key to the 'New Economy' will be an issue we return to in the concluding section. Section 7 extends discussion of the role of IP in the knowledge society, emphasizing the fundamental role of the Information and Communication Technologies (ICTs), where innovation is increasingly seen as the fuel of the New Economy, with the internet the 'electricity', and Section 8 concludes by looking forward to identify key research questions and methodological challenges to progress these debates.

2. Historical Background

One of the key questions we try to address relates to whether we are currently living through a period of fundamental change, as radical and extensive as the 'great transformation'[2] (Giddens, 1982) of the 18th and 19th centuries. This 'transformation' comprised changes to the technological, economic, political and values base of societies.

To explore this question we will examine the two historical periods that have been identified as ones of dramatic change. The first created the 'industrial/modern society', replacing the agrarian period whereas the second is attributed to creating what many typically call the 'information/knowledge society'[3] (Toffler, 1980). Considerable controversy still lingers around both these claims with some seeing linear progress (Hirst and Thompson, 1996) and gradual change rather than sharp discontinuities whereas others subscribe to more radical transformations and argue for difference rather than continuity. Drawing on economic, sociological and historical traditions and critique we seek to take stock of the debates and identify the key questions still to be addressed in an ongoing research program.

Knowledge has always been important for the development of economic and social life.[4] In the 18th and 19th century industrial revolution, and in the more recent post-1960s information revolution, we see an age-old tension between the desire for an openness to innovation and change and the spread of information that would assist this activity and the need to control the access to knowledge in order to enable those who have created new IP to gain some economic return. Without protection of some kind it is suggested that there would be no incentive for a continued investment in the time, energy and capital that is necessary for the creation of yet more ideas. However, sorting out what if anything is different in the two time periods with respect to the role of knowledge has not proved straightforward for most authors. We would argue, however, that it is simply a matter of identifying the *specific types of knowledge* in use in the relevant periods and suggesting how the legal systems are forced to adapt their 'rules of the game' as these technologies emerge and evolve.

A considerable volume of research by both sociologists and economists has been devoted to examining the industrial revolutions that took place in the 18th and 19th centuries. A substantial change came from the use of new technologies and motive power – water to coal and electricity and oil. Such technologies allow new forms of production to take place expanding the industrial base of these societies. It also changed how things were made, moving products from small craft shops to factories and assembly lines. Human labour was deskilled from craft working and 're-skilled' to skilled and semi-skilled production line work (Hobsbawm, 1975). Larger units of labour required different settlement patterns encouraging the growth of new cities. For example, in the UK in 1801 there was only one city, London, that had a population of over 100,000 and by 1901 this number had increased to 35 cities of more than 100,000 containing 25.9% of UK population (Thorns, 2002). The initial development of industrial cities was marked by tenement housing and crowded conditions that allowed workers to live close to their work, but was associated with poor living and health outcomes,[5] reflecting the unequal distribution of the cost and benefits of the new system.

Economic changes associated with the development of the industrial system were profound. The source of wealth creation shifted from land-based and raw commodity trading to products of the industrial system. The accumulation of capital from the production and sale of commodities produced by increasing large-scale manufacturing became the key driver of economic life.[6] This led to the formation of the 'Fordist' system whereby reducing the cost of commodities through mass production and paying a wage that allowed workers to consume and regulating working hours[7] to create leisure, became a recipe for expansion (Amin, 1994). The labour process was changed with the growth of scientific management – 'Taylorism'. This created an ongoing debate as to what created increased efficiency and worker satisfaction (Braverman, 1975). Was it through streamlining that the production process (time and motion study) was improved or was it through creating a strong collegial bond between workers and management and developing more of a team approach (Roethlesberger and Dickson, 1939, Human Relations School)?

In industrial societies the principal source of value was human labour allied to new technologies of production. A key social change that was suggested as critical to the creation of this new system of economic activity was the spirit of capitalism (Weber, 1930, 1947). A change took place in values as a result of the Protestantism reformation emphasizing a more individual understanding of faith and religious work. Weber argues that it was the Calvinist idea of predestination and 'election' that encouraged hard work and the achievement of economic prosperity that then indicated that they were part of the 'elect'. Weber identified what he termed an 'elective affinity' between the economic, social and religious changes that created a climate that allowed the industrial system to develop extremely rapidly (Gerth and Mills, 1948). However, Lipsey *et al.* (2005) see the Protestantism work ethic as a sub-evolution following the invention of the printing press rather than a major theme. In particular they identify five key differences between Europe and the rest of the world. The first is pluralism of authority and control. The second is the corporation in the forms of the church, guilds and universities. Third is the adoption of natural philosophy rather than the doctrine of occasionalism that leads directly into the fourth, Newtonian science that cannot exist without natural laws, and fifth, a legal system that evolves out of canon law. Therefore, the economies of India and China fell behind in terms of their rates of economic growth. What this shows is that technology on its own is insufficient to create economic growth; therefore such growth comes from a combination of influences including *changes to the values and ideas* underpinning a particular society.

3. Industrial Revolution and the Role of Uncertainty, Technology Ideas, Complementarities and Elective Affinities

It is broadly recognized (see e.g. Suatet, 2000) that innovative entrepreneurship is a significant engine of technological knowledge creation, which itself is recognized as the fundamental engine of long-run economic growth.[8] Innovative, typically profit seeking, entrepreneurs have been responsible historically for a large proportion of the innovation necessary to make new technologies commercially viable. For example, much of the mapping of the globe and the refinements to the technology of three masted sailing ships in the 15th and 16th centuries occurred because individuals were seeking new ways (routes) to obtain economic profit.[9] This entrepreneurial activity led to the development of complementary technologies in the form of the joint stock company[10] and many other related financial innovations. In fact *economic incentives* have driven a significant number of major technological innovations throughout history. Writing was invented as a result of a desire to keep records for the purposes of taxation to fund public works.[11] The steam engine was invented to pump water out of mines. Furthermore, while other such General Purpose Technologies (GPTs) have found their inspiration from non-economic motives (e.g. the computer and Internet were originally developed as military technologies) their proliferation (i.e. development and diffusion) has been the direct result of entrepreneurs exploiting economic opportunities.

To the extent that economic growth is desirable it is necessary to understand this entrepreneurial engine of economic growth. In order to do this we must understand how technological knowledge manifests and develops, how it relates to other knowledge and pre-existing technologies and economic structures such as institutions, laws and capital (physical and human). We must also understand the incentives and motivation of the entrepreneurs that drive the process of technological change. Consider the process of economic growth driven by technological change. The critical feature of this process is that it is pervaded by uncertainty. Individual pieces of technological knowledge are complementary with other pieces of technological knowledge and with the economic structure into which they get embodied. The economic growth process exploits complementarities through combinations and re-combinations of technological knowledge. Decision makers (including entrepreneurs) of the system must form expectations with respect to investment decisions that take into account these features of technological change.

Because innovation implies doing something that has not been done before, uncertainty pervades the process of technological change.

> It is often impossible even to enumerate in advance the full set of outcomes of a particular line of research. Time and money are often spent investigating specific research questions to discover whether the alley they lead up is blind or rich in potential. As a result, massive sums are sometimes spent with no positive return, while trivial expenditures sometimes produce results of great value. Furthermore, the search for one technological advance often produces different, unforeseen advances. (Lipsey and Carlaw, 2000)

Uncertainty implies that different agents may make different innovative choices with respect to the same technology, resulting in different outcomes. Sociologists have drawn attention to the unintended as well as intended consequences from technological and other innovations, which also create uncertainty as we are unable to fully predict the associated or down stream affects. The environmental effects of chemical fertilizer applications and dioxin-based sprays are good examples where the unintended consequences of these new ways of enhancing farm production have had major unforeseen consequences upon the health and well-being of local populations. Yet, it is still possible for all outcomes of technology to generate economic value because each outcome can result in a commercially viable product or service. One important point is that while some outcomes may generate more value than others, there is no uniquely optimal outcome that should be chosen above all others nor do we always measure the long-term effects in making these calculations. Another important point is that no single individual can know in advance all of the potential applications for a given technology. The set of applications that is realized after this fact is the result of many diverse experiments (resulting in innovation) conducted by many different agents.

As an illustration of the importance of complementarities, consider the following thought experiment. How much would a group or groups within society be willing to pay not to have an identifiable technology such as electricity of the computer taken away for a given period, say a year? Think about conducting this experiment for several iterations, replacing the previously removed technology and taking out another. Now contemplate how many times this experiment must be conducted before the entire annual GDP of that national state (i.e. its ability to pay) is exhausted. Our conjecture is that the number of technologies that need to be individually removed to exhaust total GDP is smaller than the total number currently in use creating that national state's GDP.

Why does this occur? It is because of technological complementarities. The removal of electricity from the production system renders several (most) other technologies in that system useless. There would be no electric light, no telephones, faxes or email, no Internet in computers, etc. The subsequent replacement of electricity and removal of the computer or Internet means that the willingness-to-pay calculation has double counted the value of these technologies.

These observations about technological complementarities reveal that there is a major issue of attributing value to *individual pieces of knowledge* about which we say more shortly. The complementary structure of technological knowledge leads directly to another observation about the innovation process. Elements of technological knowledge can be combined and recombined to make different technologies. For example, many of the components for the Wright Brothers airplane were derived from bicycle parts. Another example is found in the sequence of power technologies: water wheels were displaced by steam, which in turn was replaced by electricity. However, hydroelectricity generation uses a water wheel. This is the characteristic of knowledge that leads to the optimistic view that economic growth driven by technological change is sustainable because the combinatoric possibilities with new and existing knowledge are boundless. These combinatronic possibilities circumvent diminishing returns in the creation of knowledge. In making such combinations and adaptations of technologies to new conditions the social and cultural conditions are a major factor. In Kobe, Japan, the local Rugby Union team imported a scrum machine from New Zealand and decided to 'improve the technology' by making the machine work with less friction. However, by doing so they completely defeated the purpose of the technology. Clearly there was no transfer of the complementary cultural information about the purpose and use of the machine!

There are two important aspects of entrepreneurial behaviour with respect to innovation that must concern us. First, given the characteristics (uncertainty and complementarity) of the technological growth process, the entrepreneur plays a critical role in identifying and exploiting the innovation opportunities that new technologies present. Second, entrepreneurs are the economic mechanism which transforms technological knowledge into economic value.

Entrepreneurs are the decision-making force which generates both continuous innovation and economic value from that innovation. The innovative entrepreneur is the opportunist who recognizes the opportunities inherent in new technologies. 'In that sense, the entrepreneur gives life to the implicit [in some cases explicit] demand on the part of consumers' (Sautet, 2000, p. 60). In almost all cases it is impossible to attach probabilities to outcomes and expectations are in many cases best guesses. Thus, entrepreneurs are the risk takers who form a vital linkage in the process of technological change and economic growth, converting technology into commercial value.

With such pervasive uncertainty, how do we appraise the economic value of the IP generated from innovative entrepreneurship and contemplate mechanisms to protect such property? Both are difficult issues. Appraisal requires assigning value often to individual pieces of technological knowledge. The problem exists because the economic value of the individual pieces of knowledge is only generated when they are combined with other pieces of knowledge to form commercially valuable products and processes. Protection provides the incentive to individuals to undertake innovative research, thus overcoming the positive spillover associated with the non-rivalrous characteristic of knowledge.[12] However, it also limits the exploitation of the protected technology by subsequent innovative entrepreneurs who will themselves create innovations by applying the technology in novel ways. Thus, protection slows the diffusion of new technology and limits the value extractable from it.

Economists' accounts of how technical change arises in market economies are influenced by Schumpeter's (1942) work that recognizes the need for profit in 'rivalrous' competition. In contrast sociological accounts have featured the social and professional aspects of this process and have given more attention to the social actors involved (Nelson, 1989). Increasingly both have recognized the need for an evolutionary approach that takes account of the inter-relationship of the private (market-based) imperatives and the 'public' knowledge creation and application-based aspects of innovation. Evolutionary paths though are not smooth. They may

have significant spikes when major technological innovation occurs as is clearly
shown by the work on GPTs.

What was the value of the printing press when Gutenberg first introduced the
technology (i.e. before the standardization of the vernaculars of Europe)? The press
became much more valuable after the standardization of spelling and dialect. Should
we then appraise Gutenberg's IP before or after the standardization of languages?
Our problem with appraising the value of Gutenberg's IP is a problem that pervades
all of IP over technological knowledge. How should we appraise the value of the
individual pieces of knowledge contained in the printing press, many of which
Gutenberg did not create himself? For example, movable type was invented in
China long before the European version of the printing press was created. Other
critical pieces of knowledge, such as the alphabet and language were also used by
Gutenberg but not invented by him. This provides support for the way that ideas
and technologies interact with the social and political conditions of particular nation
states in specific time periods.

The ability to associate economic value with a particular piece of knowledge is
made difficult by the very nature of technological knowledge and the processes
that create it. However, if we are trying to get incentives for these agents of change
such that they create as much economic value from new technologies as possible,[13]
we face some major issues. Some of the value will come from giving agents the
incentive to expand the set of application technologies associated with a particular
enabling technology as quickly as possible, which implies the need for diffusion.
Some of this value implies giving agents the incentive to create the enabling
technologies in the first place. (These incentives may take the form of IP protection.)
The critical issue is the amount these agents must receive in order for each type
to undertake innovative entrepreneurial activities. This amount need not be nearly
as large as the appraised value of the technology at any given stage of production.
In fact, economic theory tells us that the number need only be sufficient to cover
the resource and development costs (including the entrepreneur's opportunity costs
and risk premium) of innovation. This minimum reward is sufficient to induce the
desired behaviour and in all cases where the innovation is commercially viable
it must be less than the total value of the technology over its useful life. The
problem then is to appraise IP to get incentives correct for innovative entrepreneurs,
which means appraising the costs of innovation and not the total potential
value.

4. Intellectual Property Protection and Controls

4.1 Patents

In exploring the role of ideas and innovation, the issue of IP is a central one as
it concerns the way in which ideas can be diffused (Rogers, 1962). In thinking
about innovation, clearly one component is the creation of new ideas, such as the
creation of new technical processors, and new ways of organizing and managing
work. One way of controlling the flow of ideas and information is to subject these

to patents and copyright restrictions (see e.g. Liebowitz and Watt, 2006; Ramello, 2006; Towse, 2006).

Economists see IP protection as desirable because it gives inventors the incentive to create new technologies in the first instance. However, such protection is potentially a double-edged sword in that it restricts the creation of innovative technologies that exploit the initial technology. For example, Watt's patent on his atmospheric steam engine effectively delayed technological innovation in the form of high-pressure steam engines for 80 years (the length of his patent).

Historically, property rights, especially with respect to IP, have played a major role in technological and economic growth. However, it is important to note that the development of property rights is as often driven by technological change as it is a cause of such change. For example, rights to water access were established only after the need for fast flowing water to run water wheels to power textile and other manufacturing factories were put in place. A modern example of this problem is the Internet's impact on privacy and copyright for music (see Liebowitz and Watt, 2006). The important lesson is that well-defined property rights may help to facilitate the creation of new technologies, but new technologies may also require changes to existing property right regimes. IP comes in a variety of forms and this variety is actually a reflection of the technological knowledge being protected.

On the surface a *patent* seems to be a fairly straightforward way to ensure IP protection. However, in practice patents have little enforcement value for many holders. Pharmaceuticals and chemicals innovations enjoy nearly complete property right protection from patents while computer software innovations obtain very little protection. There is a fundamentally different characteristic between these technologies that relates to the technological characteristics of complementarities and combinatorics. Pharmaceuticals and chemical innovations are new combinations of complementary components of knowledge that take the form of molecules. The critical feature of pharmaceuticals and chemicals is that there is a unique mapping between the particular molecular combination and the output generated by the combination. Therefore, any marginal variation to the molecular combination will result in a completely different output. This is not the case for computer software (or most other technologies). Variations in computer code can produce virtually the same output. For example, consider the number of different word processors available to consumers. Thus, patents appear to be a useful protection mechanism only for technologies where there is a unique relationship between the combination of pieces of technological knowledge and the output of the technology.

Patenting does, however, have a long history. Machlup and Penrose (1950) note that a rather well-developed patent system existed in Venice in the 15th century, and that the practice of granting monopoly privileges by the Crown or by local governments to inventors was widely followed in many parts of Europe in the 16th and 17th centuries. In England the policy of granting the privilege of monopoly under royal prerogative culminated in the Statute of Monopolies of 1624, to provide the first patent law of a modern nation. Other countries followed, after a gap of more than a century, with France and the USA enacting patent laws in 1791 and 1793, respectively.

The role of patenting during the British Industrial Revolution, however, is a controversial one. On the one hand, controlling the flow of new innovations through patenting copyrighting and use of trademarks was prevalent and some analysts see this as a factor that limited innovative activity during the industrial revolution for example, 'Evidence placed before the 1851 Select Committee ... certainly throws doubt on a strong causal connection between our early patent system and the British industrial revolution'. (Boehm and Silbertson, 1967, p. 26). However, many economists have argued that innovators are 'rational profit maximizers' and as such without the protections of IP laws there would have been little incentive for them to spend time in the research and development that creates new innovations as they would be unsure as to whether or not they would have an economic return (Drahos, 2005).

Historians' judgements of the consequences for economic development of the precocious English patent system are mixed. Some, including Fox (1947) simply associate the origins of the modern patent system in England with the location of the British Industrial Revolution. MacLeod (1988, p. 198) takes a more cautious approach. She notes that the concept of 'intellectual property' in regard of technical invention was a late development.[14] It was mentioned first in a pamphlet of 1712, and after that the term re-appears sporadically in the patent applications later in the 18th century, before being enshrined in the Act extending James Watt's patent in 1775, 'his property in the said application secured'. However, MacLeod argues that the unreformed (pre-1852) patent system was at best ineffective, or at worst, a brake on invention and its dissemination. Ashton (1955, p. 107) suggests that if Watt's Fire Engine Act had not extended the life of his steam engine patent we would have had a railway system earlier.

Ironically, Dutton (1984, p. 204) argues that the imperfect nature of the British patent system during the Industrial Revolution may have in practice approached the ideal. Inventors paid heavily and separately in England, Scotland and Ireland, for the temporary, 14 years in the first instance, and uncertain privileges of patent protection, because property rights were dependent on decisions made by the Courts, not by the Patent Office. Nevertheless, British patents offered a degree of property protection to inventors, but did not provide complete barriers to access and use by others, and this, according to Dutton, was in all probability the most appropriate for the economy as a whole during the Industrial Revolution. The balance eventually swung in the favour of patentees. Sullivan (1989, p. 436) argues that part of the increased patent activity after 1830 was a response to the increased value of patent rights due to favourable treatment of patentees in the courts. Even so, in 1850 the system, according to Boehm and Silbertson (1967, p. 19) was enormously cumbersome, and involved 10 stages, which involved obtaining the sovereign's signature twice. The Patent Law Amendment Act of 1852, which simplified the process and cheapened the price of patenting, was the outcome of the persistent lobbying by inventors in the years since 1780.

For the period 1780–1851, Dutton's instinct that an imperfect patent system approached the ideal, receives the support of classical economists from Smith to Mill, the latter stating categorically that the condemnation of monopolies ought not to extend to patents. Sentiments in favour of abolishing the patent system were not entirely absent in an era that saw the end of Bank of England and East India Company monopolies in the 1830s. Machlup and Penrose (1950, p. 15), for example, cite an editorial from the *Economist* in 1850, which argues that inventors, to establish a right of property in their invention, should give up all the knowledge and inventions of others, which is impossible. Nevertheless in Europe, only the Netherlands, in 1869, abolished patents, although its citizens could take out patents in foreign countries, while Switzerland did not enact patent legislation, after torturous debate, until 1888. Schiff (1971) argues that industrialization flourished in these two countries in the absence of a patent system.

Whether the property rights afforded to inventors during the Industrial Revolution were a lever to technological and industrial progress is, on the basis of the historiography, unclear. Indeed, Boehm and Silbertson (1967), cite Rogers' (1863) view of the century earlier debates, 'that the arguments have not gone further than a *post hoc ergo propter hoc* discussion', and express doubt there has been much subsequent advance in thinking. The reverse interpretation, that the growth of patenting after 1760 followed industrial development, does appear in the literature. Ashton (1948) postulates that the timing and the direction of Industrial Revolution patenting activity was influenced by economic conditions, including prices, costs and interest rates.

Historians remain divided on the sectoral pervasiveness of Industrial Revolution technological progress. O'Brien (1993), Harley (1993) and Crafts (1985) argue that technological progress was localized in the cotton and iron industries. Alternatively, Temin (1997) and Landes (1969) see the Industrial Revolution as broadly based. McCloskey (1988) adopted an intermediate position, claiming that around 46% of economy-wide productivity growth arose outside the 'modernized sectors'. The linkages between patents, as a measure of 'protected' inventive activity, and the disaggregate records of British industrial growth between 1780 and 1851, have the potential to inform the debates surrounding historians' conceptualizations of the Industrial Revolution. The extent, if any, to which the effects of patented inventions spilled through the industrial economy, will shed light on whether protecting inventors' property rights impinged on the economy-wide adoption of new technology. Conversely, the statistical causality tests will also show if patenting activity was stimulated by particular industrial sectors.

In a series of papers, Greasley and Oxley (1994, 1996, 1997a) use modern times-series econometric methods and macro-level real total industrial production data, to identify the origins and likely 'end' of the British Industrial Revolution, dating the period as 1780–1851. Their work uses the Crafts and Harley (1992) amended version of the Hoffman (1955) data set. Using traditional Granger-type and more recent Toda and Phillips (1991) and Toda and Yamamoto (1995) methods, Greasley and Oxley (1997b) and Oxley and Greasley (1997) also consider possible causal linkages between industrial production (output) and other aggregate level data that have traditionally been identified in the economic history literature as potential candidates for 'drivers/engines of growth'. The candidates included real wages, imports, exports, population and *patents* and affected production *processes*. In that work, bi-directional causality between patents/processes (levels or growth rates) and industrial production (levels or growth rates) was identified. Their work is the only published work we know that considers the causal relationship between British industrial production and patent activity over the period of the Industrial Revolution. In related work, however, Sullivan (1989) assumes that because increased growth of patenting *preceded* increased growth of total factor productivity (TFP), a causal relationship can be inferred. However, he does not test for causality or, importantly, consider the effects of the non-stationary nature of the data that would affect the form of chosen causality test.

Greasley and Oxley (2000) also consider the sectoral inter-relatedness of the growth of industrial output, and thus of the pervasiveness of technological progress during the Industrial Revolution period, applying co-integrating relationship methods and tests for common stochastic trends, to Hoffman's disaggregrate, sector-level data. They conclude that Industrial Revolution technological progress spread widely, but unevenly. From their perspective, the productivity shocks shaping cotton and iron goods output defined the profile of early British industrialization. These two key industries shared a common stochastic trend with a wide group of mining and metal industries, and had long-run causal links to shipbuilding, paper, malt and sugar. The output trends in other important industries, notably woollens, linens, flour and bread, were isolated from the technological progress driving the cotton and iron goods industries.

In Greasley and Oxley (2007), they add to the debates surrounding the pervasiveness and the forces shaping Industrial Revolution technological progress by investigating the causal links between patenting activity and industrial output at the sectoral level during the period 1780–1851. Using time-series methods applied to the Hoffman (1955) data set they consider the existence of bi- and multivariate causality between patents and 16 sectors of the British economy comprising copper, copper ore, beer, coal, iron and steel, woollens, worsted, tobacco products, tin, sugar, shipbuilding, malt, linen yarn, cotton yarn, cotton pieces and hemp products. Broadly, their results show that the rise in patented inventions after 1780 was a consequence, not a cause, of the Industrial Revolution. Because patenting procedures did not change materially in the period to 1851, the simple implication is that the value of protecting the IP embodied in technical inventions rose sharply during the Industrial Revolution. These findings offer support to those historians, including MacLeod (1988), who argue that inventors 'rediscovered' the patent system after 1760 and learned to use it to their best effect. Before this date, inventors did not figure prominently in the debates surrounding IP, which centred largely on the rights of authors, publishers and printers. In contrast, post-1780 the engineering lobby was the most vociferous in the campaigns for patents reform, and for cheaper and more certain protection of IP. Interestingly, the results show that patenting activity was associated particularly with the 'new' fast growth sectors of the Industrial Revolution, notably cotton and iron. Inventors responded to the specific opportunities of the Industrial Revolution, a result that coincides with Ashton's (1948) interpretation of the direction of patenting activity.

4.2 *Secrecy*

Secrecy is another illustration of how the particular characteristics of a technology imply which IP protection mechanism is best suited. IP used internally in a particular production process is often usefully protected using secrecy. Moser (2005) demonstrates, using data on 4688 English innovations at the 1851 Crystal Palace Exhibition, that industries such as watch makers rely on alternatives to patenting to protect IP, that is, secrecy, tend to be more geographically concentrated than those that do. Those industries that subsequently shift to patent protection experience a tendency to geographic diffusion. Close proximity is required to enforce secrecy and minimize 'leaks'. Similarly, in the lean (or 'just in time') production created in modern Japanese automobile manufacturing firms (particularly Toyota) the technological knowledge was completely internal to the firm's production activities. Even when American automobile manufacturing firms first visited Japanese plants to uncover the secrets of the Japanese success they misunderstood the technology. The many failed experiments in robotics and complete automation of the assembly line in the USA are a testament to this.

4.3 *First to the Market*

Being 'first to the market' is an especially effective protection mechanism for technologies that are complementary with human capital that must be acquired by the user to extract any value from the technology. For example, computer software requires a human capital investment by the user in order to be able to generate output by using the software. In this case being first to the market means that owners of software capture large segments of the market because there is a cost for consumers to switch to any competing technology that enters the market subsequently. Technologies that require users to invest in complementary human capital in order to use them are most likely to find protection by being first to the market.

4.4 *Copyright*

Historically copyright has been a relatively effective mechanism for protecting IP that is stored in a physical medium. For example, owners of IP stored in books, records, cassette tapes and CDs have been able to appropriate much of the value of their property. However, with the new technology of digitally recording music the physical medium is no longer needed and, thus, we observe the current debate about the rights of Internet web sites such as Napster breaking copyright law (see e.g. Liebowitz and Watt, 2006 for a fuller discussion of this particular issue).

There are various other mechanisms for IP protection in use today, but the above discussion is sufficient to illustrate the point that the effectiveness of the mechanism depends on the type of technology to which it is applied. This should not be surprising given what has already been said about the complementary nature of technological knowledge. *Intellectual property protection mechanisms are a kind of technological knowledge themselves that are complementary to the particular technology to which it is applied.* Given what we know about complementarities and combinatorics it should be obvious that these complementarities will manifest in different forms just as different technologies do.

It should also be obvious that the protection mechanisms will co-evolve with technology. Furthermore, as has already been noted, some technological changes undermine existing IP protection mechanisms. In a sense the technology of these protection mechanisms is rendered obsolete by Schumpeterian creative destruction. Just like technologies themselves, new IP protection mechanisms must be invented and in many cases the inventors of such mechanisms will be entrepreneurs trying to protect research investments and profits they perceive from the opportunities in the new technologies.

5. The Role of Science and Research and Development

A further critical component of the 'great transformation' was the role of science. The adoption of a natural philosophy (rather than occasionalism) within the Christian religion brought a challenge to existing authority systems and epistemologies creating a belief in 'scientific knowledge' and exploration. The basis for this was systematic enquiry based on the new methods of science – observation, objectivity, classification and theory development. The world could be better explained through these means and once understood would be easier to shape and control. Reason was to dominate over the belief in other forms of knowledge. Science expanded and as it did so did the demands on it by the growing industrial economy and society. The growth of new applied disciplines of engineering, metallurgy and mining became important and new universities based around delivering these areas of study arose – often in the new industrial cities (e.g. Manchester, Leeds and Sheffield) and were supported by public funds and civic investment. In part, the rise of these new more technologically focused institutions occurred because the older established institutions were less sympathetic to these new areas of knowledge. This raises a further interesting question that impinges on our interest in IP and the way ideas flow which is, how far is growth in knowledge limited by the institutional structures that exist at the time?

In an important contribution to the understanding of how science advances, Kuhn (1962) suggested that this was through paradigm shifts. Kuhn argued that science and technology grew not through the falsification of existing paradigms, but in fact by making a move to a new paradigm. Movements in ideas therefore occurred through 'scientific revolutions' when a new paradigm overthrows an existing one – rather than paradigms being defeated through careful and systematic study. During non-revolutionary periods 'normal' science takes place within the dominant paradigm. The work of Kuhn drew attention to the social conditions and institutional restrictions of innovation that can occur through the ways in which disciplines and areas of knowledge become dominated by powerful elites who, as the gatekeepers of knowledge, attest to the quality of work, shape the journals and decide on orthodoxy. Such systems would also strongly support a more restrictive approach to IP transfer and availability.

The role of research and development is a critical component of the innovation system and one that impinges on debates around IP rights. In many countries there is substantial public investment in R&D and this raises the issue of the new subjects and sub-disciplines within science and technology, the rise of more applied subjects and the growth of the social sciences. It also raises the issue of the ownership of knowledge created via public investment (Nelson, 1989). Knowledge, though a commodity, is different from other commodities, in that many can make use of it without degrading it.[15] However, it can also be used to create new wealth generating activity and thus limitations on its dissemination have attractions. The New Zealand New Economies Research Fund (NERF) is an example of where public money is available to support research, which it is hoped will have possible commercial applications that will stimulate new economic activity. In such cases the release of research results can be restricted and can therefore conflict with the right of the public to know the outcome of funded research activity. David (2005) identifies three principal institutional devices employed by states to encourage the provision of public R&D – these are patronage, property and procurement. Patronage is where publicly financed research is awarded on the basis of a competitive process, such as the way that the NZ Foundation of Science and Technology administers the Public Good Science Fund of $460 million. Here the assumption would be that the results are in the public domain and are available for wide distribution. However since the 1990s, as the science system has increasingly been based around Crown Research Institutes (CRIs), which operate as profit making concerns and with universities also being encouraged to adopt a more business like model, holding onto the IP by the research organization has become more attractive and significant for their overall economic performance.[16] Procurement is where the state contracts with a preferred research organization or individual and the decision as to whether or not the information is made available tends to be a decision of the contracting party rather than the researcher. This model has increasingly been adopted within NZ Government especially as the public sector reforms of the 1980s led to the downsizing of the internal research capacity within Departments and Ministries (Pool, 1999; Thorns, 2000, 2003). Here research can be 'buried' where it is of a sensitive nature and at odds with current policy directions. Release here is often dependent on the nature of Freedom of Information legislation and Statutes of Limitation. The final arrangement is that where private producers of new knowledge are granted exclusive property rights that allow them to collect fees and other forms of return for the use of their knowledge. The increasing importance of information, and the new ways that this can now be accessed, sets the context for new struggles over IP rights and controls within the second period of transition that we are considering in this paper – the 'information and knowledge revolution'.

6. Information/Knowledge Economy/Society

So far we have considered a number of themes, that is, the role of entrepreneurship, technological knowledge creation and obsolescence; intellectual capabilities and intellectual knowledge and the role of science and research and development in our historical comparisons to set the scene. Up to this point we have not considered the modern meanings and origins of the period that is (currently) referred to as (variously) the information/knowledge economy/society in any systematic or rigorous way. However, if we are to critically and, importantly, fairly, to address the fundamental question of whether we are any more of a knowledge society now than we were in Neolithic times, the Renaissance and the Industrial Revolution, we have to be sure that we are talking the same language of those authors we seek to review.

In this section we will undertake a thorough critical analysis of what current authors appear to mean when they refer to the information/knowledge economy/society; what they identify as the unique characteristics of this period etc., with a view to ascertaining whether, based upon 'their' definitions of the beast, the world is fundamentally different.

The foreshadowing of the 'new' information/knowledge economy/society can be found in the revival and development of the economies and societies of the protagonists in the Second World War built around a continuation of the pre-war pattern. The basic industries were still mining, steel production and manufacture of commodities within a 'Fordist' system of production. This system was one based around mass commodity production and strong welfare states that ensured full employment and basic social provisions such as health, education and social security (Jessop, 2000). Economic growth was assisted by the recovery required after the destruction of wartime, strong growth in population as a result of disruptions and delays to marriage and childbirth through war. Growth in population also stimulated housing and the growth of consumer spending on household appliances and motor cars, which became an increasingly significant mode of transport. However by the 1960s the boom times were ending and the restructuring of the industrial economies began that had far-reaching effects in the 1970s and 1980s. This was a time of 'de-industrialization' in the economies of North America and Western Europe (Bluestone and Harrison, 1983; Massey, 1984; Lash and Urry, 1987). Manufacturing reduced as a component of the economies and in a number of cases shifted to cheaper labour markets in Southern Europe (e.g. Spain) to Central and South America (e.g. Mexico), and into Asia (including the Asian 'tiger' economies). This began the formation of a 'new international division of labour' and was one of the factors that stimulated the debate as to whether a new 'epochal' transformation was taking place and what would be the central drivers of the former industrial manufacturing economies (Froebel *et al.*, 1980; Smith and Feagin, 1987; Thorns, 1992).

The idea that the industrial manufacturing society was starting to be transformed into an 'information society' was initiated by among others Peter Drucker (1959, 1969, 1994) and Alvin Toffler (1980) and was part of a debate about the role of information and service workers within the changing economy of the time. Manufacturing and consumer services were seen as growing as the operation of companies became more complex as they grew in size. New areas of activity emerged and new areas of expertise were called upon to run the modern corporation. Strong growth occurred in information management, finance, marketing and sales. Also the expansion of the welfare systems created an expanding 'service' population engaged in government work including education, administration, social welfare services and urban and regional planning. In many of these positions – information was a more significant requirement than it had been in the past. Analysis of the growth of 'services', as part of a shift from a 'secondary' to tertiary economy and workforce, was often difficult as separating out whether the activities of service workers were new rather than an extension of previous forms of work proved very difficult due to the way that occupations were classified and recorded in national statistical databases.

By the 1970s the understanding of the changes taking place shifted from information alone to a greater emphasis on knowledge. This occurred in the 1980s and 1990s at a time when the institutional environment was one of deregulation and liberalization that encouraged government to dismantle border controls and other forms of economic regulation.

Thus we see that technological and economic change has been allied with political and social change as it was in the 'great transformation'. This supports the argument that *we are living through a time of far-reaching changes to the basis of societies*. The key to understanding these changes is being ascribed to the place occupied by knowledge, but what exactly is this role and is it uniquely 'new'?

Stehr has suggested that

central to my thesis is that the origin, social structure and development of knowledge societies is linked first and foremost to a radical transformation to the structure of the economy. (Stehr, 1994, p. 122)

The main element of change is seen here as that from a *material* economy to a *symbolic* one. Stehr argues

The economy of the industrial society is initially and primarily a material economy and then changes gradually to a monetary economy ... and then becomes as evident recently, a symbolic economy. (1994, p. 123)

Economists as well as sociologists have also identified knowledge as a key driver of contemporary economies. Economists, however, present a wide set of definitions/characteristics of what they believe constitutes a knowledge economy and hence its drivers. Smith (2002), however, summarizes succinctly the problem one faces with such attempts:

What does it mean to speak of the 'knowledge economy' however? At the outset, it must be said that *there is no coherent definition* (emphasis added), let alone theoretical concept, of this term: it is at best a widely-used metaphor, rather than a clear concept. The OECD has spoken of knowledge-based economies in very general terms, as meaning 'those which are directly based on the production, distribution and use of knowledge and information'. This definition is a good example of the problems of the term, for it seems to cover everything and nothing: all economies are in some way based on knowledge, but it is hard to think that any are directly based on knowledge, if that means the production and distribution of knowledge and information products. (pp. 6–7)

Economists tend to focus on the idea of Knowledge Based Economies (KBEs) which could be seen as a subset of the knowledge society, and limit the focus to the changed role of knowledge in economic activity. For example the OECD defined a KBE as

Economies which are directly based on the production, distribution and use of knowledge and information. (OECD, 1996)

In the Asia-Pacific Economic Co-operation (APEC, 2000) definition this is broadened somewhat to talk about how in such an economy all sectors are being reconstituted around a higher input of 'knowledge', but fundamentally the circularity persists.

In a series of papers Quah (2002a, b) and Coyle and Quah (2002) raise the idea of the New Economy as a *weightless economy*. This terminology is inherently 'Quah' and has not resulted in widespread adoption even though it has more concreteness than several other leading brands:

The weightless economy,[17] comprises four main elements: 1. Information and communications technology (ICT), the Internet. 2. Intellectual assets: Not only patents and copyrights but also, more broadly, namebrands, trademarks, advertising, financial and consulting services, and education. 3. Electronic libraries and databases: Including new media, video entertainment, and broadcasting. 4. Biotechnology: Carbon-based libraries and databases, pharmaceuticals.

Central to many authors' views on the New Economy is the importance of digital technologies, the Internet, computers, information and the globalized networks these technologies enable. To Talero and Gaudette (1996),

the information economy – is emerging where trade and investment are global and firms compete with knowledge, networking and agility on a global basis. A corresponding new society is also emerging with pervasive information capabilities that make it substantially different from an industrial society: much more competitive, more democratic, less centralized, less stable, better able to address individual needs, and friendlier to the environment.

Where does all this take us in our understanding of what the knowledge economy is and whether it is fundamentally different from the past? Appendix 1 below highlights a range of definitions/ideas that currently exist. All explicitly or implicitly have a central role for 'knowledge' in economic activity. We would suggest, however, that historically this is not *fundamentally* 'new'. The entrepreneurs of the Industrial Revolution used 'knowledge' to create new products. Fundamental constraints on the quantity and quality of the these products during this (and later industrial) period included importantly land, raw material and production technologies (factories and machines) governed by scarcity, rivalry and diminishing returns. However, what is 'new' now is the type of technologies in which the economy and society exist – digital technologies, built around ICTs. The issue to economists is whether these technologies create a fundamentally new technical environment where, for example, diminishing returns and inflationary tendencies are 'a thing of the past'.[18] To Gordon (1998) this has led to the growth of the 'Goldilocks Economy' where

> Freed from the restraint of restrictive monetary policy that had choked earlier expansions, and with its fires stoked by the lowest medium-term and long-term nominal interest rates in three decades, the economy charged ahead and achieved a state of high growth-noninflationary bliss that some have dubbed the 'Goldilocks economy' (neither too hot nor too cold, but just right).

Although it is clear that economists talk of knowledge, Stehr criticizes them for not giving the role of knowledge sufficient attention in their work:

> A close examination of the literature in economics indicates, however, that the function of knowledge and information in economic activity is, for the most part, ignored by economists. Either that, or they introduce knowledge as an exogenous variable, as an expense and generally treat it as a black box. (1994, p. 123)

However, although there has been considerable recent growth in the study of knowledge, the view of Adhikari and Sales (2001, p. 2–3) is that concepts such as the knowledge society are also incomplete and imprecise for they are found wanting in exact meaning and are of partial and sectarian relevance. McLennan (2003, p. 4) notes that in much of the literature concerning the knowledge society there has been an absence of a sustained discussion concerning definitional issues. Others, such as Ungar (2003), argue that the idea of the knowledge society is itself a gloss, as it is frequently evoked but rarely ever defined or explored in a systematic way. Moreover, Ungar continues, it is used merely as an extension of the 'more concrete' concept of the knowledge economy. Indeed, it seems apparent that the concept of the knowledge society needs additional clarity so as to differentiate it from other, similar concepts. In the view of Knorr Cetina (cited in Adhikari and Sales, 2001, p. 15), there is a need for a sociological concept of knowledge growth that brings into focus knowledge itself, 'breaking open and specifying the processes that make up the 'it'.' In other words, a more sociological approach to knowledge needs to identify the social processes in which knowledge is generated and from which it is turned into a commodity.

If the term 'knowledge economy' is primarily concerned with knowledge as a commodity and the value of intellectual labour in the creation of wealth, then the term 'knowledge society' should concern the social climate in which the knowledge economy resides. In other words, the knowledge society concept should relate to the much broader social context that both motivates and mediates the development and exchange of knowledge. This point is elucidated by McLennan (2003, p. 7) who notes that while some persistently equate the knowledge economy with the knowledge society, in actuality they are concepts that run in two different directions. McLennan notes that while the concept of the knowledge economy involves a 'strenuous reductionism', the concept of the knowledge society generally accepts that there are broader social and cultural factors that underlie the techno-economic momentum central to the post-industrial order and acknowledges knowledge's intrinsic value beyond its worth as a commodity.[19] This conceptual position is antithetical to that of the knowledge economy that merely conceives of knowledge as an object of economic value. Knorr Cetina and Preda (2001, p. 30) refer to this an as exteriorized perspective of knowledge whereby knowledge viewed as a commodity is regarded merely as a product or a research finding. Such an approach to knowledge growth overlooks social and cultural factors, which may be pertinent to how knowledge is generated and valued. This, on the other hand, appears to be what the concept of the knowledge society is attempting to address. Rather than viewing knowledge growth in purely reductionist terms, the concept of the knowledge society acknowledges that there are social and cultural factors that may influence knowledge growth at any point of time. As Thorlindsson and Vilhjalmsson (2003, p. 99) note, although the concept of the knowledge society is not yet well developed, it generally acknowledges that while science, innovation and expertise are the moving forces of economic development, social forces may intervene at any stage. This often relates to issues with power: those who own knowledge and the politics of knowledge-exchange.

In discussion of the current 'transformation of capitalism' knowledge as a key driver of production has been cited; typical of this view is that

> Capitalism is undergoing a transformation from a mass production system, where the principal source of value was human labour to a new era of innovation mediated production, where the principal component of value creation productivity and economic growth is knowledge. (Houghton and Sheehan, 2003, p. 2)

The key element in the transformative properties of the knowledge society is identified as 'information' and here the major factor has been the ICT revolution and in particular the growth of the Internet and more recently digitization. This makes the access to information easier and quicker, extends its global reach and makes it considerably harder to control. For all these reasons Castells has suggested that

> What is new in our age is a new set of information technologies. I contend they represent a greater change in the history of technology than the technologies associated with the Industrial Revolution, or with previous Information Revolution (printing). (Castells, 2000a, p. 10)

Castells has further suggested that the Internet is the 'electricity of the information age' (2001, 2004). There has been a phenomenal increase in the expansion of the Internet within a very short space of time. In 1989 there were 159,000 Internet hosts and this has grown to 43 million by 2000 (Houghton and Sheehan, 2003). However, one must not ignore the fact that there have also been massive gains in computational capacity of Complementary Metal Oxide Semiconductor (CMOS) logic design. This has been far more rapid and for a much longer period of time than the expansion of the Internet. Some would argue that the expansion of the Internet would not have been possible without the efficiency advances of microchips. What the IT revolution has brought about is the ability to manipulate, store and transmit large quantities of information at very low cost (Houghton and Sheehan, 2003). ICT and digital technology through the power of the modern computer and the next generation of high-speed computers with storage in terabytes rather than gigabytes have created new possibilities in the storage, surveillance, linking and processing of data sets that previously were unconnected. This extends possibilities from the tracking of criminals and terrorists across the globe, to profiling markets for products by small geographical areas (Geographic Information Systems (GIS) and other applications) to tracing benefit frauds (Lyon, 2003). New networking opportunities are created through this enhanced connectivity that generates new forms of knowledge and leads to a whole range of new economic activities associated with the creation, storage and retrieval of information.

The new computer and digital technologies have started to transform the way that work gets done across all sectors, but particularly within the 'knowledge generating' areas of science and technology. We can see here the growing impact in the last decade of E-Science and E-Social Science based on collaborations built around shared information transmitted via the new fibre optic superhighways and satellites – creating a much more globally connected world. These transformations are at least partially attributable to particular characteristics of the technology, namely, the sending and receiving capabilities of communication at a very large number of dispersed nodes, generating a network externality and the non-rivalrous nature of the commodity being exchanged, *information*. This stimulates the demand for new software products and creates new networks, information clusters and incubators that have become key nodes of innovation. The managing of these new information systems has led to knowledge management becoming a critical area of contemporary business development and practice.

We need here to distinguish between the data – which are the units recorded, information which is processed data and knowledge which is what can be created from the information. What this indicates is that in 'knowledge societies' some would argue that we have a new principle, 'knowledge' that creates a new source of added value. This leads into the wider debate that has emerged about different forms of capital. Bourdieu (1986) has extended understanding of capital to include alongside economic capital, cultural capital, and subsequently social capital has also been distinguished (Cunningham, 2005; Pillay, 2005; Marinova and Raven, 2006).

Human capital in knowledge societies has also been reinterpreted and seen to be of increased importance. Knowledge is now a commodity to exchange and create new wealth generating opportunities; thus those with desired 'human capital' become sought after. Bell (1973) sees this shift leading to the end of the industrial working class and its gradual replacement by a post-industrial proletariat consisting of poorly unionized, part time, casual workers. Such a core peripheral pattern of employment creates new patterns of social inequalities with the new 'knowledge' class as one of its significant components. Such a class is global in its importance and it significantly increases the value of and need for new skills and capabilities that in turn has impacted upon the way education is thought of and delivered. Drucker (1969) drew attention to the importance of teamwork in a knowledge society, and he drew a distinction between people who work with their hands and people who worked with their minds and thought. Increasingly, in the knowledge society he argues the dominant class of people is likely to be those who work with their minds.

Contemporary society is coming to *depend more and more* on knowledge in economic production, political regulation and everyday life (Stehr, 1994; Castells, 1997). With the spread of knowledge and the demonstrated loss of scientific legitimacy through a growing realization that there are many areas where there is still limited understanding, a greater questioning and scepticism towards experts is becoming more prevalent. This is part of the wider post-modern critique of the enlightenment scientific paradigm and a move away from meta-narratives and linear theories to embrace a greater range of understandings about how social change takes place. Many now see path-dependent and complexity theories providing greater insights into change than more determinist approaches, either technologically driven explanations or ones that assumed a linear pathway such as forms of modernization theory (Urry, 2003; Law and Urry, 2004). The idea of the knowledge society is not a new form of technological determinism, but rather a new argument about 'elective affinity'. Social actors have greater capacities for self-interpretation and action than have been acknowledged in past theories of change (Giddens, 2001). For Castells 'the information technology revolution did not create the network society. But without information technology, the Network Society would not exist' (Castells, 2000a, p. 139). In a knowledge society it is suggested that the wealth of a company is increasingly embodied in its creativity and information. The place of the creative industries cannot be relegated to a footnote, but now it needs to be seen as an integral component of the 'knowledge'-based industries (O' Brien *et al.*, 2002).

Alongside these views that information technology has created new social and economic conditions thus creating a social transformation, are a range of sceptics who consider that there is insufficient evidence for such an assertion (May, 2002). Much of this critique turns on the view that the argument is based on technological determinism through the assertion that 'technological changes bring in their wake major shifts in societies which use them' (May, 2002, p. 24). Bimber (1995) draws attention to three strands of technological determinism: the normative, nomological and unintended. Most accounts of the shift to the *information society* stress the first two rather than the unintended as they are stressing the positive move towards a new social and economic organization of knowledge and practice of accumulation. Sociological work adopting less determinist views has stressed continuity rather than rupture; thus the information 'revolution' becomes part of the continuing development and utilization of technologies to change the ways that we do things both intentionally and unintentionally (Mumford, 1966; May, 2002). This suggests that we should adopt an approach to the 'knowledge society and economy' that sees it as part of a continuingly evolving history of connection between specific national and international contexts, technological innovations and economic, social, political and cultural opportunities that either facilitate or resist innovation and change.

The other strong link that has been made is between the knowledge society and globalization. Globalization, rather like the knowledge society, is subject to controversy (Scholte, 2000; Holton, 2005). There is some agreement that what we are now seeing is a much greater connectedness across the globe created by the possibilities arising from the IT revolution. This compresses time and space and allows new ways of working drawing upon globally connected workers. This makes national boundaries and forms of control much more difficult and potentially creates challenges to local and national cultures through the penetration of globalized entertainment, information, ideas and practices. The world through a range of new media has now become accessible and available as never before. Competitiveness is now within a global environment that emphasizes free trade and weaker national borders to allow the freer flow of capital and labour. A greater importance is attached to flexibility in labour markets that brings an end to stable employment and predictability of career paths. Growing inequality has resulted at both the global and local levels with a growing gap between rich and poor at the national and individual level.

7. Intellectual Property in the Knowledge Society

One of the major themes that runs through the current literature on the knowledge economy/society is the role of innovation created via human capital with '*a greater reliance on intellectual capabilities*' in production and consumption. These issues are increasingly seen by some as the 'fuel' of the New Economy, with the Internet, *enabled by electricity*, as the 'energy/motive power'. In this section we will focus upon the role of IP in modern societies, an area that is typically ignored or subsumed in simple *economy*-based discussions.

For advanced societies a greater emphasis appears to be placed upon a culture of innovation and a focus on how this can be generated. The power of the Internet and the connectivity that it allows poses new threats to the control of IP and for some raises issue as to whether it is still possible to protect the flow of information at all. Computer systems are vulnerable to security breaches and ensuring the security of such systems has become a significant growth industry in itself as web-based activity extends into all aspects of life from work through to shopping, banking, recreational and leisure activities including gambling and downloading music and video MP3 files onto iPods (see e.g. Liebowitz and Watt, 2006).

The speed of innovation also raises further questions with respect to the protection of IP in the contemporary environment where in some areas, with the current speed of diffusion, the shelf life of new products may be only a matter of months. Computer systems and software are subject to frequent upgrades and changes making it potentially a 'greedy technology' that constantly demands investment to keep it 'current'.

The importance of networks and clusters within the new environment has led to the creation of new territorial and virtual clusters of innovation, for example, Silicon Valley in California and New York's Manhattan's Silicon Alley (see Graham, 2004). Knowledge can now thus be created in 'virtual' research communities that can gain intellectual capital through the participation of cross-national teams working through computer-based collaborative technologies. Such innovations have led to new linkages between universities and commercial enterprises looking to make use of the new knowledge areas such as genetics and genetic engineering, biotechnology and nanotechnology. Universities now operate in the new 'enterprise and business environment' in which they are also interested in the commercialization of the IP of their researchers (see Verspagen, 2006). This raises questions as to who owns the IP created (Delanty, 2001). Digital access, broadband and Internet connectivity become the key aspects of inclusion in the new knowledge creating activities and thus become of increased importance. Being part of the 'advanced networks' to allow fast and extended linkages across national systems and globally are now seen as keys to research and development and maintaining global competitiveness. For example, the NZ Government's decisions to invest in the Advanced Network providing gigabytes of connectivity across universities and CRIs was stimulated by the desire to keep the New Zealand R&D sector globally competitive. Such Advanced Networks are now present in 40 other countries, so the absence within New Zealand creates problems for our scientists – the Advanced Network will 'ensure our scientists are able to catch up with their partners and participate in the exciting world of modern science' (Jarvie, 2005, p. 2). However, there is still a digital divide with the levels of connectivity across and within nations differing that creates a new set of inequalities. For example a recent UNCHS report talks about

> Enclaves of 'super connected' people, firms and institutions, with their increasingly broadband connections to elsewhere via the internet, mobile phones and satellite TVs and their easy access to information services, often cheek by jowl with much larger numbers of people with at most rudimentary access to modern communications technologies and electronic information. (UNCHS - United Nations Centre on Human Settlement, 2001, p. 6)

The OECD countries have the highest rates of telephone, mobile phone subscribers and Internet and broadband connections and as with many other forms of technology those with the lowest incomes, globally and locally, have the most restricted access to the benefits of the technology.

Sociologists have typically focused on the issues associated with power and the limitation of access and the reasons why material might be withheld. Do such restrictions assist in maintaining the power and position of the dominant sectors within society and thus contribute to the maintenance or creation of social inequalities? Information on the new superhighway of the Internet is mostly public and therefore freely available as long as the potential user is connected. Open source software was central to the original creators of the Internet as they were about facilitating interchange and not restricting access to information. Acknowledging the power issues are crucial to a sociological understanding of the role of knowledge in society and therefore to the understanding of IP. The concept of IP refers to a number of protections for human creations including patents, trademarks and copyrights (amongst others).

In the shift to a knowledge-based economy, whereby ideas gain economic value, it is believed that the existence of intellectual property rights (IPRs) are absolutely vital in order to prevent others from producing and selling copies of your own ideas (Kenny, 1996, p. 701). Owing to their abstract nature, intellectual technologies are difficult to control and may 'escape' the clutches of their creators to become public goods, to be used and manipulated by others (Kenny, 1996, p. 702). Acknowledging this, it is apparent that assigning IPRs is an exercise in knowledge management aimed at restricting the accessibility of knowledge in order to preserve or enhance its value as a commodity; or in Fuller's words (2001, p. 188), with the assignment of IPRs, knowledge is 'captured' and then delivered as a service. IPRs, in this case, are directly concerned with the privatization of knowledge for monetary gain.

Globally there is a significant digital divide with levels of connectivity that are very different across nations and within nations (UNDP, Mansell *et al.*, 2002). One of the changes to IP under the knowledge society is that knowledge has itself increasingly become a commodity, a product that can be traded. The ideas as well as the people creating them are valuable. The cost of excluding people from information can also be high as it can limit innovation or can result in the appropriation of information by the few. The shift to greater emphasis upon ideas and their creators increases the value of the well-educated and trained section of the population giving rise to 'brain drains and brains gains'. The declining and ageing of the intellectual workforce in the European economies is one of the growing pressures on migration from the less developed countries of their innovative and highly qualified and trained people. This has implications for the digital and other aspects of the knowledge divide and is one factor in the continuing inequalities between the wealthier and poorer nations.

One of the key differences 'knowledge as a commodity' has with other commodities is that it is not reduced by use; rather there is evidence that it is a collective product that is enhanced by many users. This raises a further challenge to determining IP as many of the 'innovations' and 'inventions' within a knowledge society are the products of large international, multidisciplinary teams; thus ascribing IP to individuals becomes increasingly difficult. Research and development funding has also had to adjust to these new times and there has been a move towards longer funding cycles and a greater emphasis on inter- and multi-disciplinarity that crosses not only the traditional sciences but also recognizes the contribution of the social science and humanities.

The forms of protection include both statutory systems of protection such as patents from the 15th century, and copyright, to the 18th century, trademarks and design protection. The new global environment has focused attention increasingly on international agreements as a new way of trying to enforce IP protection. Examples here are the passing of a directive on the legal protection of databases by the European Union (EU) in 1996. Since then the EU has continued to work for a treaty on this issue. The World Intellectual Property Organization administers currently 23 treaties on Intellectual Property and WTO members are required to abide by the standards set out in the agreement on the Trade Related Aspects of Intellectual Property Rights (TRIPS) (David, 2005; Drahos, 2005). These various agreements and statutes have given rise to the growth of national and international bureaucracies and forms of administration. In all these contemporary debates we can see the interconnection of economic, legal and political arguments and decision making surrounding the need for and ways to control the flow of ideas.

The globalization of IP protection has largely benefited the advanced economies, particularly the USA and EU. Such protections are part of the ways that these countries and the corporations based in them but operating globally seek to maintain their dominance. Here the increased prominence of transnational companies, many of which have a turnover greater than many nation states, as key global players is increasingly significant (Held, 2000). The awareness of the value of IP amongst developing countries and indigenous people has also stimulated attention to the protection of such IP from the activities of global corporations. An example here would be the recent UNESCO convention on cultural indigenous knowledge protection (see also Marinova and Raven, 2006). Some of these attempts at protection, however, come up against WTO free trade agendas and the desire of the advanced countries to include trade in services and ideas within the general debates surrounding freer trade across the globe. Interestingly, the development of the Internet, especially in its earliest stages, was not through commercial imperatives, but more as a result of the work of researchers and enthusiasts exploring the possibilities of a new form of communication. The ethos of this group was about openness, hence the open source nature of much of the Internet. It is interesting to note that high-tech developments in ICT have occurred largely in the absence of IP protections.

As David (2005) notes, there has also been a long running moral argument about the accessibility of information. Advocates for the openness of government and commercial activity to public scrutiny suggest this is best achieved by the free flow of information and the encouragement of debate on social improvement. Those who support a more open system of exchange generally favour a move towards a greater balance between the interests of the IP holders and users. Drahos (2005, p. 149) argues that

> The current problem facing knowledge economies is that their law-making processes have been heavily influenced by owners of intellectual property. As a result the rights of owner have strengthened.

Thus, the debate about openness and free dispersal of knowledge versus restriction and exclusivity is not new. In recent times, however, international law has focused on strengthening exclusivity of IP rights rather than making knowledge more accessible, for example, the Digital Millennium Copyright Act (1998). Prosecuting and policing the increasingly borderless transmission of information is proving difficult. The solution that is being sought is the harmonization of IP rights laws. However, this is likely to provide the greatest advantage to the developed countries. Alternatively the rights and participation of users could be strengthened creating a more even contest around the access to and use of knowledge. Increasing knowledge becomes the key resource for future economic growth. As a consequence, the struggle over IPRs will intensify making it even more important that we undertake robust analysis of whether IP protection facilitates or restricts the flow of new innovations and creative activities in twenty-first century societies.

8. Conclusions

The concepts of knowledge society and economy are clearly related as both leverage off the idea of transformation to create fundamentally different features of society and economy. Both see information as having a special and significantly different place. Speed and forms of storage and transmission emerge as key elements in its newness. Information as a central driver of production requires new forms of organization favouring the more flexible and responsive idea of networks rather than institutional structures. Thus we see a new form of society emerging characterized as a 'network' society where flows and movement and less certainty are characteristic. Forms of explanation have shifted from linear causality to a greater appreciation of path dependency and complexity. Combinations of technologies and social and cultural practices mediated by local and global political relations are now part of what has to be considered to explain the growth of new forms of technological and economic activity. This favours explanations that explore the past as a way of understanding the present. It requires a deeper and sustained empirical analysis than is seen in much of the debate about either the knowledge society, knowledge economy or information society.

There are substantial challenges facing work in this area. These are both at the theoretical and methodological level. A more consistent set of definitions is required and more robust measures are derived from the theory rather than from what is currently or conveniently available. For an economist the question has been: is the 'knowledge economy' a *fundamentally* new economic paradigm, with new drivers or is it just '*hype*'? Whereas sociologists have asked: is the 'knowledge society' *fundamentally* different from what preceded it? The first issue we face is one of potentially viewing a *process* rather than an *outcome*. The period of the 'great transformation' has occurred and although one might debate the relative importance of patents as a cause or effect of the Industrial Revolution, in the absence of new evidence the historical events have occurred. For those studying the 'knowledge society' the twin problems of definitional limitations and potential lack of a complete historical lens complicate analysis. We may simply conclude 'the world is no different to the past' simply because change is incomplete.

Assuming, for the moment, we can revolve the definitional issues of what constitutes the knowledge economy or the knowledge society and what set of changes is 'fundamental', what evidence could we call upon to test such hypotheses, in particular the role and consequences of innovation, IP, its creation and protection?

Innovative entrepreneurship operating in a world of uncertainty, where profit seeking innovation creation leads to new product creation with and from new technologies, where IP has an important role to play, could equally describe the Industrial Revolution or the Information Revolution. The technologies differ and the relative mix of land, labour, capital and knowledge differs, but the general paradigm has explanatory power. The historical forms of IP protection remain in place although the mix of users differs. It is interesting to note that one of the simplest and less formal, secrecy, with resultant geographic proximity, has made a resurgence when faced with the challenges of protecting digital goods. New challenges for IP protection arise with the rise of 'digital goods', but this technology generated the need for a technologically new IP protection system that is not, in itself, new. The actual goods produced differ, the *relative* role of knowledge-led produced goods differs, but is the economic world *fundamentally* different?

What has the weightless economy done to workers, firms, ownership and control? The traditional neoclassical theory of the firm (Grossman, Hart, Moore) puts ownership of physical capital to the fore. Do we have a robust theory of the firm in a knowledge economy? We would suggest not. If and until knowledge-only-driven weightless goods production can be explained by the traditional theory of the firm, the possibility remains of not rejecting the notion that the knowledge economy represents a fundamentally new economic paradigm where the 'old rules' do not apply.

In the old economy, reading, writing and the access to books was what divided the 'haves' from the 'have-nots'. Those with these basic skills were identifiably different from those without. Here access to a knowledge base of trusted information was potentially 'exclusive' – the knowledge was typically expensive to acquire (books or education), but the knowledge itself was 'trustworthy'. The modern analogy is access to the Internet and ICTs more generally. The 'digital divide' is in part about access and acquisition of information, much as it always was. However, the added dimension, above simple access, is about the trustworthiness of the available information. Information is cheap to acquire, but the trustworthiness of its content is low. As in the past, information remains data without the human capital ('wisdom') to create knowledge from combination. Reputation of the provider acts as a screen, with the role of trademarks and brands coming to the fore as they have in the past.

In terms of societal transformation that could be fundamental are the ways that work, leisure and relationships across a whole range of aspects of life are being changed by the impact of digital technologies and new forms of connectedness. Here speed and availability via computers, Internet and cellular technologies is potentially transformative, opening up new ways of knowing and choosing and organizing aspects of life from shopping, to travel, to working practices to dating, gambling and selecting and listening to music on the iPod. The technologies in their broadest sense also create new means of sifting and sorting populations from the web base 'Up My Street' systems in the UK to the marketers' databases on tastes and preferences to police and social welfare databases on where at-risk populations are concentrated (Burrows and Ellison, 2004). The new technologies of storage and retrieval also raise issues around protection and authentication of material; we now have the Wiki encyclopaedia alongside more established ones claiming its place as a repository of knowledge. Such sources create new challenges to the establishment of authenticity and accuracy of the text. The growth of more 'open source' ways of discovery also poses challenges to established gatekeepers of knowledge and have been seen to open the way to more democratic practices of knowledge dissemination and use. However, will these constrain innovation by undermining its commercial value or enhance it? This is the old debate in the new clothes of the 21st century digital and Internet world. To move forward we need a clear understanding of the key elements of change in past transformations to guide us in determining the present and possible future transformations. In finding a way forward it is important to acknowledge both the continuities with the past and the discontinuities and to further see how technological innovations and economic, social, political and cultural opportunities both facilitate or resist innovation and change.

Acknowledgement

The authors acknowledge the funding from the New Zealand Marsden Fund for the research that contributed to this paper.

Notes

1. Hausman, 'Real options and damages in Intellectual Property cases'; Verspagen, 'University research, intellectual property rights and European innovation systems'; Towse, 'Copyright and artists: A view from cultural economics'; Marinova and Raven, 'Indigenous knowledge and Intellectual Property: A sustainability agenda'; Ramello, 'What's in a sign? Trademark law and the economic theory'; Liebowitz and Watt, 'How to best ensure remuneration from creators in the market for music? Copyright and its alternatives'.
2. One might argue with this terminology 'great transformation' in that it may have been no 'greater' than the move to settled agriculture in Neolithic times or the transformation that ensued with the invention of writing.
3. Again, one might challenge this rather contrived demarcation of history if we identify the creation of writing and the printing press as the 'first information society'.
4. Lipsey *et al.* (2005) argue that the evolution of technological knowledge has driven economic growth and social transformation since at least the Neolithic agricultural revolution.
5. However, there is a body of literature that would argue that the lowest classes of serfs and roaming labour were far better off in industrial working activities than they were in the feudal agricultural system.
6. 'When a man's wages went up in the eighteenth century the first beneficial effects might be expected to occur in the brewing industry, and in the commercialisation of sport and leisure ... gambling, boxing, horse racing and the like. When a woman's wages went up the first commercial effects would be expected in the clothing industries, which provided consumer goods for the home. Her increased earnings released her desire to compete with her social superiors – a desire pent up for centuries or at least restricted to a very occasional excess' (McKendrick, 1974).
7. '...workers that had once been forced to work out of poverty or coercion ... now men are forced to labour because they are the slaves to their own wants' (Steuart, 1767).
8. Other engines of technological change include basic science, public and to some extent privately funded research. Worker 'learning by doing' using and adapting human curiosity.
9. Though much was State sponsored.
10. Here technological innovation is being used more broadly than simply 'physical' technologies (see Lipsey *et al.*, 2005).

11. One could also argue that this shows the importance of the political process linked ultimately to the development of the Nation State.

12. Knowledge is non-rivalrous in the sense that one individual's use of knowledge does not preclude another's use of the same knowledge in the same way that one person's consumption of a loaf of bread precludes another's consumption of the same loaf of bread.

13. This assumes that economic and social objectives are themselves aligned – an heroic assumption.

14. Intellectual property laws and patents are synonymous in these earlier periods, but this is certainly not the case today where IP is protected via a range of other legal means.

15. Knowledge is typically 'non-rivalrous'.

16. See here the paper by Verspagen (2006) in this issue.

17. The 'weightless economy', as compared with the label 'weighty economy' of the industrial era.

18. The view of Lipsey *et al.* (2005) is that it is the ongoing creation of new technologies that frees us from diminishing returns and not any specific technology in any period of time. ICTs may be a suffient technology to achieve this at this point in time, but it is not necessary in the light of other new GPTs that might arrive.

19. However, it is easy to conceive of the knowledge economy as simply being encompassed, or nested within, the concept of the knowledge society.

References

Abramovitz, M. and David, P. A. (2001) *Two centuries of American macroeconomic growth. From exploitation of resource abundance to knowledge-driven development.* Stanford Institute for Economic Policy Research, August, SIEPR Discussion Paper 01-05. Stanford.

Adhikari, K. and Sales, A. (2001) Introduction: New directions in the study of knowledge, economy and society. *Current Sociology* 49(4): 1–25.

Amin, A. (ed.) (1994) *Post Fordism: A Reader*. Oxford: Blackwell.

Ashton, T. S. (1948) Some statistics of the industrial revolution in Britain. *The Manchester School* 16: 214–223.

Ashton, T. S. (1955) *An Economic History of England*. London: Meuthen.

Asia-Pacific Economic Cooperation (2000) Towards knowledge-based economies in APEC. November. Singapore.

Australian Bureau of Statistics (2002) *Measuring a knowledge-based economy and society: An Australian framework*. Canberra: Discussion Paper.

Bell, D. (1973) *The Coming of Post Industrial Society*. New York: Basic Books.

Bimber, B. (1995) Three faces of technological determinism. In M. R. Smith and L. Marx (eds), *Does Technology Drive History: The Dilemma of Technological Determinism* (pp. 79–100). Cambridge, MA: MIT Press.

Block, F. (1985) Postindustrial development and the obsolescence of economic categories. *Politics and Society* 14: 71–104, 416–441.

Bluestone, B. and Harrison, B. (1983) *The Deindustrialisation of America*. New York: Basic Books.

Boehm, K. and Silberstson, A. (1967) *The British Patent System*. Cambridge, UK: Cambridge University Press.

Bohme, G. and Stehr, N. (eds) (1986) *The Knowledge Society*. Dordrecht: Reidel.

Bourdieu, P. (1986) The forms of capital. In J. G. Richardson (ed.), *Handbook of Theory and Research for the Sociology of Education* (pp. 241–258). New York: Greenwood.

Braverman, H. (1975) *Labor and Monopoly Capital: Degradation of Work in the Twentieth Century*. New York: Monthly Review Press.

Brint, S. (2001) Professionals and the 'knowledge economy': Rethinking the theory of postindustrial society. *Current Sociology* 49(4): 101–132.

Browne, F. (2000) Discussing the papers of Gordon and Felderer. *Oesterreichische Nationalbank 28. Volkswirtschaftliche Tagung Das neue Millennium – Zeit für ein neues ökonomisches Paradigma?*

Burrows, R. and Ellison, N. (2004) Towards a social politics of neighbourhood informatization. Paper presented to the British Sociological Association Conference. UK: York University, March 2004.

Castells, M. (1996) *The Rise of the Network Society, Vol. 1. The Information Age*. Oxford: Blackwell.

Castells, M. (1997) *The Power of Identity*. Oxford: Blackwell.

Castells, M. (2000a) Material for an exploratory theory of the network society. *British Journal of Sociology* 51(1): 5–24.

Castells, M. (2000b) The contours of the network society. *Foresight: The Journal of Futures Studies, Strategic Thinking and Policy* 2(2): 151–157.

Castells, M. (2001) *The Internet Galaxy*. Oxford: Oxford University Press.

Castells, M. (2004) *The Network Society: A Cross Cultural Perspective*. Northampton, MA: Edward Elgar.

Choi, S. Y. and Whinston, A. B. (2000) *The Internet Economy: Technology and Practice*. Austin, TX: SmartEcon Publishing.

Council of Economic Advisors (2002) Economic Report to the President 2002. Washington, DC: US Government Printing Office.

Coyle, D. and Quah, D. (2002) Getting the measure of the new economy. *ISociety*.

Crafts, N. F. R. (1985) *British Economic Growth During the Industrial Revolution*. Oxford: Oxford University Press.

Crafts, N. F. R. and Harley, C. K. (1992) Output growth and the British industrial revolution. *Economic History Review* 45: 703–730.

Cunningham, S. (2005) Knowledge and cultural capital. In D. Rooney, G. Hearn and A. Ninan (eds), *Handbook on the Knowledge Economy* (pp. 93–101). Northampton, MA: Edward Elgar.

Danabalan, D. V. (1999) Knowledge economy and knowledge society – Challenge and opportunities for human resource management. Paper presented at the Workshop on Human Resource Management organised by the Public Service Department, Malaysia, in cooperation with the Commonwealth Secretariat Langkai, 12–14 November 1999.

David, P. (2005) Does the new economy need all the old IPR institutions and more? In L. Soete and B. ter Weel (eds), *The Economics of the Digital Society* (pp. 113–151). Northampton, MA: Edward Elgar.

David, P. and Foray, D. (2002) Economic fundamentals of the knowledge society. *Policy Futures in Education* 1(1): 20–49.

Delanty, G. (2001) *Challenging Knowledge; the University in the Knowledge Society*. Philadelphia, PA: Open University Press.

Department of Trade and Industry (UK) (1998) Building the knowledge driven economy: Analytical report. London.

Drahos, P. (2005) Intellectual property rights in the knowledge economy. In D. Rooney, G. Hearn and A. Ninan (eds), *Handbook on the Knowledge Economy* (pp. 139–151). Northampton, MA: Edward Elgar.

Drucker, P. (1959) *Landmarks of Tomorrow*. London: Heineman.

Drucker, P. (1969) *The Age of Discontinuity: Guidelines to Our Changing Society*. London: Heineman.

Drucker, P. (1994) The age of social transformation. *Atlantic Monthly* 174: 53–80.

Dutton, H. I. (1984) *The Patent System and Inventive Activity during the Industrial Revolution*. Oxford: Oxford University Press.

Editors (2000) Editors' summary. *Brookings Papers on Economic Activity* 2000(1): ix–xxxii.

Elmeskov, J. (2000) New sources of economic growth in Europe? *Oesterreichische Nationalbank 28. Volkswirtschaftliche Tagung Das neue Millennium – Zeit für ein neues ökonomisches Paradigma?*

European Commission (2000) European Competitiveness Report 2000. Luxembourg.

European Commission (2001) European Competitiveness Report 2001. Luxembourg.

Foray, D. (2004) *The Economics of Knowledge.* Cambridge, UK: Cambridge University Press.

Foss, N. J. (2002) Economic organization in the knowledge economy: An Austrian perspective. In N. J. Foss and P. G. Klein (eds), *Entrepreneurism and the Firm: Austrian Perspectives on Economic Organization* (pp. 48–71). Cheltenham, UK: Edward Elgar.

Foss, N. J. (2005) *Strategy, Economic Organization, and the Knowledge Economy: The Coordination of Firms and Resources.* Oxford: Oxford University Press.

Froebel, F., Heinrichs, J. and Kreye, D. (1980) *The New International Division of Labour.* Cambridge, UK: Cambridge University Press.

Fuller, S. (2001) A critical guide to knowledge society newspeak: Or, how not to take the great leap backward. *Current Sociology* 49(4): 177–201.

Fox, H. G. (1947) *Monopolies and Patents.* Toronto: University of Toronto Press.

Gerth, H. and Mills, C. W. (1948) *From Marx to Weber: Essays in Sociology.* London: Routledge and Kegan Paul Ltd.

Gibbon, M., Limoges, C., Nowotny, H., Schwartzman, S., Scot, P. and Trow, M. (1994) *The New Production of Knowledge: The Dynamics of Science and Research in Contemporary Societies.* London: Sage.

Giddens, A. (1982) *Sociology: A Brief but Critical Introduction.* London: Macmillan.

Giddens, A. (2001) *The Global Third Way Debate.* Cambridge, UK: Polity Press.

Godin, B. (2004) The New Economy: What the concept owes to the OECD. *Research Policy* 33: 679–690.

Gordon, R. J. (1998) Foundations of the Goldilocks economy: Supply shocks and time-varying NAIRU. *Brookings Papers on Economic Activity* 1998(2): 21–40.

Gordon, R. (2000) Does the New Economy measure up to the great inventions of the past? *Journal of Economic Perspectives,* 14(4): 49–74.

Graham, S. (ed.) (2004) *The Cybercities Reader.* London: Routledge.

Greasley, D. and Oxley, L. (1994) Rehabilitation sustained: The industrial revolution as a macroeconomic epoch. *Economic History Review* 47: 760–768.

Greasley, D. and Oxley, L. (1996) Technological epochs and British industrial production, 1700–1992. *Scottish Journal of Political Economy* 43: 258–274.

Greasley, D. and Oxley, L. (1997a) Endogenous growth or big bang: Two views of the first industrial revolution. *Journal of Economic History* 57: 935–949.

Greasley, D. and Oxley, L. (1997b) Causality and the first industrial revolution. *Industrial and Corporate Change* 7: 33–47.

Greasley, D. and Oxley, L. (2000) British industrialization 1816–1860: A disaggregate time series perspective. *Explorations in Economic History* 37: 98–119.

Greasley, D. and Oxley, L. (2007) Patenting, intellectual property rights and sectoral outputs in Industrial Revolution Britain, 1780–1851. *Journal of Econometrics* (to appear).

Harley, C. K. (1993) Reassessing the industrial revolution: A macro view. In J. Mokyr (ed.), *The British Industrial Revolution: An Economic Perspective* (pp. 171–226). Boulder, CO: Westview.

Harris, R. (2001) The knowledge-based economy: Intellectual origins and new economic perspectives. *International Journal of Management Reviews* 3(1): 21–40.

Hassan, R. (2003) Network time and the new knowledge epoch. *Time and Society* 12(2/3): 225–241.

Held, D. (2000) *A Globalizing World? Culture, Economics, Politics.* London: Routledge.

Hirst, P. and Thompson, G. (1996) *Globalization in Question.* Cambridge, UK: Polity Press.

Hobsbawm, E. (1975) *Age of Capital.* London: Weidenfeld and Nicholson.

Hoffmann, W. H. (1955) *British Industry 1700–1950.* Oxford: Blackwell.

Holton, R. (2005) *Making Globalization.* Basingstoke, UK: Palgrave/Macmillan.

Houghton, J. and Sheehan, P. (2003) A primer in the knowledge economy. Centre for Strategic Economic Studies, Victoria University of Technology, Melbourne.

Ittner, C. D., Lambert, R. A. and Larcker, D. F. (2003) The structure and performance consequences of equity grants to employees of new economy firms. *Journal of Accounting and Economics* 34: 89–127.

Jarvie, C. (2005) *The Advanced Network.* Ministry of Science and Technology, Wellington.

Jessop, B. (2000) The state and the contradictions of the knowledge-driven economy. In J. R. Bryson, N. D. Henry and J. Pollard (eds), *Knowledge, Space, Economy* (pp. 63–78). London: Routledge.

Kenny, M. (1996) The role of information, knowledge and value in the late 20th century. *Futures* 28(8): 696–707.

Kling, R. and Lamb, R. (2000) *IT and Organizational Change in Digital Economies: A Sociotechnical Approach.* In E. Brynjolfsson and B. Kahin (eds), *Understanding the Digital Economy – Data, Tools, and Research.* Cambridge, MA: MIT Press.

Knorr Cetina, K. (1999) *Epistemic Cultures. How the Sciences Make Knowledge.* Cambridge, MA: Harvard University Press.

Knorr Cetina, K. and Preda, A. (2001) The epistemization of economic transactions. *Current Sociology* 49(4): 27–44.

Kuhn, T. (1962) *The Structure of Scientific Revolutions.* Chicago: University of Chicago Press.

Landes, D. S. (1969) *Prometheus Unbound.* Cambridge, UK: Cambridge University Press.

Lane, R. E. (1966) The decline of politics and ideology in a knowledge society. *American Sociological Review* 31: 649–662.

Lash, S. and Urry, J. (1987) *The End of Organised Capitalism.* Oxford: Polity Press.

Law, J. and Urry, J. (2004) Enacting the social. *Economy and Society* 33(1): 390–410.

Law, J. and Urry, J. (1987) *The End of Organised Capitalism.* Oxford: Polity Press.

Law, J. and Urry, J. (2004) Enacting the social. *Economy and Society* 33(1): 390–410.

Leadbeater, C. (1999) *Living on Thin Air: The New Economy.* Harmondsworth: Viking and Penguin.

Liebowitz, S. and Watt, R. (2006) How to best ensure remuneration from creators in the market for music. *Journal of Economic Surveys* 20: 513–545.

Lipsey, R. G. and Carlaw, K. I. (2000) Technology policy: basic concepts. In C. Edquist and M. McKelvey (eds), *Systems of Innovation: Growth, Competitiveness and Employment* (pp. 421–455). UK: Edward Elgar.

Lipsey, R. G., Carlaw, K. I. and Bekar, C. (2005) *Economic Transformations: General Purpose Technologies and Long Term Economic Growth.* Oxford, UK: Oxford University Press.

Lyon, D. (2003) *Surveillance After September 11.* Cambridge, UK: Polity Press.

Machlup, F. and Penrose, E. (1950) The patent controversy in the nineteenth century. *Journal of Economic History* 10: 1–29.

MacLeod, C. (1988) *Inventing the Industrial Revolution.* Cambridge: Cambridge University Press.

Makarov, V. (2004) The knowledge economy: Lessons for Russia. *Social Sciences* 35(1): 19–30.

Mansell, R., Samarajiva, R. and Mahan, A. (2002) *Networking Knowledge for Information Societies: Institutions and Intervention.* Delft, Netherlands: Delft University Press.

Marginson, S. (2006) Putting the 'public' back into the public university. *Thesis Eleven*, 84: 44–59.

Marinova, D. and Raven, M. (2006) Indigenous knowledge and intellectual property: A sustainability agenda. *Journal of Economic Surveys* 20: 587–605.

Marshall, A. (1890) *Principles of Economics*. Vol. 1. London: Macmillan.

Massey, D. (1984) *Spatial Divisions of Labour*. London: Macmillan.

May, C. (2002) *The Information Society: A Sceptical View*. Cambridge, UK: Polity Press.

McCloskey, D. N. (1988) Bourgeois virtue and the history of P and S. *Journal of Economic History* 58: 297–317.

McKendrick, N. (1974) Home demand and economic growth: a new view of the role of women and children in the Industrial Revolution. In N. McKendrick (ed.), *Historical Perspectives: Studies in English Thought and Society in Honor of J. H. Plumb* (152–210). London: Europa Publications.

McKenna, B. and Rooney, D. (2005) Wisdom management: Tensions between theory and practice in practice. A paper given at the Second Annual International Conference on 'Knowledge Management in Asia Pacific – Building a Knowledge Society: Linking Government, Business, Academia and the Community,' November 28–29, Wellington.

McGuckin, R. H. and van Ark, B. (2002) Performance 2001: Productivity, Employment, and Income in the World's Economies, The Conference Board, Report No. 13, January.

McLennan, G. (2003) Sociologists in/on 'knowledge society'. A paper based upon a presentation given for the Sociological Associated of Aotearoa/New Zealand Sociological Conference, Auckland.

Micklethwait, J. and Wooldridge, A. (2003) *A Future Perfect: The Challenge and Promise of Globalization*. New York: Random House.

Moser, P. (2005) *Do patent laws help to diffuse innovations? Evidence from the geographic localization of innovation in production in 19th century England*. MIT Sloan and NBER Working Paper.

Mumford, L. (1966) *Technics and Human Development, Vol. 1 of Myth of the Machine*. London: Secker and Warburg.

Munro, D. (2000) The knowledge economy. *Journal of Australian Political Economy* 45: 5–17.

Nassehi, A. (2004) What do we know about knowledge: An essay on the knowledge society. *Canadian Journal of Sociology* Summer edition: 439–450.

NCHS (2001) *Cities in a Globalizing World*. London: Earthscan.

Neef, D. (1998) The knowledge economy: An introduction. In D. Neef (ed.), *The Knowledge Economy* (pp. 1–12). Boston: Butterworth-Heinemann.

Nelson, R. (1989) What is private and what is public about technology? *Science, Technology, and Human Values* 14(3): 229–241.

Nokkala, T. (2004) Knowledge economy discourse dominant reality in higher education? ESIB European Student LINK, Number 3/December 2004 – Issue 28. Available from http://www.esip.org/newsletter/link/2004-03/knowledge.php.

Notes (2001) Antitrust and the information age: Section 2 monopolization analyses in the new economy. *Harvard Law Review* 114(5): 1623–1646.

Nowotny, H., Scott, P. and Gibbons, M. (2001) *Rethinking Science: Knowledge and the Public in an Age of Uncertainty*. Cambridge: Polity.

O'Brien, L., Opie, B. and Wallace, D. (2002) Knowledge, innovation and creativity: Designing a knowledge society for a small country. *Ministry of Research Science and Technology*: Wellington.

O'Brien, P. K. (1993) Introduction: Modern conceptions of the industrial revolution. In P. K. O'Brien and R. Quinault (eds), *The Industrial Revolution and British Society* (pp. 1–20). Cambridge, UK: Cambridge University Press.

OECD (1996) The knowledge-based economy. Organisation for Economic Cooperation and Development, Paris.

OECD (2000) A new economy? The changing role of innovation and information technology in growth. 3 July. Paris.

Oxley, L. and Greasley, D. (1997) Vector autoregression, cointegration and causality: Testing for causes of the British industrial revolution. *Applied Economics* 30: 1387–1397.

Piazolo, D. (2001) The digital divide. *CESifo Forum* 2(3): 29–34.

Pillay, H. (2005) Knowledge and social capital. In D. Rooney, G. Hearn and A. Ninan (eds), *Handbook on the Knowledge Economy* (pp. 82–90). Northampton, UK: Edward Elgar.

Pool, I. (1999) Social sciences and an evidence based public policy. Royal Society New Zealand Miscellaneous Series 54, 62-73, Wellington.

Powell, W. W. and Snellman, K. (2004) The knowledge economy. *Annual Review of Sociology* 30: 199–220.

Progressive Policy Institute (nd) The New Economy Index. Available from http:/www.neweconomyindex.org/.

Quah, D. (2002a) Digital goods and the New Economy. LSE Economics Department, December. London.

Quah, D. (2002b) Technological dissemination and economic growth: Some lessons for the New Economy. LSE Economics Department, January.

Quah, D. (2003) The weightless economy. Available from http://econ.lse.ac.uk/staff/dquah/tweirl0.html.

Ramello, G. (2006) What's in a sign? Trademark law and the economic theory. *Journal of Economic Surveys* 20: 547–565.

Roethlisberger, F. J. and Dickson, W. J. (1939) *Management and the Worker*. Cambridge, MA: Harvard University Press.

Rogers, E. M. (1962) *Diffusion of Innovations*. New York: Free Press.

Rogers, J. E. T. (1863) On the rationale and working of the patent laws. *Journal of the London Statistical Society* 26: 125.

Rooney, D., Hearn, G., Mandeville, T. and Joseph, R. (2003) Public policy in knowledge-based economies: Foundations and frameworks. Cheltenham, UK: Edward Elgar.

Samuelson, P. and Varian, H. R. (2001) The 'New Economy' and information technology policy. University of California, Berkeley. Version: July 18, 2001.

Sautet, F. E. (2000) *An Entrepreneurial Theory of the Firm*. London and New York: Routledge.

Schiff, E. (1971) *Industrialisation without Patents: The Netherlands, 1869–1912, Switzerland 1850–1907*. Princeton, NJ: Princeton University Press.

Schiller, H. I. (1991) *Who Knows: Information in the Age of the Fortune 500*. Norwood, NJ: Ablex.

Scholte, J. A. (2000) *Globalization: A Critical Introduction*. Basingstoke, UK: Palgrave/Macmillan.

Schumpeter, J. A. (1942) *Capitalism, Socialism and Democracy*. New York: Harper.

Smith, K. (2002) *What is the 'knowledge economy'?* Knowledge Intensity and Distributed Knowledge Bases, United Nations University, Institute for New Technologies, Discussion Paper Series, 2002–2006, June 2002. Maastricht.

Smith, P. S. and Feagin, J. R. (1987) *The Capitalist City: Global Restructuring and Community Politics*. Oxford, UK: Basil Blackwell.

Stehr, N. (1994) *Knowledge Societies*. London: Sage.

Stehr, N. (2001) *The Fragility of Modern Societies: Knowledge, and Risk in the Information Age*. London: Sage.

Steuart, J. (1767) *An Inquiry into the Principles of Political Economy*. London. Reprinted, edited and with an introduction by A. S. Skinner (1966). Edinburgh: Oliver and Boyd.

Sullivan, R. J. (1989) England's 'Age of Invention': The acceleration of patents and patentable invention during the industrial revolution. *Explorations in Economic History* 26: 424–452.

Talero, E. and Gaudette, P. (1996) Harnessing information for development: A proposal for a World Bank group strategy. Available from http://www.worldbank.org/html/fpd/harnessing/index.html#contents.

Temin, P. (1997) Two views of the British industrial revolution. *Journal of Economic History* 57: 63–82.

The Enterprise Development Website (2005) The knowledge economy. Available from http://www.enterweb.org/know.htm.

Thompson, G. F. (2004) Getting to know the knowledge economy: ICTs, networks and governance. *Economy and Society* 33(4): 562–581.

Thorlindsson, T. and Vilhjalmsson, R. (2003) Introduction to the special issue: Science, knowledge and society. *Acta Sociologica* 46(2): 99–105.

Thorns, D. C. (1992) *Fragmenting Societies*. London: Routledge.

Thorns, D. C. (2002) *The Transformation of Cities*. Basingstoke, UK: Palgrave/Macmillan.

Thorns, D. C. (2003) The challenge of doing sociology in a global world: The case of Aotearoa/New Zealand. *Current Sociology* 51(6): 689–708.

Toda, H. Y. and Phillips, P. C. B. (1991) *Vector autoregression and causality: A theoretical overview and simulation study*. Working Paper No. 977. New Haven, CT: Cowles Foundation.

Toda, H. Y. and Yamomoto, T. (1995) Statistical inference in vector autoregressions with possibly integrated processes. *Journal of Econometrics* 66: 225–250.

Tofler, A. (1980) *The Third Wave*. London: Collins.

Towse, R. (2006) Copyright and artists: A view from cultural economics. *Journal of Economic Surveys* 20: 567–585.

Ungar, S. (2003) Misplaced metaphor: A critical analysis of the 'knowledge society.' *The Canadian Review of Sociology and Anthropology* 40(3): 331–347.

Urry, J. (2003) *Global Complexity*. Cambridge, UK: Polity Press.

Verspagen, B. (2006) University research, intellectual property rights and European innovation systems. *Journal of Economic Surveys* 20: 607–632.

Wadhwani, S. B. (2001) The New Economy: Myths and realities. The Travers Lecture, delivered at London Guildhall University on 20 March.

Weber, M. (1930) *The Protestant Ethic and Spirit of Capitalism*. London: Allen and Unwin.

Weber, M. (1947) *The Theory of Economic and Social Organisation*. New York: Free Press.

Webster, K. (1995) *Theories of the Information Society*. London: Routledge.

Appendix 1. Definitions of a Knowledge Economy

Knowledge Economy

Houghton and Sheehan (2003)

In an agricultural economy land is the key resource. In an industrial economy natural resources, such as coal and iron ore, and labour are the main resources. A knowledge economy is one in which knowledge is the key resource (p. 1).

David and Foray (2002)

The crux of the issue lies in the accelerating (and unprecedented) speed at which knowledge is created, accumulated and, most probably, will depreciate. This trend has resulted *inter alia* in intense scientific and technological progress (p. 21).

Munro (2000)

The phrase 'knowledge economy' will be shown to be a concoction of five different approaches: information technology (usually considered to encompass computing and communication technologies); information networks, new industry processes (including innovation, research and development, and technological diffusion); the human capital approach; and a new approach to capital accumulation through the privatization and commercialization of knowledge (p. 5).

Powell and Snellman (2004)

We define the knowledge economy as production and services based on knowledge-intensive activities that contribute to an accelerated pace of technical and scientific advance, as well as rapid obsolescence. The key component of a knowledge economy is a greater reliance on intellectual capabilities than on physical inputs or natural resources (abstract).

Rooney *et al.* (2003)

We take the term knowledge economy to mean that part of the economy that creates wealth essentially through intellectual activity... (p. 16)

Foss (2002)

Whatever we think of this journalistic concept, it arguably does capture real tendencies and complementary changes. These include, on the organization side, a shrinking of the corporate boundaries and new ways of structuring these, falling firm sizes and a flattening of internal organization; increased differentiation of tastes on the demand side; acceleration of innovation and technological development on the supply side; and changes in the composition of labour on the input side (p. 48).

The Enterprise Development Website (2005)

For the last two hundred years, neo-classical economics has recognized only two factors of production: labour and capital. This is now changing. Information and knowledge are replacing capital and energy as the primary wealth-creating assets, just as the latter two replaced land and labour 200 years ago. In addition, technological developments in the 20th century have transformed the majority of wealth-creating work from physically-based to 'knowledge-based'. Technology and knowledge are now the key factors of production. With increased mobility of information and the global work force, knowledge and expertise can be transported instantaneously around the world, and any advantage gained by one company can be eliminated by competitive improvements overnight. The only comparative advantage a company will enjoy will be its process of innovation – combining market and technology know-how with the creative talents of knowledge workers to solve a constant stream of competitive problems – and its ability to derive value from information. We are now an information society in a knowledge economy.

Nokkala (2004)

One of the buzzwords featuring prominently in the higher education policy documents, and used to legitimize the Lisbon agenda, the Bologna process as well as committing education to the GATS agreement, is the concept of knowledge economy or knowledge society. It is often used to illustrate the shift from an economy based on the low skills industrial production to knowledge intensive production and services as the back bone of the economy, or the shift from a fordist to a post-fordist society, marked by denationalization and transnationalization of state regulation, transnational flow of capital and ensuing global competition. The discourse of knowledge economy emphasizes the shift to knowledge intensive high skills labour force, international circulation of brains, life long learning, transferable skills and competences and knowledge management as a key individual and organizational capacity. In the age of globalization, the knowledge economy discourse has become a way to characterize the new relationships between the state, society and economy and rendered higher education increasingly important for the international competitiveness of the nation states through their central tasks of generation, application and dissemination of knowledge and training high skilled labour force.

Foss (2005)

More specifically, it (the knowledge economy) is concerned with important parts of the theorizing that has emerged within the strategy and organization fields to accommodate the emergence of the knowledge economy, or, more precisely, accommodate those tendencies that we may think of as characterizing the knowledge economy. Among these – real, alleged, and imagined – tendencies is the increasing importance of human-capital inputs, the generally increasing importance of im-material assets and scientific knowledge in production, the increasing importance of immaterial products, the need to control in-house an increasing number of technologies (even if product portfolios are shrinking) and in general to tap an increasing number of knowledge nodes, not just internally but also through an increasing number of alliances and network relations with other firms as well as public research institutions. These tendencies – that in turn co-evolve with a host of other tendencies that may be placed under the knowledge-economy heading, such as increasing competitive pressure and an increasing extent of the market stemming from increased deregulation and internationalization, increasing technological modularity, improved methods of measurement and cost allocation, and the increasing importance of ICT – profoundly impact on economic organization and competitive advantages (pp. 1–2).

Smith (2002)

What does it mean to speak of the 'knowledge economy' however? At the outset, it must be said that there is no coherent definition, let alone theoretical concept, of this term: it is at best a widely-used metaphor, rather than a clear concept. The OECD has spoken of knowledge-based economies in very general terms, as meaning 'those which are directly based on the production, distribution and use of knowledge and information'. This definition is a good example of the problems of the term, for it seems to cover everything and nothing: all economies are in some way based on knowledge, but it is hard to think that any are directly based on knowledge, if that means the production and distribution of knowledge and information products (pp. 6–7).

Leaving aside such general definitional problems there seem to be four basic views about the changed significance of knowledge: Firstly, there are those who believe that knowledge is quantitatively and in some sense qualitatively more important than before as an input. Peter Drucker, for example, suggests that 'Knowledge is now becoming the one factor of production, sidelining both capital and labour'. Along the same lines, the OECD has suggested that '...the role of knowledge (as compared with natural resources, physical capital and low-skill labour) has taken on greater importance. Although the pace may differ, all OECD economies are moving towards a knowledge-based economy'. Secondly, there is the idea that knowledge is in some way more important as a product than it has been hitherto – that we are seeing the rise of new forms of activity based on the trading of knowledge products. Thirdly, there is the view that codified knowledge (as opposed to tacit, person-incorporated skills) is in some ways more significant as a component of economically relevant knowledge bases. Thus Abramowitz and David argue that 'Perhaps the single most salient characteristic of recent economic growth has been the secularly rising reliance on codified knowledge as a basis for the organization and conduct of economic activities...'. Finally, there are those who argue that the knowledge economy rests on technological changes in ICT, since innovation in computing and communications changes both physical constraints and costs in the collection and dissemination of information. So for some, the rise of ICT technologies and the complex of ICT industries is coterminous with the move to a knowledge society. Lundvall and Foray argue a more sophisticated view: 'Even if we should not take the ICT revolution as synonymous with the advent of the knowledge-based economy, both phenomena are strongly interrelated ... the ICT system gives the knowledge-based economy a new and different technological base which radically changes the conditions for the production and distribution of knowledge as well as its coupling to the production system' (pp. 7–8).

Knowledge-Based Economies

Foray (2004)

... essentially, economies in which the proportion of knowledge-intensive jobs is high, the economic weight of information sectors is a determining factor, and the share of intangible capital is greater than that of tangible capital in the overall stock of real capital (p. ix).

... a scientific development corresponding to the emergence of a new economic subdiscipline of which the research object – knowledge – poses new theoretical and empirical problems; and a historical knowledge heralding the advent of a particular period in the growth and organization of economic activities. I stress the importance of this twofold change, which some authors fail to recognize. For them, the only new development of any relevance is theoretical, and the historical period in which they are living follows earlier periods without any discontinuity whatsoever. Because one believes, on the contrary, in the dual nature of the economics of knowledge – as a discipline and as a historical period – it is naturally around that duality that this volume is organized. By convention, so as not to confuse the two phenomena, I call the discipline 'the economic of knowledge' and the historical period 'the knowledge-based economy' (p. xi).

Harris (2001)

... the notion that economic wealth is created through the creation, production, distribution and consumption of knowledge and knowledge-based products (p. 22).

Rooney *et al*. (2003)

... a knowledge-based economy to be an economy in which knowledge is the most important productive factor (p. 16).

Australian Bureau of Statistics (2002)

The term 'knowledge-based economy' was coined by the OECD and defined as an economy which is 'directly based on the production, distribution and use of knowledge and information' (OECD, 1996). The Asia-Pacific Economic Co-operation (APEC) Economic Committee extended this idea to state that in KBE 'the production, distribution and use of knowledge is the main driver of growth, wealth creation and employment across all industries' (APEC, 2000). According to this definition, a KBE does not rely solely on a few high technology industries for growth and wealth production. Rather, all industries in the economy can be knowledge intensive, even so called 'old economy' industries like mining and agriculture. Further, the APEC Economic Committee states that 'the knowledge required by a knowledge-based society is wider than purely technological knowledge; for example it includes cultural, social and managerial knowledge'.

OECD (1996)

... economies which are directly based on the production, distribution and use of knowledge and information (p. 7).

Asia-Pacific Economic Cooperation (2000)

A Knowledge-Based Economy is an economy in which the production, distribution, and use of knowledge is the main driver of growth, wealth creation and employment across all industries. In this context, being a KBE means more than simply having a thriving 'New Economy' or 'information economy' that is somehow separate from a stagnant 'old economy'. In a truly knowledge-based economy, all sectors have become knowledge-intensive, not just those usually called 'high technology'. Important features of an ideal KBE include: an openness to trade, new ideas and new enterprises; sound macroeconomic policy; the importance attached to education and lifelong learning; and the enabling role of information and telecommunications infrastructure. Note that the knowledge required by a knowledge-based society is wider than purely technological knowledge; for example, it includes cultural, social, and managerial knowledge. The knowledge possessed by an organization is much more than the information written in its files, and includes its culture, the way in which people interact within the organization, knowledge about the contacts they use to gain information from outside, and so on. The organization's knowledge consists of its capability in integrating information with experience and expertise to take action. This assimilation is no mean feat; as one wit put it: 'Today we are drowning in information but starving for knowledge' (p. vii).

Neef (1998)

The phrase (knowledge based economy) has been used enthusiastically to describe a new interconnected economy and the positive effect of newly emerging technologies in the workplace and home. Equally, it has been used to lament the effect of downsizing on the blue-collar sectors of the labor force. For some, 'knowledge-based economy' describes the ever-increasing proportion of the nation's GNP dedicated to computerization and high-technology electronics industries. For others, it is the impetus behind 'knowledge management' – adaptation of traditional organizational structures in a way that better accommodates the highly skilled 'knowledge workers' who populate the high-performance workplace and provide complex problem-solving services. The knowledge-based economy is a phrase that has been used to describe both a coming age of global prosperity and a coming economic apocalypse (p. 1).

Knowledge-Driven Economy

Department of Trade and Industry (1998)

... knowledge driven economy is one in which the generation and the exploitation of knowledge has come to play the predominant part in the creation of wealth. It is not simply about pushing back the frontiers of knowledge; it is also about the more effective use and exploitation of all types of knowledge in all manner of economic activity.

Weightless Economy

Quah (2003)

Instead, it is the weightless economy where the economic significance of knowledge achieves greatest contemporary resonance. The weightless economy, in this view, comprises four main elements: 1. Information and communications technology

(ICT), the Internet. 2. Intellectual assets: Not only patents and copyrights but also, more broadly, namebrands, trademarks, advertising, financial and consulting services, and education. 3. Electronic libraries and databases: Including new media, video entertainment, and broadcasting. 4. Biotechnology: Carbon-based libraries and databases, pharmaceuticals.

Harris (2001)

... economic value seems to be increasingly concentrated in non-material objects (p. 23).

Knowledge Economy/ Weightless Economy

Danabalan (1999)

Knowledge economy is the ability to create, distribute and exploit knowledge and information for increasing economic wealth and improvement in the quality of life. It is also described as the 'weightless economy', in comparison with the label 'weighty economy' of the industrial era.

Goldilocks Economy

Gordon (1998)

Freed from the restraint of restrictive monetary policy that had choked earlier expansions, and with its fires stoked by the lowest medium-term and long-term nominal interest rates in three decades, the economy charged ahead and achieved a state of high growth-noninflationary bliss that some have dubbed the 'Goldilocks economy' (neither too hot nor too cold, but just right) (pp. 297–298).

Thus far, I have characterized the major surprise in the Goldilocks economy as the low rate of inflation given the low rate of unemployment, and indeed, this has been the focus of the media as well. Stated another way, the real questions about the Goldilocks economy are why inflation has been so low relative to changes in wages and why the unemployment rate has declined when utilization has not increased (p. 300).

Information Economy

Harris (2001)

... focuses on the important role that information and communication have come to play in the modern economy (p. 23).

Taler and Gaudette (1996)

A new kind of economy – the information economy – is emerging where trade and investment are global and firms compete with knowledge, networking and agility on a global basis. A corresponding new society is also emerging with pervasive information capabilities that make it substantially different from an industrial society: much more competitive, more democratic, less centralized, less stable, better able to address individual needs, and friendlier to the environment (abstract).

Revolutionary advances in information technology reinforce economic and social changes that are transforming business and society. From this revolution emerges a new kind of economy – the information economy – in which information is the critical resource and the basis for competition. Old ways of doing business will be challenged and sometimes defeated (section 1, p. 1, How is information shaping the economy and society?).

Digital Economy

Department of Trade and Industry (1998)

The 'digital economy' is shorthand for the transformational impact which information and communication technologies (ICTs) are having on every single aspect of business activity.

New Economy

Ittner *et al.* (2003)

Talks about New Economy firms by which it means 'organizations competing in the computer, software, internet, telecommunications, or networking fields'.

Quah (2002a)

Digital goods are bitstrings, sequences of 0s and 1s, that have economic value. They are distinguished from other goods by five characteristics: digital goods are non-rival, infinitely expansible, discrete, aspatial and recombinant. The New Economy is one where the economics of digital goods importantly influence aggregate economic performance.

As documented elsewhere in this Handbook (and attested to by journalistic frenzy in the late 1990s' dotcom boom) the New Economy means different things to different observers. Possible dimensions to the New Economy range from e-commerce, e-government, the Internet, the productivity paradox, knowledge-intensive work, social mass-mobilization, and globalization, all the way through auction proliferation, electronic payment systems, venture capital financing saturation, and business restructuring. In less guarded moments, popular conception held that with the New Economy, inflation might be forever conquered, explosive income growth might be hereafter the norm, and stock markets be always stratospheric (p. 4).

Quah (2002b)

This paper attempts to draw lessons for the New Economy from what economists know about technology dissemination and economic growth. It argues that what is most notable about the New Economy is that it is knowledge-driven, not just in the sense that knowledge now assumes increasing importance in production, thereby raising productivity. Instead, it is that consumption occurs increasingly in goods that are like knowledge – computer software, video entertainment, gene sequences, Internet-delivered goods and services – where material physicality matters little. That knowledge is aspatial and nonrival is key. Understanding the effective exchange and dissemination of such knowledge-products will matter more than resolving the so-called productivity paradox (abstract).

Coyle and Quah (2002)

Definitions of the 'New Economy' tend to cluster into two main types. The first equates the New Economy with ICT and its sectoral consequences; either on certain core industry sectors, mainly professional services, or wider economic effects on all economic structures, mainly through cost reduction and networking enabling processes. The second sees the New Economy as the post-industrial economy as a whole. Equal emphasis is placed on symbolic analysis and frontline services as areas for employment growth (p. 6).

Samuelson and Varian (2001)

Some have asserted that the 1990s witnessed the emergence of a 'New Economy'. That term dates back to the 1980s when it referred to an economy driven by services rather than manufacturing. The fear then was that the services economy would result in slow growth, rising prices, and low-wage jobs. In 1996 Michael Mandel published an article in Business Week called 'The Triumph of the New Economy' which emphasized the development of a technology-driven, fast-growing, low-inflation economy, which he referred to as 'the New Economy'. The latter connotation came to dominate popular discussion, although economists as a whole remain somewhat sceptical of the concept.

Abramovitz and David (2001)

The term 'New Economy' itself acquired a variety of quite different connotations: for many commentators, it continues to refer primarily to the altered macroeconomic configuration that saw an accelerating rate of growth of real GDP and a steadily falling unemployment rate which, unexpectedly, did not give rise to inflationary pressures on wages and prices. Some connected this with evidence of the revival of labour productivity growth that became increasingly visible in the aggregate statistics for the private sector, and emphasized that as the key development heralding a permanent escape from the US economy's poor performance record during the preceding two decades. For others, however, the productivity growth picture beneath the aggregate level was less than entirely clear, and the core of the 'New Economy' was peculiarly associated with the growth of output and employment in 'hi-tech' industries, particularly those involving information technologies and computer mediated telecommunications, and with the on-going restructuring of business organizations and markets that are driven by advances in the latter (ICTs). The high and rising stock market valuations of companies in this sector, and the wave of venture capital that poured into new enterprises launched after 1993 to exploit the commercial possibilities of the explosively expanding Internet, seemed for still other observers to be the very essence of what was new and positive in these developments. Indeed, in the exuberance that marked the century's close, the Nasdaq stock market index came to be identified with the New Economy, whereas the comparatively weak performance of the Dow-Jones index was disparaged as representative of 'the Old Economy' (p. 116).

Micklethwait and Wooldridge (2003)

The New Economy is difficult to define, largely because it encompasses three things. The first, now fortunately gone for good, had to do with the stock market in the 1990s: that it somehow justified crazy equity prices. But the other two things have survived the bubble. The second has to do with the organization of business: the idea that corporate life, particularly in America, is being transformed by the Internet and by Internet companies. This seems very hard to quarrel with. The third, most complicated debate has to do with macroeconomics and how its laws and assumptions need to be rewritten in the light of all this new technology and, to a lesser extent, globalization (p. 107).

Progressive Policy Institute (nd)

The term New Economy refers to a set of qualitative and quantitative changes that, in the last 15 years, have transformed the structure, functioning, and rules of the economy. The New Economy is a knowledge and idea-based economy where the keys to job creation and higher standards of living are innovative ideas and technology embedded in services and manufactured products. It is an economy where risk, uncertainty, and constant change are the rule, rather than the exception.

Notes (2001)

The world is currently undergoing a fundamental economic transformation. A combination of technological developments – powerful personal computers, high-speed telecommunications, and the Internet – has created a new market environment variously referred to as the 'information economy', the 'network economy', the 'knowledge economy', or simply the 'New Economy'. This New Economy is anchored primarily in the production, processing, and dissemination of such information goods as software, content, or expertise. To be sure, there is nothing new about the existence of information goods; music and books, for example, have existed as information goods for quite some time. What is new, however, is the dominance of information goods in the total marketplace and the present pace of major technological advances. The technological revolution impacts the cost and distribution of such goods in a way that fundamentally alters how their purveyors must operate (pp. 1627–1628).

OECD (2000)

The term 'New Economy' has been used extensively in recent years to describe the workings of the US economy and in particular the part of its economy that is linked to ICT. It reflects a view that something has changed and that the economy now works differently. Few studies clearly define the term 'New Economy' and it seems to mean different things to different people. The three main characteristics of the New Economy appear to be the following: The New Economy may imply higher trend growth. Due to more efficient business practices linked to ICT use, the New Economy may experience a pick-up in trend growth, due to higher MFP growth. The New Economy may affect the business cycle. ICT, in combination with globalization, may change the short-run trade-off between inflation and unemployment and lower the NAIRU (non-accelerating inflation rate of unemployment). As a result, the economy can expand for a longer period without inflationary pressures emerging. In this view, ICT puts downward pressure on inflation, while increased global competition keeps wage inflation in check. More extreme views have argued that the New Economy may mean the end of the business cycle. The sources of growth are different in the New Economy. Certain parts of the New Economy may benefit from increasing returns to scale, network effects and externalities. The value of communications networks and Internet applications, for instance, increases as more people are connected. This situation entails considerable spillovers, and these contribute to higher MFP growth and fuel further growth. These three characteristics are closely related and the US experience of the past decade provides some support for all, although there is no support for extreme claims about the end of the business cycle (p. 17).

Godin (2004)

The New Economy referred to data that indicated the appearance of new economies in the USA and in a number of smaller OECD countries not very 'vibrant' in terms of entrepreneurship. What characterized new economies was the acceleration of trend growth and productivity. Technologies, particularly information and communication technologies (ICT), were believed to be at the heart of the phenomenon (p. 679).

Today, alongside the OECD, it is the European Commission that most faithfully pursues work on productivity gaps between Europe and the USA in its annual reports on competitiveness (European Commission, 2000, 2001). The failure to close the gap appears, according to the commission, what characterizes the New Economy in the USA: higher employment rates and higher labour productivity as a consequence of investments in information and communication technologies (ICT) (pp. 667–668).

Editors (2000)

The authors examine the data for 'New Economy' companies, defined as those engaged in the manufacture of computers or other electronics products or in software or telecommunications, and 'old economy' companies; they also examine the data by manufacturing industry (p. xix).

'New Economy' proponents credit the success to the information revolution, which they see as driving a fundamental transformation of the economy that will lead to faster productivity growth for many years. Sceptics of this view acknowledge the importance of the high rates of investment stimulated by the computer revolution, but attribute much of the economy's success to a series of favourable but temporary shocks (p. xx).

Thompson (2004)

Of course, in large part this depends upon how one defines the idea of a 'New Economy'. The difficulties here are legion. Just to give two examples, the US Council of Economic Advisors (2002, pp. 58–60) restricts its analysis very much to the dominance of ICTs, whereas an analysis for the Bank of England by Wadhwani (2001, p. 495) includes a wider set of structural changes, including 'globalization', intensifying product market competition, financial market liberalization, changes in labour market flexibility and other factors. Both these argue that there is a 'New Economy' in the USA and possibly the UK, but not elsewhere. In addition, McGuckin and van Ark (2002), for the US Conference Board, see a New Economy only appearing in the USA, as US productivity figures soar away from the rest of the world (p. 565).

Wadhwani (2001)

There is no generally accepted definition of what one means by the NE. Recall that the term NE, in the early 1980s, implied an economy that was driven by services rather than manufacturing. Then, the worry was that a service-driven economy was going to create poor, low-wage jobs. More recently, the use of the term NE has been transformed radically. Unsurprisingly, there are those who see the NE as being synonymous with an acceleration in the diffusion of Information and Communications Technology (see, e.g. Gordon, 2000). However, I regard that as a rather narrow definition. Recall that John Travers was, of course, active in the free trade movement during the mid-19th century. Indeed, much that might be different about the economy today relates not just to ICT advances, but also to the effects of globalization, intensifying product market competition, labour market reform, financial market liberalization and several other factors (pp. 5–6).

Browne (2000)

My own preferred definition relates instead to features of the aggregate macro economy itself rather than to technology – three features are isolated for attention.

1. A permanently raised potential growth rate of the economy (using the 1970s, 1980s and early 1990s as a benchmark) attributable predominantly to the revolution in the Information and Communications Technologies (ICT); 2. The second feature is a permanent reduction in structural and frictional unemployment to which it is argued the ICT also contributes through a number of channels; 3. The third feature is a permanent reduction in the variation in the growth rate of output in the 1990s, and possibly to some extent in the 1980s, relative to previous decades (p. 210).

Elmeskov (2000)

The conjunction of a number of economic developments in the USA has contributed to an impression that something fundamental may have changed in that country. These developments include: strong non-inflationary growth, coupled with high labour utilization; the spread of information and communication technology (ICT); and microeconomic evidence of continued restructuring of production processes. Taken together, these developments have been seen as representing the emergence of a 'New Economy' (p. 57).

Internet Economy

Choi and Whinston (2000)

... the Internet economy is defined as that part of the economy that deals with information goods such as software, online contents, knowledge-based goods, the new media and supporting technology industries that provide computers and network devices.

Multiple Terms

Knowledge economy, knowledge-based economy, innovation economy, high-technology civilization, knowledge society, information society

Makarov (2004)

The term 'knowledge economy' was coined by the Austrian-American economist Fritz Machlup (1962) in reference to one of the sectors of the economy. Today this term, together with the term 'knowledge-based economy', is used to designate a type of economy in which knowledge plays a crucial role and the production of knowledge is the main source of growth. Such widely used concepts as 'innovation economy', 'high-technology civilization', 'knowledge society' and 'information society' are close to the knowledge economy concept (p. 19).

Digital economy, information economy, knowledge-based economy, weightless economy, virtual economy, Internet economy, electronic commerce, e-commerce, e-conomy, New Economy

Piazolo (2001)

Various catchwords have been coined to capture the essence of the economy-wide consequences resulting from an increased use of processed digital information and from the application of the Internet for a wide array of services (software programming, webpage maintenance, ticket and hotel reservations, on-line information and support, ordering facilities, publishing, indexing or abstracting etc.) as well as transactions (delivering music, movies, documents, literature or software in digital form). The following catchwords aim at different characteristics of this phenomenon but are frequently used as synonyms: 'digital economy', 'information economy', 'knowledge-based economy', 'weightless economy', 'virtual economy', 'Internet economy', 'electronic commerce', 'e-commerce', 'e-conomy', or maybe more capacious 'New Economy'. Some authors have tried to assign distinguishing concepts to this variety. For example, Kling and Lamb (2000) suggest to use the term 'information economy' to include all informational goods and services like publishing, research, legal and insurance services, entertaining, and teaching in all of its forms, and the term 'digital economy' to address (only) the goods and services whose development, production, sale, or provision is critically dependent upon digital technologies. Furthermore, the term 'New Economy' is associated for them to the possible consequences of the information economy and the digital economy, namely high growth, low inflation, and low unemployment. However, in many papers – including the present one – the concept of the 'New Economy' is wider and includes the characteristics of the 'information economy' and of the 'Internet economy' as subsets. In the following, the term 'New Economy' describes an economy where both final output and intermediate input predominantly consist of information and where the modern (digital) information and communication technologies provide world-wide access to almost any available information. These new technologies might have the potential to enable an increase in the productivity of conventional business practices, but also facilitate the establishment of new processes and products. Consequently, the evolution of the New Economy should not be considered as being restricted to the information sector, but as a far reaching process that might alter and extend the products and production processes within the whole economy. This means also that the consequences of being excluded from the progress of the New Economy might be rather detrimental for (developing) countries (p. 29).

Appendix 2. Definitions of a Knowledge Society

Knowledge Society

Rooney *et al.* (2003)

A knowledge society is a broader term than 'knowledge economy' or 'knowledge-based economy' in that it encompasses more intellectual activity than narrow economic, commercial and industrial concern (p. 16).

Fuller (2001)

'Knowledge society', 'knowledge management', and especially the burgeoning employment prospects of 'chief knowledge officers' ('CKOs') are peculiar signs of what is supposedly distinctive about our times. To those innocent of social theory, it should be perfectly obvious that knowledge has always played an important role in the organization and advancement of society. In that sense, saying that we live in a 'knowledge society' would seem to be no more informative than saying that we live in a 'power society' or a 'money society' or a 'culture society' (p. 177).

Lyotard's image of the knowledge society comes closest to a knowledge dispersion, in which a competitive labour market reduces 'skill' to a scarce locally relevant knowledge, the value of which may be expected to change (and may even be converted to non-human capital) according to market conditions. Thus, your knowledge is most valuable if it complements that of others in your immediate situation, thereby enabling all of you to collaborate in activities that will benefit each of you individually (p. 179).

Marginson (2006)

In sum, Habermas's theorization of the public sphere, which is heterogeneous to the public/private goods distinction drawn from political economy, is suggestive of the forms of life associated with democratic public political projects inside the university. Community, criticism and social awareness might make a platform for regenerating a public university that has been boxed into a losing position by status competition. Habermas's later focus on communicative action points to the potential of an institution combining high communicative competence with specialized expertise. This is a more fertile, open-ended notion of the 'knowledge society' or 'knowledge economy' than accounts that subordinate the university to global economic competitiveness (p. 54).

Hassan (2003)

Prior to the rise of the industrial revolution, all societies, be they tribes, bands, empires or civilizations, were always already 'knowledge societies'. These produced forms of everyday and specialized knowledges, some that are still with us, some that are irretrievably lost, that correspond to each society's 'structures of organization' and the temporalities that suffused them. The arrival of the industrial revolution changed this world of perpetual flux of temporalities and knowledges forever, and humanity embarked upon what we can see in retrospect was the first knowledge epoch (p. 228).

Thorlindsson and Vilhjalmsson (2003)

The label 'knowledge society' is rooted in the belief that science, innovation and expertise are the moving forces of social and economic development. It is backed up by increasingly popular buzzwords such as 'knowledge organizations', 'knowledge management', 'knowledge workers' and 'intellectual capital'. Knowledge work and knowledge management within the knowledge society organizations imply continuous knowledge production and revision of existing knowledge, emphasizing the skills and expertise of workers. The production of knowledge is not limited to higher education and academic research settings. Furthermore, the notion of the autonomy of science is under increasing attack, as science becomes an important part of political debate and economic policy. Social forces outside academia attempt to gain control over science, shape its nature, channel its course, and control the social and economic consequences of its findings (Nowotny *et al.*, 2001) (p. 99).

The concept of knowledge society rejects a linear view of science from basic to applied. Instead, it portrays science as a complex non-linear process where social forces intervene at any stage. However, it is safe to say that the concept is not well developed. A central source of ambiguity is 'knowledge' itself. Although its importance is stressed in every definition, there is neither consensus nor clarity about its meaning. Contemporary society contains all sorts of knowledge. Some is developed in scientific settings and published in scientific journals scrutinized by academic peers. Some is developed by various communities of workers in their worlds of everyday work (pp. 99–100).

Although the definition of 'knowledge society' can include all these different kinds of knowledge, there is a strong tendency to focus on the most prestigious or credible kinds, namely scientific knowledge, produced and certified by scientists, as well as professional knowledge, acquired by formal credentials of university-educated professors, such as engineers, psychologists, medical doctors, lawyers and similar experts. In this narrower sense, knowledge is suppose to be reliable and even true, practical and powerful, and give competitive edge in individual and economic strife, war and politics. Its relationship to science and technology is meant to set it apart from other, more ordinary forms of knowledge (p. 100).

Today, science and its products influence people's daily lives to the extent that some scholars have come to view science as the main defining characteristic of contemporary societies (Nowotny *et al.*, 2001). Second, science is increasingly contextualized, i.e. influenced by social, economic and political forces that shape the direction of scientific activity and grasp control over its applications. In the process, science becomes less of a demarcated subsystem of society, and more of a transgressive system with fluid and porous boundaries (Gibbons *et al.*, 1994; Nowotny *et al.*, 2001) (p. 100).

Adhikari and Sales (2001)

Today it is clearer that efforts to construct a definition and theory of the knowledge society which concentrate on the manifest features of a particular historical moment generally express analytical perspectives that lead to 'self-exemplifying' explanatory positions in which, to borrow a phrase, the 'logic of the society becomes the logic of the theory' (Bohme and Stehr, 1986, p. 17). Consequently, such non-processual approaches are unable to adequately take in the dynamic of knowledge as also the sources of the constitution of the knowledge–economy–society relation, inter-temporal and inter-country differences in the constitutive processes, and the variable interrelation between social forms such as states, economic organization, educational systems and the professions. They tend towards identification with modern, western society (or, more exactly, with some of its parts) and to restrictive theoretical use for investigating knowledge-related societal variation and temporal change over a wider field (p. 1).

Although knowledge society and kindred concepts (e.g. knowledge economy, information society/economy) refer primarily to the problem of 'what distinguishes a knowledge society ... from its historical predecessors' (Bohme and Stehr, 1986, p. 19), as procedures for distinguishing the contrasting, prior phases of the operation of knowledge in the economy and connected social structures, such as tradition-modern, western/non-western, pre-industrial/industrial/postindustrial and so forth, they are not methodologically distinct (p. 5).

Is knowledge society to be understood now as a theoretical construct of academic sociologists to represent those transitions which cannot be accommodated by the traditional tenets of industrial society theory? Or, is it rather to be distinguished, in its combination of in various ways with the political criteria of national governments and supranational entities for the conceptual ordering of coming developments in advanced capitalist society, by its ideological and utopian uses as a goal, but also by its low instrumental value for goal implementation (p. 17).

In none of the contributions does *knowledge society* (and its variants) interpreted as an already realized historical state, suffice as an adequate construct for the description and differentiation of the present mode of this relation in western society; nor in the explanation of continuities and change in knowledge conceived like a natural force as a 'variable' acting upon economy and society. Instead, the crucial aim is to identify the specificity of sociological processes around knowledge, their organizationally embedded operation, and the sense in which knowledge processes, structures and forms are constituted by and constitutive of society and economy at the same time (p. 22).

Nassehi (2004)

One of the most successful self-descriptions of contemporary modernity is the concept of knowledge society (Stehr, 1994). At first sight this characterization has in mind knowledge as the most leading productive power in our apparently post-industrial epoch. But a closer view shows that on one hand, knowledge has indeed become a propelling power not only in economic affairs. On the other hand, knowledge is increasingly more reflexive and explicit, making it increasingly unreliable. Even scientific knowledge cannot guarantee security. As a matter of fact, science refers to the contingency of all knowledge because it has to explicitly reflect on how to achieve it. But as we know from the sociology of science, scientific knowledge also produces cultured routines, methods, and conventions which are able to cover up the latent functions of those limitations of observation for the every-day life of research (Knorr Cetina, 1999). Only this limitation enables science to produce 'true knowledge' (p. 5).

We are accustomed to accounting for the idea of the knowledge society with the accentuation of knowledge as the decisive resource, especially in technical and economic terms (p. 5).

Above all it has to be recognized that expert cultures no longer have the power to present definite knowledge without alternatives. From the perspective of demand for professional expertise, knowledge begins to get insecure and ambiguous because one can always find tomorrow another expert with a different expertise than the one he or she believed today. Thus in the so-called knowledge society, the 'truth' of expertise has to be identified by the audience of demanders, not by the suppliers of knowledge. For the latter, this means that their expertise has to switch from the 'objective' conditions of their knowledge to their social conditions. They have to take into account for whom and under what expectations expertise is required – and the expected forms of criticism and needs seem to become the most important source of what can be expected to win currency as knowledge (p. 7).

Talking about the knowledge society hints at the fact that knowledge has become a problem, one which cannot be solved by more or better knowledge. Not knowledge is falling into short supply, but security that we once gathered from knowledge (p. 7).

Stehr (1994)

One of the first authors to employ the term 'knowledge society' is Robert E. Lane (1966, p. 650). He justifies the use of this concept by pointing to the growing societal relevance of scientific knowledge which defines a knowledgeable society, in a 'first approximation', as one in which its members

(1) inquire into the basis of their beliefs about man, nature and society; (2) are guided (perhaps unconsciously) objective standards of veridical truth, and at the upper levels of education, follow scientific rules of evidence and inference in inquiry; (3) devote considerable resources to this inquiry and thus have a large store of knowledge; (4) collect, organize, and interpret their knowledge in a constant effort to extract further meaning from it for the purposes at hand; (5) employ this knowledge to illuminate (and perhaps modify) their values and goals as well as to advance them. Just as the 'democratic' society has a foundation in governmental and interpersonal relations, and the 'affluent society' a foundation in economics, so the knowledgeable society has its roots in epistemology and the logic of inquiry.

In other words, Lane's conception of a knowledgeable society is tied rather closely to the promise of a particular theory of science and reflects, also, the great optimism of the early 1960s which suggested that science would somehow allow for the possibility of a society in which common sense would be replaced by scientific reasoning (p. 5).

Bell also employs the term 'knowledge society' in the context of his discussion of the emergence of *post-industrial* society, a designation he prefers. Bell at times uses the concept knowledge society interchangeably with the notion of 'post-industrial society' (pp. 5–6).

I choose to label the now emerging form of society as a 'knowledge' society because the constitutive mechanism or the identity of modern society is increasingly driven by knowledge (p. 6).

The appearance of 'knowledge societies' does not occur suddenly; it represents not a revolutionary development, but rather a gradual process during which the defining characteristic of society changes and a new one emerges (p. 6).

Contemporary society may be described as a knowledge society based upon the penetration of all its spheres of life by scientific knowledge (p. 9).

In the knowledge society, most of the wealth of a company is increasingly embodied in its creativity and information. In short, the point is that for the production of goods and services, factors other than 'the amount of labor time or the amount of physical capital become increasingly central' (Block, 1985, p. 95) to the economy of industrial societies (p. 10).

Much of the discussion about the information society is animated by a concern with the 'production, processing, and transmission of a very large amount of data about all sorts of matter – individual and national, social and commercial, economic and military' (Schiller, 1981, p. 25) (p. 12).

Bell (1973, p. 212) argues that post-industrial society is a knowledge society for two major reasons: (1) 'the sources of innovation are increasingly derivative from research and development (and more directly, there is a new relationship between science and technology because of the centrality of theoretical knowledge)', and (2) 'the weight of the society – measured by a larger proportion of Gross National Product and a larger share of employment – is increasingly in the knowledge field' (p. 14).

Ungar (2003)

The idea of a knowledge society is a gloss, since it is frequently evoked but seldom defined or explored in a systematic way. All too often, it emerges as an extension of the more concrete knowledge economy, or is simply deduced from the existence of information technology and the sheer quantity of available information (p. 4).

I employ Webster's (1995, p. 218) heuristic concept of the 'informatization of life' to differentiate the knowledge society from the knowledge economy. The informatization of life holds that the development of specialized occupational knowledges does not constitute a knowledge society. Informatization necessitates a broader diffusion of knowledge, including social processes that foster socially relevant knowledge among an educated public (p. 4).

The informated workplace typically provides employees with the technology, applications, networks, data bases, training and technical assistance required to carry out their specialized tasks. Hence a knowledge economy – and of course society – does not just depend on the efforts of individuals, but on the institutional arrangements and the social expectations for being knowledgeable and using knowledge (p. 5).

Following Lane's lead, a knowledge society at the institutional level can be regarded as one that provides for the widespread distribution and access to knowledge (and hence minimizes secrecy); provides access in forms or displays that are as interpretable as feasible; promotes and sponsors public discussion of ideas and issues, including networks and venues for doing so; recognizes and rewards the public use of knowledge; and employs such knowledge in decision-making processes (p. 5).

Perhaps the greatest problem with the knowledge society is that it is an unfruitful metaphor, an unenlightening addendum to the idea of the knowledge economy. Whereas the latter continues to attract interest, commentary and linguistic innovation, the former remains sterile (p. 8).

McLennan (2003)

Charles Leadbeater, for example, a much-quoted proponent of KS ideas, argues that we are now 'living on thin air', that is to say, in an economy which operates as a system of 'distributing intelligence', and which generates products, like Coke cans, the substance and value of which is *constituted by knowledge* where once they were mostly *composed of materials* (Leadbeater, 1999, pp. 8–10) (p. 4).

Of course, they say, any human form of organization is in some sense a knowledge society. But what is uniquely distinctive about the current informational regime is that, in Nico Stehr's rendering (2001, p. ix), 'we increasingly arrange and produce the reality within which we exist on the basis of our knowledge'. Manuel Castells, for his part, summarises that what is new in the information age is not the importance of knowledge per se, but rather 'the action of knowledge upon knowledge itself. (Castells, 1996, p. 17) (p. 4).

Further illegitimate elisions in KS discourse include all-purpose talk about the 'knowledge revolution', when it is often the transformation of knowledge *communication* rather than knowledge *production* that is being characterized; and the persistent equation of knowledge *economy* with knowledge *society*. The latter merger has two possible connotations, but they run in opposite directions. One involves a strenuous reductionism – something that is not, incidentally, much favoured in KS-style figurings of epistemological complexity – whereby cultural and social forms are seen as the functional prerequisites of an endogenous *techno-economic* momentum at the heart of the post-industrial order. The other connotation, which emphasizes knowledge society in a broad sense, is about intrinsic *socio-educative* goals: that it is intrinsically good to be educated and informed in an ongoing, self-realising kind of way (p. 7).

This is an economy/society which is populated by an increasingly reflexive and active citizenry of 'wired workers', those who know that knowledge is the principle factor of production, and who own know-how is now the most valuable form of property that economic organizations have recourse to. These people work with

computers in non-hierarchical settings, and they have engaged in problem solving
activities rather than repetitive tasks (p. 11).

Network Society

Castells (2000b): 'the contours of the network society'

I do think we live in a new society already, not in the future but right now. I
call that the network society, not the information society for the reasons that I
hope will become apparent soon. What is new about this society is something very
simple to start with – the technology. The technology is new. It does not mean
that the technology produces society. Technology is part of the society. It is one
inextractable dimension of the society at large (p. 152).

The fact that we have new technologies allows possibilities of social and
economic organization that did not exist before. In other words, the information
technologies are not the cause of the social transformation, but without these
technologies the processes that lead to social transformation could not happen.
Hence, it is a different argument that this new technology is not a sufficient but a
necessary condition for the kind of society we live in, the network society (p. 152).

What is new in this society is the prevalence of networks. It means that we have
entered not only a new technological paradigm, but a new form of organizational
structure for everything we do. We have shifted from the vertically organized,
standardized, rationally structured, hierarchically structured forms of activity to
networking forms of activity. A network is simply a set of interconnected nodes.
Networks have always existed, so this is not a new form of organization. Networks
have now generalized and are generalizing their presence in economy, society,
politics and culture because of the new technologies. Here is the conversion between
social change and technological change (p. 152).

We should abandon the notion of information society per se because it is
ambiguous. It does not capture the essence of what is happening. If we say
information technology society we are much closer to what is happening. On the
other hand, it would imply technological determinism, which would assume that
information technology determines society (p. 156).

Post-Industrial Society

Brint (2001)

In the case of postindustrial society, two economic changes were regarded as
particularly important. The first of these had to do with the increasing importance
on non-profit services. Bell argued that as societies develop they move from a
reliance on agriculture and mining (primary sector) to a reliance on manufacturing
(secondary sector) and finally to a reliance on services. Further, the pattern of
services-based industrial growth follows a trajectory of population wealth. Industrial
centres move from services related to the production and movement of goods (such

as transportation and repair) to personal services (such as restaurants, hotels, travel, entertainment) and, at the last stage, to knowledge-based services providing access to the 'good life', especially health, higher education, recreation and government (p. 108).

Wisdom

McKenna and Rooney (2005)

... wisdom is that which: coordinates knowledge and judgments about the 'fundamental pragmatics of life' around such properties as (1) strategies and goals involving the conduct and meaning of life; (2) limits of knowledge and uncertainties of the world; (3) excellence of judgment and advice; (4) knowledge with extraordinary scope, depth, and balance; (5) search for a perfect synergy of mind and character; and (6) balancing the good or well-being of oneself and that of others. Such a characterization, then, implies that wisdom includes both rational (scientific) intellectual practices and 'other' more transcendent and unscrutinizable (tacit) mental processes like imagination, intuition, creativity and so on. Fundamental to our theorization of 3 wisdom is a commitment to ethical behaviour, consistent with its Aristotelian (secular) and Thomistic (religious) European origins (p. 2–3).

9

HOW DOES COUNTRY RISK AFFECT INNOVATION? AN APPLICATION TO FOREIGN PATENTS REGISTERED IN THE USA

Suhejla Hoti and Michael McAleer

1. Introduction

Innovation can occur at a national level under a wide range of settings. Trends in patent registration have frequently been used to describe a country's technological capabilities, and have acted as a proxy for innovation (see e.g. Pavitt, 1988; Patel and Pavitt, 1995; Marinova, 2001). Having the world's largest economic and financial market, the USA has consistently been a destination for registering patents by innovative American and foreign companies, as well as by individuals who have aspired to commercialize new technologies. Consequently, the patents registered by the US Patent and Trademark Office (PTO) represent an excellent source of information regarding technological strengths and market ambitions for countries (for further details, see Chan *et al.*, 2004).

The leading innovative countries internationally have several common traits, including economic, financial and political stability, which are reflected in various measures of country risk. Country risk broadly refers to the economic and financial conditions and political stability of a country. It is an overall measure of country creditworthiness, indicating the capacity of a country to service its foreign financial obligations, based on its economic, financial and political performance.

The purpose of the paper is to examine, for the first time, the relationship between the economic, financial and political country risk ratings, on the one hand, and innovation, as measured by a country's registered patents, on the other. This paper analyzes monthly country risk ratings and registered patent trends (as a proxy for innovation) for the top 12 foreign patenting countries in the US market from 1975 to 1997, namely Australia, Canada, France, Germany, Italy, Japan, Korea, the Netherlands, Sweden, Switzerland, Taiwan and the UK. As reported in Chan *et al.* (2004) and Hoti *et al.* (2006), Japan is ranked first in terms of foreign patents registered in the USA, followed by Germany. Patent registrations from each of these countries have increased steadily over time, but at different rates.

Most of the research on granted patents in the USA have examined snapshot images representing the patent activities for a particular time period, based on a single year or aggregated annual information base. While broader, the country risk literature does not seem to have taken account of measures of innovation as determinants of country risk. Indeed, there has been extensive country risk measuring activity by numerous risk rating agencies, such as Moody's, Standard and Poor's, Euromoney, Fitch IBCA, and International Country Risk Guide (ICRG), which combine quantitative and qualitative information regarding economic, financial and political conditions of a country into associated risk ratings. Although these agencies use different methods of deriving country risk ratings, to date they have all failed to accommodate measures of innovation in their rating systems. Hence, it is important to analyze the relationship between country risk and innovation.

Higher innovation reflects higher technological capabilities and growth opportunities in a country which, in turn, leads to higher country risk ratings or creditworthiness. On the other hand, higher country risk ratings lead to higher foreign investment and capital flowing into a country which, in turn, lead to higher growth and technological advancement, and hence to higher innovation. This finding would be particularly important for less-developed countries, which need high country risk ratings to attract foreign investments in order to promote economic growth and innovation. One way for these countries to improve their country risk ratings is by increasing their efforts in technological innovation.

The plan of the paper is as follows. Section 2 describes the data used, namely economic, financial and political risk ratings as reported by the ICRG, and registered patents in the USA by the 12 countries. The econometric model is described in Section 3, while the empirical results regarding the relationship of country risk ratings and registered patents across the 12 countries are discussed in Section 4. The US leading effects will also be analyzed in this section. Some concluding remarks are given in Section 5.

2. Patent Registrations and Country Risk Ratings

2.1 *General Trends*

In the current state of world affairs, the economic and financial wealth and political power of the USA are decisive for its dominant position in the international financial community and political status. As argued by Chan *et al.* (2004), for over two centuries the USA has adopted the patent system as a mechanism for market protection and stimulation of innovative activities. Long before it became the world's largest market, the USA was developing a patent system that has steadily attracted parties from around the world who were interested in developing technologies and in establishing trade links.

A patent is an intellectual (or industrial) property that confers to its owner or holder monopoly rights to a product or process over a stipulated period of time. Such applications are granted on the basis of innovation and non-obviousness. Trending patterns over time of patent filings and successes have been discussed by McAleer *et al.* (2005), Chan and McAleer (2006), and Hoti *et al.* (2006). Overall, the patent office in the USA receives by far the largest number of foreign applications, with almost one half of all patents in the USA being granted to foreigners. This makes clear the important role of the US market as a world leader in innovation.

This paper investigates for the first time the relationship between innovation (as approximated by patents registered in the US Patent and Trademark Office) and the economic, financial and political risk ratings of a country. Monthly patent registrations and country risk ratings are analyzed for the top 12 foreign countries, namely Australia, Canada, France, Germany, Italy, Japan, Korea, the Netherlands, Sweden, Switzerland, Taiwan and the UK. The patenting behaviour of these 12 countries was examined in Chan *et al.* (2004) for the period January 1975 to December 1997. Of the 12 countries, Japan has the largest number of US patents held by foreigners, followed by Germany. The highest number of patents per capita (or patent intensity) is held by Switzerland, followed by Japan and Sweden. Although France and Italy hold large numbers of patents, they nevertheless have low patent intensities.

The economic, financial and political risk attributes of the selected 12 countries have also been examined by Hoti and McAleer (2005). They used the monthly economic, financial, political and composite risk ratings compiled by the ICRG agency for the period January 1984 to May 2002. ICRG ratings for the 12 countries are all very high reflecting well-established and advanced economic, financial and political systems, and hence low associated risk.

The ICRG has provided economic, financial, political and composite risk ratings for 93 countries on a monthly basis since January 1984. As of June 2006, the four risk ratings were available for a total of 140 countries. The ICRG rating system comprises 22 variables that represent three major components of country risk, namely economic (5 variables), financial (5 variables) and political (12 variables). Using each set of variables, a separate risk rating is created for the three components, on a scale of 0–100. The three component risk ratings are then combined to derive a composite risk rating as an overall measure of country risk. Each of the five economic and financial components accounts for 25% of the total, while the 12 political components account for 50% of the composite risk rating. The lower (higher) is a given risk rating, the higher (lower) is the associated risk.

Figures 1–5 show the trends in foreign patenting in the USA and the four risk ratings for the 12 countries for the period January 1984 to December 1997. All the countries exhibit increasing trends with a peak occurring towards the end of the sample. For the empirical analysis conducted in this paper, these extreme observations have been replaced by the annual average of the years when these observations occur. The economic, financial, political and composite risk ratings for the 12 countries in Figures 2–3 exhibit different patterns across the various countries. No general trend is observed for any of the four ratings, unlike the time-series patterns in the foreign patents. The financial risk ratings do not vary at all for long periods, while the composite risk ratings reflect the trends of both the economic and political risk ratings. Overall, the three risk ratings improved substantially in the second half of the sample period for Australia, Canada, France, Germany, Italy, Japan, the Netherlands, Sweden and the UK, while Korea and Taiwan exhibit increasing trends throughout the sample period.

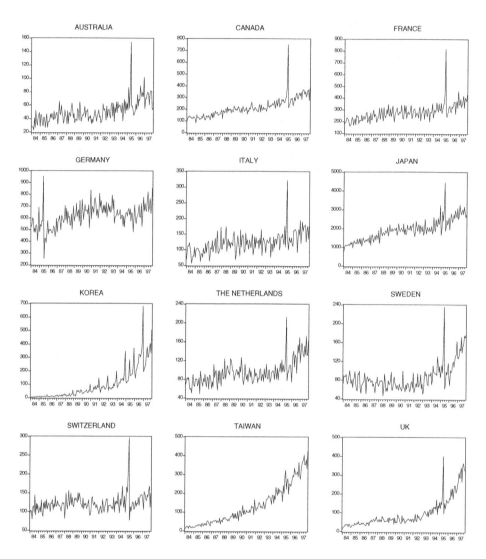

Figure 1. Trends in Registered Patents for 12 Countries.

2.2 Descriptive Statistics

In this paper, the patenting behaviour of the 12 countries is examined in connection with their economic, financial and political performances as reflected in the economic, financial, political and composite ICRG risk ratings. The data were for the period January 1984 to December 1997 for all countries, apart from Korea, where country risk data started in March 1985, and Germany, for which the data are available from October 1990. Descriptive statistics for monthly patent registrations

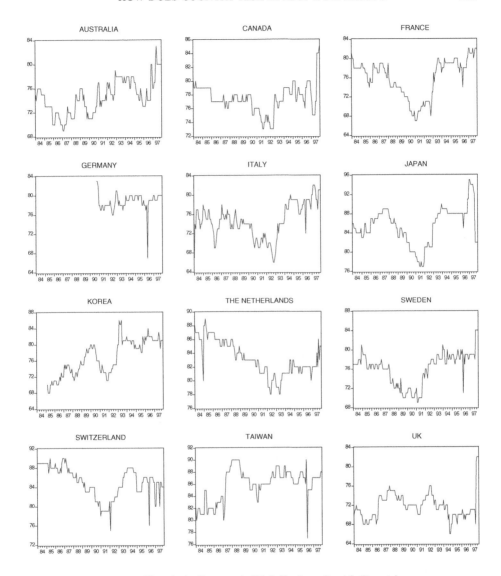

Figure 2. Trends in Economic Risk Ratings for 12 Countries.

and economic, financial, political and composite risk ratings for the 12 countries, as well as for the USA, are reported in Tables 1–5.

In Table 1, the mean number of US patents varies substantially across countries, ranging from 50.78 for Australia to 1934.81 for Japan, with a total US mean patents of 9432.61. As discussed above, Japan clearly holds the largest number of US patents held by foreigners, followed by Germany. The median, maximum and minimum patent figures also vary substantially across countries, with standard deviations simply reflecting the different mean magnitudes. Apart from Germany,

Table 1. Descriptive Statistics for Registered Patents by Country.

Descriptive Statistics	Australia	Canada	France	Germany	Italy	Japan	Korea	The Netherlands	Sweden	Switzerland	Taiwan	UK	USA
Mean	50.78	213.68	280.38	618.04	122.91	1934.81	96.09	95.70	86.79	122.18	133.79	98.38	9432.61
Median	48.50	200.00	271.00	621.50	121.00	1883.50	54.50	91.50	78.50	119.00	104.00	66.00	9102.00
Maximum	154.00	751.00	819.00	954.00	322.00	4454.00	683.00	213.00	236.00	297.00	426.00	402.00	16911.00
Minimum	23.00	82.00	164.00	255.00	57.00	789.00	1.00	50.00	47.00	78.00	10.00	12.00	4940.00
Std. Dev.	16.26	79.95	71.42	96.77	32.58	571.40	114.75	25.14	29.05	23.04	104.22	79.52	2601.71
Skewness	1.96	2.12	2.75	−0.11	1.47	0.75	1.94	1.32	1.86	2.92	0.91	1.81	0.80
Kurtosis	11.82	13.73	20.81	4.16	10.06	4.31	7.42	5.78	7.65	22.04	2.81	5.78	3.11
Observations	168	168	168	168	168	168	168	168	168	168	168	168	168

Sources: http://164.195.100.11/netahtml/search-adv.htm and http://www.census.gov/cgi-bin/ipc/idbsprd (Chan *et al.*, 2004).

Table 2. Descriptive Statistics for Economic Risk Ratings by Country.

Descriptive Statistics	Australia	Canada	France	Germany	Italy	Japan	Korea	The Netherlands	Sweden	Switzerland	Taiwan	UK	USA
Mean	74.54	77.42	75.94	78.72	74.61	85.49	76.70	83.18	76.10	85.04	85.87	71.75	75.48
Median	74.00	77.00	77.50	79.00	75.00	86.00	76.50	83.00	77.00	86.00	87.00	72.00	75.50
Maximum	83.00	85.00	82.00	83.00	82.00	95.00	86.00	89.00	84.00	90.00	90.00	82.00	81.00
Minimum	69.00	73.00	67.00	67.00	66.00	77.00	68.00	78.00	69.00	75.00	77.00	66.00	64.00
Std. Dev.	2.81	2.02	3.94	1.82	3.57	3.85	4.32	2.50	3.33	3.23	2.67	2.61	2.61
Skewness	0.27	0.38	−0.63	−2.79	−0.19	−0.19	−0.05	0.15	−0.41	−0.64	−0.67	1.19	−0.50
Kurtosis	2.57	4.98	2.31	21.34	2.50	2.93	1.89	2.24	2.64	2.76	2.88	6.32	4.23
Observations	168	168	168	87	168	168	154	168	168	168	168	168	168

Source: International Country Risk Guide (2005).

Table 3.   Descriptive Statistics for Financial Risk Ratings by Country.

Descriptive Statistics	Australia	Canada	France	Germany	Italy	Japan	Korea	The Netherlands	Sweden	Switzerland	Taiwan	UK	USA
Mean	84.91	91.49	88.08	94.70	85.99	96.73	87.25	93.07	88.34	99.37	92.70	94.17	96.33
Median	86.00	92.00	88.00	94.00	82.00	96.00	94.00	94.00	88.00	100.00	96.00	94.00	98.00
Maximum	92.00	96.00	96.00	100.00	94.00	100.00	96.00	96.00	94.00	100.00	98.00	100.00	98.00
Minimum	71.00	79.00	74.00	75.00	76.00	90.00	62.00	71.00	68.00	88.00	76.00	72.00	73.00
Std. Dev.	4.26	4.07	4.47	5.07	6.19	3.53	11.74	3.42	5.34	1.93	6.33	5.62	3.87
Skewness	−0.80	−0.76	−0.64	−1.99	0.30	−0.54	−1.34	−5.00	−1.04	−3.84	−1.01	−1.25	−4.97
Kurtosis	3.10	3.23	3.50	8.87	1.43	1.90	3.06	30.51	4.68	19.21	2.66	6.24	29.44
Observations	168	168	168	87	168	168	154	168	168	168	168	168	168

Source: International Country Risk Guide (2005).

Table 4. Descriptive Statistics for Political Risk Ratings by Country.

Descriptive Statistics	Australia	Canada	France	Germany	Italy	Japan	Korea	The Netherlands	Sweden	Switzerland	Taiwan	UK	USA
Mean	81.85	82.75	79.62	80.64	75.30	84.83	69.47	86.90	84.98	90.76	76.97	81.24	82.81
Median	81.00	82.00	80.00	82.00	75.00	86.00	66.00	87.00	86.00	93.00	77.00	80.00	83.00
Maximum	90.00	88.00	85.00	87.00	86.00	94.00	83.00	93.00	90.00	97.00	83.00	91.00	95.00
Minimum	74.00	78.00	74.00	73.00	66.00	75.00	59.00	82.00	78.00	84.00	71.00	74.00	74.00
Std. Dev.	3.91	2.56	2.09	3.51	5.03	4.70	7.51	3.33	3.99	4.11	2.80	4.22	4.41
Skewness	0.38	0.75	−0.06	−0.76	0.21	−0.10	0.16	0.16	−0.18	−0.35	−0.32	0.71	0.56
Kurtosis	2.15	2.72	3.54	2.68	2.18	1.99	1.44	1.89	1.44	1.70	3.14	2.48	3.34
Observations	168	168	168	87	168	168	154	168	168	168	168	168	168

Source: International Country Risk Guide (2005).

Table 5. Descriptive Statistics for Composite Risk Ratings by Country.

Descriptive Statistics	Australia	Canada	France	Germany	Italy	Japan	Korea	The Netherlands	Sweden	Switzerland	Taiwan	UK	USA
Mean	80.79	83.60	80.82	83.68	77.80	87.97	75.72	87.51	83.60	91.48	83.13	82.10	84.36
Median	80.88	83.25	81.00	84.00	78.00	88.00	75.75	87.25	83.50	91.63	84.00	82.00	84.13
Maximum	87.00	87.50	85.00	87.50	83.50	92.00	84.75	92.25	87.75	95.75	87.25	87.75	91.25
Minimum	76.00	80.75	77.75	79.50	70.75	82.75	62.50	84.00	77.75	86.00	77.25	77.25	80.00
Std. Dev.	2.54	1.57	1.34	2.03	2.73	2.22	6.63	2.11	2.04	2.40	2.50	2.45	2.17
Skewness	0.01	1.01	−0.08	−0.44	−0.38	−0.10	−0.60	0.41	−0.14	−0.26	−0.80	0.30	0.94
Kurtosis	2.37	3.53	2.78	2.56	2.97	2.26	2.13	2.00	2.23	2.10	2.61	2.14	4.13
Observations	168	168	168	87	168	168	154	168	168	168	168	168	168

Source: International Country Risk Guide (2005).

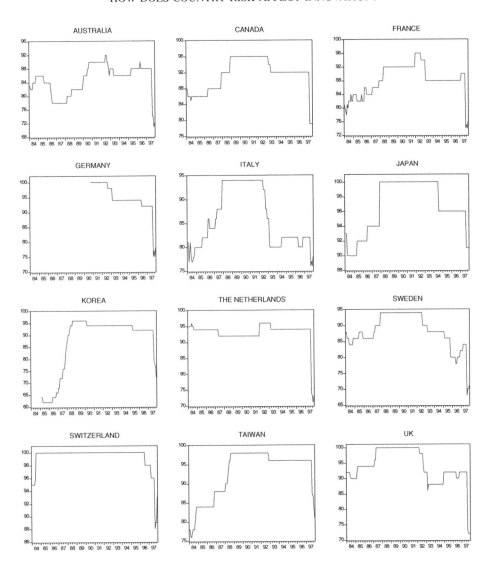

Figure 3. Trends in Financial Risk Ratings for 12 Countries.

patents according to countries are positively skewed, with kurtosis ranging from 2.81 for Taiwan to 22.04 for Switzerland.

The mean economic risk ratings in Table 2 are very high and do not vary considerably across the 13 countries, ranging from 71.75 for the UK to 85.49 for Japan. Similarly, the median, maximum, minimum and standard deviations of economic risk ratings vary slightly across countries. The ratings can be positively or negatively skewed, with a wide range of kurtosis. Similar comments hold for the descriptive statistics in Tables 3–4 for the financial, political and composite risk

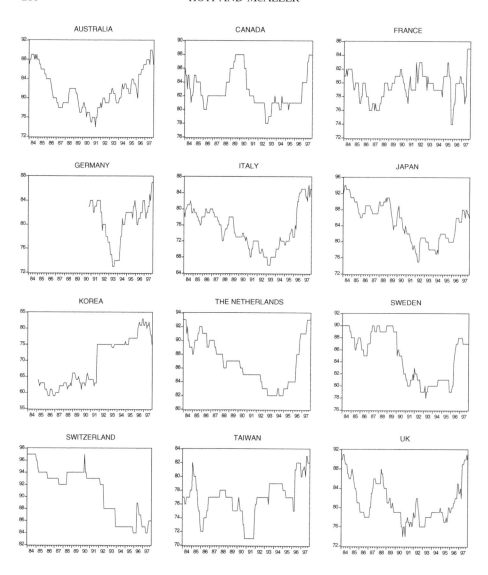

Figure 4. Trends in Political Risk Ratings for 12 Countries.

ratings. The mean risk ratings vary from 84.91 (Australia) to 99.37 (Switzerland) for the financial risk ratings, 69.47 (Korea) to 90.76 (Switzerland) for the political risk ratings and 77.80 (Italy) to 91.48 (Switzerland) for the composite risk ratings.

2.3 *Correlation Coefficients*

Correlation coefficients between the 13 countries by data series are calculated and reported in Tables 6–10, while the correlation coefficients between the 5 data series

Table 6. Country Correlation Coefficients for Registered Patents.

Correlation Coefficients	Australia	Canada	France	Germany	Italy	Japan	Korea	The Netherlands	Sweden	Switzerland	Taiwan	UK	USA
Australia	1.000	0.831	0.741	0.280	0.674	0.778	0.685	0.710	0.694	0.642	0.717	0.754	0.842
Canada		1.000	0.873	0.420	0.772	0.914	0.776	0.826	0.779	0.661	0.851	0.867	0.971
France			1.000	0.428	0.866	0.849	0.674	0.810	0.721	0.720	0.684	0.748	0.895
Germany				1.000	0.400	0.486	0.415	0.338	0.215	0.130	0.443	0.371	0.446
Italy					1.000	0.761	0.579	0.736	0.621	0.612	0.617	0.665	0.790
Japan						1.000	0.792	0.814	0.690	0.632	0.856	0.829	0.955
Korea							1.000	0.729	0.767	0.373	0.909	0.867	0.828
The Netherlands								1.000	0.751	0.602	0.735	0.800	0.840
Sweden									1.000	0.584	0.740	0.853	0.814
Switzerland										1.000	0.393	0.518	0.680
Taiwan											1.000	0.921	0.890
UK												1.000	0.903
USA													1.000

Table 7. Country Correlation Coefficients for Economic Risk Ratings.

Correlation Coefficients	Australia	Canada	France	Germany	Italy	Japan	Korea	The Netherlands	Sweden	Switzerland	Taiwan	UK	USA
Australia	1.000	0.336	0.471	0.172	0.285	0.404	0.387	0.064	0.458	0.298	0.283	0.229	0.067
Canada		1.000	0.677	0.362	0.655	0.383	0.566	0.503	0.587	0.532	0.124	0.131	0.073
France			1.000	0.231	0.869	0.852	0.796	0.317	0.773	0.704	0.328	-0.130	-0.193
Germany				1.000	0.272	0.202	0.069	0.226	0.089	0.292	0.359	0.009	0.252
Italy					1.000	0.735	0.644	0.529	0.581	0.582	0.101	-0.241	-0.328
Japan						1.000	0.791	0.088	0.587	0.658	0.270	-0.422	-0.441
Korea							1.000	0.079	0.623	0.680	0.199	-0.253	-0.313
The Netherlands								1.000	0.233	0.104	-0.191	0.111	-0.140
Sweden									1.000	0.573	0.277	0.242	0.105
Switzerland										1.000	0.456	-0.210	0.055
Taiwan											1.000	0.152	0.400
UK												1.000	0.531
USA													1.000

Table 8. Country Correlation Coefficients for Financial Risk Ratings.

Correlation Coefficients	Australia	Canada	France	Germany	Italy	Japan	Korea	The Netherlands	Sweden	Switzerland	Taiwan	UK	USA
Australia	1.000	0.938	0.891	0.905	0.612	0.650	0.860	0.854	0.704	0.781	0.955	0.900	0.908
Canada		1.000	0.951	0.978	0.715	0.811	0.888	0.822	0.859	0.821	0.944	0.898	0.916
France			1.000	0.937	0.754	0.757	0.793	0.786	0.830	0.712	0.877	0.878	0.844
Germany				1.000	0.778	0.823	0.854	0.759	0.906	0.838	0.918	0.917	0.887
Italy					1.000	0.596	0.390	0.243	0.781	0.374	0.582	0.847	0.488
Japan						1.000	0.744	0.593	0.870	0.697	0.726	0.624	0.720
Korea							1.000	0.924	0.747	0.873	0.950	0.710	0.951
The Netherlands								1.000	0.573	0.846	0.878	0.625	0.906
Sweden									1.000	0.695	0.770	0.778	0.784
Switzerland										1.000	0.817	0.650	0.845
Taiwan											1.000	0.861	0.945
UK												1.000	0.802
USA													1.000

Table 9. Country Correlation Coefficients for Political Risk Ratings.

Correlation Coefficients	Australia	Canada	France	Germany	Italy	Japan	Korea	The Netherlands	Sweden	Switzerland	Taiwan	UK	USA
Australia	1.000	0.531	0.251	0.230	0.804	0.648	0.831	0.670	0.714	−0.693	0.843	0.810	0.728
Canada		1.000	0.280	0.565	0.718	0.659	0.187	0.827	0.745	−0.145	0.326	0.807	0.642
France			1.000	0.084	0.151	0.156	0.173	0.297	0.291	0.098	0.298	0.329	−0.047
Germany				1.000	0.587	0.515	−0.035	0.622	0.526	0.142	−0.121	0.375	0.297
Italy					1.000	0.806	0.588	0.900	0.932	−0.356	0.588	0.792	0.792
Japan						1.000	0.588	0.785	0.786	−0.289	0.409	0.619	0.642
Korea							1.000	0.398	0.505	−0.688	0.861	0.585	0.503
The Netherlands								1.000	0.922	−0.096	0.419	0.823	0.617
Sweden									1.000	−0.176	0.551	0.775	0.718
Switzerland										1.000	−0.707	−0.421	−0.603
Taiwan											1.000	0.692	0.608
UK												1.000	0.685
USA													1.000

Table 10. Country Correlation Coefficients for Composite Risk Ratings.

Correlation Coefficients	Australia	Canada	France	Germany	Italy	Japan	Korea	The Netherlands	Sweden	Switzerland	Taiwan	UK	USA
Australia	1.000	0.352	0.509	−0.187	0.613	0.771	0.787	0.691	0.449	−0.687	0.751	0.361	0.401
Canada		1.000	0.046	0.365	0.710	0.459	−0.074	0.618	0.445	−0.353	0.019	0.631	0.391
France			1.000	−0.217	0.119	0.268	0.477	0.239	0.505	−0.289	0.609	0.218	0.125
Germany				1.000	0.373	−0.131	−0.462	0.348	0.224	0.233	−0.523	0.372	0.104
Italy					1.000	0.595	0.251	0.841	0.509	−0.503	0.217	0.659	0.426
Japan						1.000	0.606	0.693	0.374	−0.626	0.581	0.181	0.538
Korea							1.000	0.391	0.196	−0.544	0.877	−0.040	0.367
The Netherlands								1.000	0.626	−0.383	0.349	0.669	0.478
Sweden									1.000	−0.090	0.308	0.573	0.440
Switzerland										1.000	−0.507	−0.214	−0.154
Taiwan											1.000	0.057	0.399
UK												1.000	0.103
USA													1.000

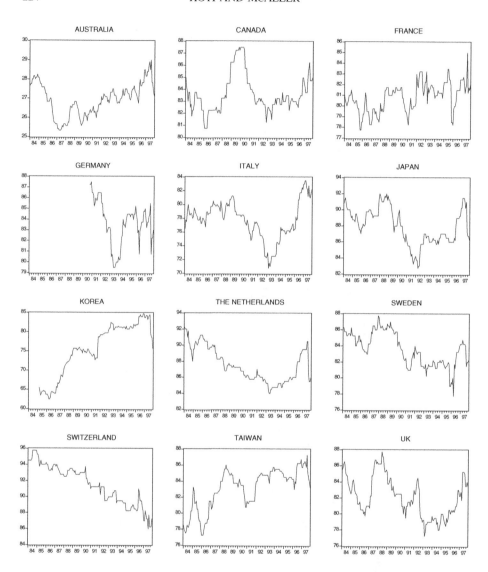

Figure 5. Trends in Composite Risk Ratings for 12 Countries.

by country are given in Table 11. The correlation coefficients between the number of patents held by the 12 countries, as well as the USA, are reported in Table 6. The 78 correlation pairs are positive and are generally very high, indicating a strong positive relationship between the innovative activities of the 12 countries. Germany, followed by Italy and Switzerland, has generally the lowest patent correlations with the rest of the countries, including the USA. Patents held by Canada, Japan and the UK are strongly correlated with the total for the USA.

Table 11.   Correlation Coefficients between Registered Patents and Risk Ratings by
Country.

Patents	Economic	Financial	Political	Composite
Australia	**0.389**	0.145	0.187	**0.312**
Canada	0.138	**0.201**	−0.014	0.163
France	**−0.649**	−0.033	−0.172	0.167
Germany	−0.004	−0.092	0.159	0.079
Italy	**0.327**	−0.003	0.073	0.173
Japan	**0.219**	**0.331**	**−0.438**	**−0.238**
Korea	**0.615**	**0.263**	**0.783**	**0.660**
The Netherlands	**−0.274**	**−0.351**	0.048	**−0.186**
Sweden	**0.559**	**−0.700**	0.005	**−0.225**
Switzerland	−0.099	−0.113	**−0.345**	**−0.351**
Taiwan	**0.337**	**0.432**	**0.517**	**0.653**
UK	0.135	**−0.571**	0.192	−0.126
USA	0.148	**−0.496**	**−0.277**	**−0.458**

Unlike the results in Table 6, the correlation coefficients for the four risk ratings across the 13 countries in Tables 7–10 can be positive and negative. The correlations for the economic risk ratings in Table 7 are much lower than the correlations in Table 6, indicating a weaker relationship between the countries in terms of their economic risk attributes. However, Table 8 reports strong correlation coefficients, and hence relationships, between the financial risk ratings for the 13 countries, while the magnitude of the correlation coefficients between the political risk ratings varies across country pairs in Table 9. Similarly, the degree of correlation between the composite risk ratings varies substantially across the country pairs. These results imply that, in general, the 12 countries, as well as the USA, are closely related in terms of their innovative activities and financial risk traits, and less so in terms of their economic, political and composite risk ratings.

It is also worth analyzing the degree of relationship between innovative activities and the four risk ratings for the 13 countries. Table 11 reports the correlation coefficients between patents and the economic, financial, political and composite risk ratings for each country. The magnitudes of the correlation coefficients between patents and the four risk ratings vary across the countries and risk ratings. Of the 52 correlation coefficients, only 28 exceed 0.200. Moreover, 13 of these 28 correlations are negative. Patents held by Korea and Taiwan are, in general, strongly correlated with the four risk ratings. For Australia, patents are mildly correlated with the economic and composite risk ratings, while for Canada this is the case only with financial risk ratings.

There is a high negative correlation between patents and economic risk ratings for France, and a weaker but positive correlation for Italy. For Japan, patents are positively correlated with economic and financial risk ratings, but are negatively correlated with political and composite risk ratings. Patents held by the Netherlands are negatively correlated with economic and financial risk ratings, while for Sweden they are positively correlated with economic risk ratings, but negatively correlated with financial and composite risk ratings. Strong negative correlations also hold between patents and political and composite risk ratings for Switzerland, between patents and financial risk ratings for the UK, and between patents and financial, political and composite risk ratings for the USA.

These findings are interesting as innovative advancements (respectively, higher country risk ratings) are expected to lead to higher risk ratings (respectively, innovative advancements) for a country. Moreover, the low correlation coefficients in 24 cases indicate no relationship between innovative advancements and country risk ratings. Hence, it is important to model the relationship between patents and economic, financial and political risk ratings for the 12 countries. The effect of the US market performance in the innovative activities of the 12 countries is also taken into account.

3. Conditional Mean Model

The primary purpose of the remainder of the paper is to model the relationship between innovation, as approximated by patent registrations, and country risk attributes, as measured by country risk ratings, for the top 12 performing countries in the USA patent market. The effect of the US market leading performance in the innovative activities of the 12 countries is also taken into account.

Consider the following model for the number of patents held in the USA by a foreign country i, P_{it}:

$$P_{it} = \beta_{0i} + \beta_{1i}\text{ERR}_{it} + \beta_{2i}\text{FRR}_{it} + B_{3i}\text{PRR} + \beta_{4i}P_{\text{USA}t} + \varepsilon_{it} \qquad (1)$$

where

ERR_{it} is the economic risk rating for country i at time t;

FRR_{it} is the financial risk rating for country i at time t;

PRR_{it} is the political risk rating for country i at time t;

P_{USAt} is the total number of patents registered in the USA Patent and Trademark Office (as a proxy for the level of innovation in the USA) at time t;

ϵ_{it} is a random disturbance term, which is independently and identically distributed, with mean zero and constant variance;

$t = 1, \ldots, T$ is the number of monthly observations, where $T = 168$ for all countries apart from Germany ($T = 87$) and Korea ($T = 154$).

4. Empirical Results

Using monthly data on registered patents and economic, financial and political risk ratings for Australia, Canada, France, Germany, Italy, Japan, Korea, the Netherlands, Sweden, Switzerland, Taiwan and the UK, the conditional mean is modelled in each case as the specification given in equation (1). The conditional mean parameters

Table 12. Conditional Mean Estimates for the Number of Patents Held in the USA by a Foreign Country.

Countries	Intercept β_0	Country Risk Attributes Effects			US Effect	Adjusted R^2
		β_1	β_2	β_3	β_4	
Australia	37.899	−0.756	−0.040	0.333	0.005	0.641
	(1.397)	(−2.087)	(−0.151)	(1.699)	(13.565)	
Canada	−265.32	2.603	1.575	−1.241	0.025	0.933
	(−2.562)	(2.704)	(3.343)	(−2.247)	(39.377)	
France	433.850	−1.886	−0.751	−1.779	0.021	0.756
	(3.442)	(−2.868)	(−1.296)	(−1.773)	(23.453)	
Germany	544.487	−1.294	−0.316	2.748	0.002	0.033
	(1.179)	(−0.354)	(−0.135)	(1.166)	(0.474)	
Italy	−92.673	0.380	0.973	0.322	0.008	0.556
	(−1.916)	(0.747)	(3.626)	(1.127)	(13.793)	
Japan	−1805.203	−7.752	22.075	4.635	0.197	0.929
	(−2.987)	(−2.425)	(5.688)	(1.252)	(24.196)	
Korea	−363.773	0.443	−2.066	4.056	0.034	0.806
	(−2.660)	(0.217)	(−5.204)	(3.232)	(4.972)	
The Netherlands	−98.159	0.341	−0.230	1.301	0.008	0.704
	(−1.636)	(0.543)	(−0.655)	(2.811)	(15.387)	
Sweden	−143.895	1.501	−1.158	1.774	0.007	0.802
	(−2.031)	(3.017)	(−2.880)	(5.282)	(12.852)	
Switzerland	−374.725	1.112	2.017	1.473	0.007	0.249
	(−2.115)	(1.870)	(2.384)	(2.047)	(4.982)	
Taiwan	−330.346	−1.136	−0.092	2.897	0.037	0.892
	(−2.294)	(−0.809)	(−0.136)	(2.518)	(16.746)	
UK	−273.912	0.644	−2.049	3.497	0.025	0.892
	(−2.435)	(0.662)	(−4.051)	(4.225)	(13.250)	

Notes: The t-ratios (given in parentheses) have been computed using the Newey-West Heteroscedasticity and Autocorrelation (HAC) consistent standard errors.

for the number of patents held by the 12 leading countries as reported in Table 12 are estimated using the least squares method in the EViews 5.0 econometric software package (Quantitative Micro Software LLC).

As reported in Table 12, the adjusted R^2 values are generally very high, the exceptions being Germany and Switzerland, with adjusted R^2 values of 0.033 and 0.249, respectively. In these two cases, the conditional mean model does not seem to be empirically adequate. However, of the remaining 10 countries, Canada and Japan have the highest adjusted R^2 values of 0.933 than 0.929, respectively, followed by Taiwan and the UK, both at 0.892, and Korea and Sweden, with 0.806 and 0.802, respectively. The remaining four countries are France, the Netherlands, Australia and Italy, with adjusted R^2 values of 0.765, 0.704, 0.641 and 0.556, respectively.

The impact of the country risk attributes on the number of patents varies across the 12 countries. Based on the statistical significance of the β_1 coefficient estimates, the economic risk ratings have a significant impact only for Australia, Canada, France, Japan and Sweden. However, contrary to expectations, economic risk ratings seem to have a negative impact on the number of patents held by Australia, France and Japan. The economic risk rating is measured by the ICRG on the basis of five economic risk attributes, namely GDP per capita, real annual GDP growth, annual inflation rate, budget balance as percentage of GDP, and current account balance as percentage of GDP. This means that a decline in any one, or a combination, of the economic risk attributes will increase the country's incentives towards innovative activities in order to improve its economic performance.

Based on the statistical significance of the β_2 coefficient estimates, the financial risk ratings have an important effect on the number of patents held for Canada, Italy, Japan, Korea, Sweden, Switzerland and the UK. Of these 7 cases, the financial risk ratings have an adverse effect on the patents held by Korea, Sweden and the UK. Again, this finding would seem to be against the prior belief that higher country risk ratings are associated with higher innovative activities in a country. Financial risk ratings are measured by the ICRG on the basis of five financial risk attributes, namely foreign debt as a percentage of GDP, foreign debt service as a percentage of exports in goods and services, current account as a percentage of exports in goods and services, net liquidity as months of import cover, and exchange rate stability. As in the previous case, this would seem to imply that a decline in any or a combination of the financial risk attributes encourages technical change and innovation in a country as a way of improving its financial performance.

In terms of the political risk ratings, the β_3 parameter estimates are statistically significant in 7 cases, namely Canada, Korea, the Netherlands, Sweden, Switzerland, Taiwan and the UK. Except for Canada, political risk ratings have a strong positive impact on the number of patents held by these countries. As expected, an increase in political risk ratings for a country reflects improvements in the ICRG political risk attributes, namely government stability, socio-economic conditions, investment profile, internal and external conflicts, corruption, military in politics, religious tensions, law and order, ethnic tensions, democratic accountability and bureaucratic quality. In these cases, strong and stable political and legal landscapes lead to higher economic incentives to innovate, as would be expected.

Finally, the influential impact of the innovation in the US market for the 12 countries is determined based on the statistical significance of the β_4 parameter estimates. Apart from Germany, the US market is a significant leader in innovation for all the countries considered. This is also to be expected, given the dominant position of the USA in the global market and in international affairs.

Overall, from Table 12, the economic, financial and political risk ratings have had a considerable impact on the innovative activities of the 12 countries. Total US patent applications also appear to be influential in terms of inducing technical change and innovation in the 12 countries.

5. Conclusions

Innovation can occur at a national level under a wide range of settings. However, the leading innovative countries internationally have several common traits, including economic, financial and political stability, which are reflected in various measures of country risk. Country risk broadly refers to the economic and financial conditions and political stability of a country. It is an overall measure of country creditworthiness, indicating the capacity of a country to service its foreign financial obligations based on its economic, financial and political performance.

The purpose of the paper was to examine, for the first time, the relationship between the economic, financial and political country risk ratings, on the one hand, and innovation, as measured by a country's registered patents, on the other. This paper analyzed the monthly country risk ratings and registered patent trends for the top 12 foreign patenting countries in the US market from 1975 to 1997, namely Australia, Canada, France, Germany, Italy, Japan, Korea, the Netherlands, Sweden, Switzerland, Taiwan and the UK.

Higher innovation reflects higher technological capabilities and growth opportunities in a country which, in turn, leads to higher country risk ratings or creditworthiness. On the other hand, higher country risk ratings lead to higher foreign investment and capital flowing into a country which, in turn, lead to higher growth and technological advancement, and hence to higher innovation. For this reason, the correlation coefficients between registered patents and country risk ratings were computed for the 12 countries. The magnitude of these coefficients varied across both countries and risk ratings. Of the 52 correlation coefficients, only 28 exceeded 0.200. Moreover, 13 of these 28 correlations were negative.

Finally, the level of innovation (as approximated by the number of registered patents) was modelled on the basis of the economic, financial and political risk ratings, as well as the total US patent applications, for each of the 12 countries. The empirical results showed that economic, financial and political risk ratings have had considerable impact on the innovative activities of the 12 countries. Total US patent applications also appeared to be influential in terms of inducing technical change or innovation in the 12 countries. Such issues have not previously been addressed in the literature on country risk and innovation.

Acknowledgement

The authors wish to acknowledge the financial support of the Australian Research Council.

References

Chan, F. and McAleer, M. (2006) Trends in U.S. patent activity. In D. Slottje (ed.), *Economic Damages in IP Matters: A Hands-On Guide to Litigation* (pp. 15–25). New York: Wiley.

Chan, F., Marinova, D. and McAleer, M. (2004) Trends and volatilities in foreign patents registered in the USA. *Applied Economics* 36: 585–592.

Hoti, S. and McAleer, M. (2005) *Modelling the Riskiness in Country Risk Ratings*. Contributions to Economic Analysis Series, Vol. 273. Amsterdam: Elsevier.

Hoti, S., McAleer, M. and Slottje, D. (2006) Intellectual property litigation activity in the USA. *Journal of Economic Surveys* 20: 715–729.

International Country Risk Guide (2005) The PRS Group, New York.

Marinova, D. (2001) Eastern European patenting activities in the USA. *Technovation* 21(9): 571–184.

McAleer, M., Slottje, D. and Wee, P. (2005) *Patent Activity and Technical Change in U.S. Industries*. Contributions to Economic Analysis Number 273, Amsterdam: North-Holland.

Patel, P. and Pavitt, K. (1995) Divergence in technological development among countries and firms. In J. Hagedoorn (ed.), *Technical Change and the World Economy: Convergence and Divergence in Technology Strategies* (pp. 147–181). Aldershot: Edward Elgar.

Pavitt, K. (1988) Uses and abuses of patent statistics. In A. F. J. van Raan (ed.), *Handbook of Quantitative Studies of Science and Technology* (pp. 509–536). Amsterdam: Elsevier.

10

INTELLECTUAL PROPERTY LITIGATION ACTIVITY IN THE USA

Suhejla Hoti, Michael McAleer and Daniel Slottje

1. Introduction

The world famous Coca Cola brand has recently been valued at roughly $72.5 billion.[1] This valuation is just $2 billion ahead of Microsoft, due mainly to Microsoft's rise in recognition and a decline by Coca Cola. For both companies, the brand name or trademark carries incredible economic power and prestige. There is increasing recognition by world bodies that intellectual property (IP), whether manifested in patents, trademarks, copyrights or trade secrets, is highly valuable and must be protected like any other asset. This recognition has resulted in robust IP enforcement that would have been unheard of as recently as one decade ago. According to a 2003 survey by the American Intellectual Property Lawyers Association, the average costs of patent and trademark litigation are $2 million and $600,000, respectively, and for other types of IP litigation the average cost is between $500,000 and $800,000 (see Slottje and Whitaker (2005) for further discussion).

Notorious dens of IP piracy such as China, India and Brazil have begun to realize that, as their own economies mature, the intellectual capital being created domestically within each country is valuable and must be protected. A natural consequence is the concurrent enforcement and protection of their own IP if mutual respect and protection of IP is to exist. According to the Northern Ireland Office Media Centre, the US Government's Strategy for Targeting Organized Piracy and the Organization for Economic Development (OECD) has estimated that counterfeiting and piracy costs companies in the UK billions of pounds annually, and perhaps as much as $638 billion each year internationally.[2] The World Health Organization (WHO) estimates that at least 6% of the pharmaceuticals sold worldwide every year are counterfeit, and are valued at more than $30 billion.[3] According to the same Northern Ireland Office Media Centre citation, in some countries the vast majority of the software and musical recordings sold are counterfeit versions. The OECD estimates that the total costs of counterfeiting are equivalent to between 5% and 7% of world trade.[4]

As these statistics make clear, focusing on piracy issues and protection of IP is becoming a central focus of diplomacy and trade talks internationally, with most nations having a significant stake in how this problem is resolved. The USA is an interesting natural laboratory as patent, trademark and copyright litigation battles have been raging domestically for some time. This paper describes some of the trends and IP litigation activities that are transpiring in the USA, where IP enforcement is taken very seriously.

The plan of the remainder of the paper is as follows. Section 2 discusses the information age and IP enforcement. Section 3 describes the primary forms of IP as being patents, trademark, copyrights and trade secrets. An overview is given of the different types of IP assets, how US law enforces the property rights inherent in each type of asset, and how damages may be calculated when each type of asset is presumed to be infringed. Section 4 presents an empirical analysis of how the IP litigation activity in the USA has changed over time. Some concluding comments are given in Section 5.

2. The Information Age and IP Enforcement

The concurrent phenomena of growing worldwide recognition of the true value of IP assets, increasing patent protection through litigation, the attendant demands made by patent holders for royalties on patented IP, and strengthened copyright enforcement and trademark recognition initiatives, have begun to create interesting economic situations. For example, Hausman and Leonard (2006) consider what happens to economic incentives to innovate when the legal landscape is changed, while Hoti and McAleer (2006) examine how country risk affects innovation with reference to foreign patents registered in the USA.

Technological advances have caused the relative prices of some consumer electronics to fall, while royalties on these goods have risen. A classic example is the DVD player, which can be purchased in the USA for under $29, but the royalties paid on the components that comprise the DVD player could cost more.

In response to this increasingly frequent situation, patent pools have arisen. A patent pool is a cooperative arrangement that allows the holders of several patents, all of which are necessary for the development of a product or process (such as a DVD player), to license or assign their rights at a single price.[5] The patent pool is common in the biotech field, and is becoming more frequent among consumer electronics products. The US Patent and Trademark Office (USPTO) has created white papers on the subject and explained when the use of patent pools may be appropriate.[6] Nations such as China have started bringing antitrust suits, arguing that such cooperative arrangements are anticompetitive, while large companies such as Philips, Sony and Pioneer that create the cooperative arrangements argue they are necessary to keep royalty costs in check. An important fact is that the increased recognition of the value of IP has led to stronger enforcement of IP protection, an increase in IP litigation, and growing policy actions that are focused on how that protection should be manifested. As a consequence, IP issues are beginning to have a significant impact on how firms behave and interact with each other, and how countries behave with respect to the safekeeping of their respective IP portfolios.

In the following section we discuss the four main forms of IP assets, the legal remedies that are available to enforce IP ownership and the basic damages theory relating to each form of IP.

3. Patents, Trademarks, Copyrights and Trade Secrets

The primary forms of IP are patents, trademark, copyrights and trade secrets. A patent is an intellectual (or industrial) property that confers to its owner or holder monopoly rights to a product or process over a stipulated period of time. Applications are granted on the basis of innovation and non-obviousness (see Besen and Raskind, 1991). McAleer *et al.* (2005) and Chan and McAleer (2006) have discussed the trending patterns over time of patent filings and successes. US Code Section 284 forms the basis for damages awarded by a Court for the infringement of a patent and states:

> Upon finding for the claimant the court shall award the claimant damages adequate to compensate for the infringement, but in no event less than a reasonable royalty for the use made of the invention by the infringer, together with interest and costs as fixed by the court.[7]

This law has led to two primary damages remedies for patent holders, namely lost profits and reasonable royalties. Lost profits are the profits that would have accrued to the patent holder but for the alleged infringement. A reasonable royalty is the royalty that would have been paid by the patentee to the patent holder if the two parties had engaged in a hypothetical negotiation between a willing buyer and a willing seller. US case law has shaped how these economic fictions are to transpire.

In Panduit Corp. v. Stahlin Bros. Fibre Works, 575 F.2d 1152 (6th Cir. 1978), the Court established that a plaintiff seeking lost profits damages must prove demand for its patented product, the absence of acceptable non-infringing substitutes, sufficient manufacturing and marketing capability to exploit the demand, and the amount of the lost profit. In Georgia-Pacific Corp. v. US Plywood-Champion Papers, Inc., 318 F. Supp. 116 (S.D.N.Y. 1970), the Court enumerated 15 separate factors to consider when determining a reasonable royalty (cf. Perry and Slottje, 2003). The first 13 factors address issues regarding comparable agreements, the parties, the hypothetical license, the technology, and the accused products. The 14th factor allows for the introduction of expert testimony to guide the finder of fact. The final factor states that a reasonable royalty is one arrived at between the parties in a hypothetical negotiation, which takes place on or about the first date the alleged infringement has occurred. Slottje (2006) contains a number of essays by leading economists that lay out precisely how one is to calculate damages in patent cases in great detail.

According to the USPTO, a trademark is a word, phrase, symbol or design, or a combination of words, phrases, symbols or designs, that identifies and distinguishes the source of the goods of one party from those of others. The Lanham Act refers to trademarks as:

> any word, name, symbol, or device, or any combination thereof (1) used by a person, or (2) which a person has a bona fide intention to use in commerce and applies to register on the principal register established...to identify and distinguish his or her goods, including a unique product, from those manufactured or sold by others and to indicate the source of the goods, even if that source is unknown.

The purpose of a trademark is 'to guarantee a product's genuineness. In effect, the trademark is the commercial substitute for one's signature'.[8] The primary body of law regarding trademarks, as found in Section 15 of the US Code, is influenced by the Lanham Act.[9] Enacted in 1946, the Lanham Act has since undergone revisions and updates to make it relevant to the issues surrounding the current uses of trademarks.

The goal of trademark law is to prevent deception and customer confusion, and to protect property interests in trademarks.[10] As Inglish (2006) notes, case law is not as strong and clear with respect to precedent for the calculation of damages related to trademark infringement, as the role the Panduit test or Georgia-Pacific factors play in patent infringement matters, but there is some guidance. In addition, some of the general concepts of damages calculations from other types of IP or commercial damages disputes are useful for their relevance to the realm of trademark infringement damages. The Lanham Act provides for the recovery of (1) defendant's profits, (2) any damages sustained by the plaintiff and (3) the costs of the action.[11] An interesting twist is that some believe the plaintiff has only to prove the defendant's sales and to deduct the relevant costs, with the defendant having to prove that other factors accounted for the sales. A comprehensive discussion of this issue is given in Inglish (2006).

Title 17 of the US Code Section 102 defines a copyright as:

> ...original works of authorship fixed in any tangible medium of expression, now known or later developed, from which they can be perceived, reproduced or otherwise communicated, either directly or with the aid of a machine or device.... This includes pictorial, graphic and sculptural works.

Title 17 of the US Code Section 504(b) forms the basis for damages awarded by the Court for the infringement of a copyright, and states:

> The copyright owner is entitled to recover...any profits of the infringer that are attributable to the infringement and are not taken into account in computing actual damages. In establishing the infringer's profits, the copyright owner is required to present proof only of the infringer's gross revenue, and the infringer is required to prove his or her deductible expenses and the elements of profit attributable to factors other than the copyrighted work.

This means that the real burden of proof is on the infringer (or defendant) to show how other factors beside the copyright have impacted on sales of the product in question. This notion of damages as defined by the courts provides a natural application of econometric methods to an appropriate determination of damages (for an interesting example, see Basmann and Slottje, 2003).

Finally, a trade secret is defined under The Uniform Trade Secrets Act of 1985 (see Sickles and Ayyar, 2006) as:

> information, including a formula, pattern, compilation, program device, method, technique, or process, that: (i) derives independent economic value, actual or potential, from not being generally known to, and not being readily ascertainable by proper means by, other person who can obtain economic value from its disclosure or use, and (ii) is the subject of efforts that are reasonable under the circumstances to maintain its secrecy.

Sickles and Ayyar (2006) also note there are five main measures of damages in trade secret cases:

1. The value of the trade secrets to the plaintiff at the time they were first misappropriated if they have been destroyed, otherwise their diminution;
2. The plaintiff's lost profits as a result of lost sales;
3. The price erosion of the plaintiff's products caused by the defendant's unlawful competition, called price erosion with causality;
4. The defendant's unjust enrichment, expressed by the value of the trade secrets to the defendant at the time of taking, but also considering:
   i. Plaintiff is entitled to disgorgement of defendant's profits,
   ii. Profits from sales made possible by product development or collateral sales connected to the misappropriation,
   iii. Research and development costs avoided by defendant;
5. A royalty on gross sales that the defendant would hypothetically pay to legally license the use of the trade secrets. The royalty payment should restore the plaintiff's lost profits.

The discussion above has provided an overview of the different types of IP assets, how US law enforces the property rights inherent in each type of asset, and how damages may be calculated when each type of asset is presumed to be infringed.

4. An Empirical Analysis of IP Litigation Activity in the USA

In this section some aspects of IP litigation activity in the USA will be presented for various sub-periods of 1980–2005, specifically the leading 20 significant awards and settlements for copyrights, trademarks and trade secrets, leading 20 patent damage awards, leading 20 significant patent damage settlements, leading 25 countries receiving US patents, leading 10 countries receiving US patents as a percentage of the total, US patent applications filed and granted, trademark applications filed and granted, IP cases commenced in US District Courts, patent cases commenced in US District Courts, trademark cases commenced in US District Courts, and copyright cases commenced in US District Courts.

Table 1. Leading 20 Significant Awards and Settlements, Copyrights/Trademarks/Trade Secrets, 1990–2005.

Parties	Awards	Date	Source	IP
Cadence Design Systems v. Avant	$495,700,000	Nov-02	Wall Street Journal	Trade Secret
Lexar Media v. Toshiba	$465,400,000	Mar-05	Associated Press	Trade Secret
All Pro Sports Camps v. Walt Disney	$240,000,000	Aug-00	National Law Journal	Trade Secret
Philip Morris v. Otamedia	$173,000,000	Mar-05	Associated Press	Trademark
DSC Comm. v. Next Level Comm.	$137,732,000	Oct-97	51 USPQ2d 1173	Trade Secret
Atlantic Recording v. Media Group	$136,200,000	Aug-02	National Law Journal	Copyright
Bancorp Services v. Hartford Life	$118,338,000	Mar-02	National Law Journal	Trade Secret
Qwest Communications v. OneQwest	$117,000,000	Dec-02	National Law Journal	Trademark
Pioneer Hi-Bred v. Cargill	$100,000,000	May-00	Wall Street Journal	Trade Secret
Injection Research v. Polaris	$90,000,000	Aug-98	National Law Journal	Trade Secret
Avery Dennison v. Four Pillars	$80,160,000	Aug-00	National Law Journal	Trade Secret
Orthofix v. Electro-Biology	$64,170,000	Sep-01	National Law Journal	Trademark
UMG Recordings v. MP3.com	$53,400,000	Dec-00	National Law Journal	Copyright
Data General v. Grumman Systems	$52,300,000	Sep-94	Press Release	Copyright
Neon Systems v. New Era of Networks	$39,000,000	Jun-01	Press Release	Trademark
Caliper Technologies v. Aclara	$37,500,000	Jan-01	National Law Journal	Trade Secret
Polteco v. Smith & Nephew Richards	$37,500,000	Jan-92	National Law Journal	Trade Secret
NMPA v. Napster	$36,000,000	Sep-01	Associated Press	Copyright
Super Vision v. Opti-Tech	$33,100,000	Sep-02	National Law Journal	Trade Secret
Columbia Pictures v. Feltner	$31,680,000	Apr-99	National Law Journal	Copyright

Source: FTI (available at http://www.fticonsulting.com/web/services/Intellectual_Property_Charts_and_Statistics.html}.

Table 1 presents the leading 20 significant awards and settlements for copyrights, trademarks and trade secrets for the period 1990–2005. Of the 20 awards and settlements, the largest number is 11 for trade secrets, followed by five copyright cases and four trademark cases. The leading three awards and settlements are for trade secrets. Only one of the leading 10 is a copyright case. The amounts range from almost half a billion US dollars to slightly in excess of US$30 million, and demonstrate the importance of litigation activity for copyrights, trademarks and trade secrets. The primary source of these cases is the National Law Journal.

The leading 20 patent damage awards are given for the period 1980–2005 in Table 2. Although the largest damage award, at almost US$1 billion, is significantly higher than those presented in Table 1, the following four highest damage awards are comparable to the leading two awards and settlements in Table 1. The leading source of these damage awards is the Wall Street Journal, followed by the National Law Journal and the IP Law Bulletin.

As compared with the leading 20 patent damage awards in Table 2, Table 3 presents the leading 20 significant patent damage settlements for the period 1980–2005. The leading four damage settlements are at least US$1 billion, and the median damage settlement is in excess of US$325 million, as compared with the median value of around US$190 million in damage awards. Thus, patent damage settlements are typically much greater than patent damage awards. The leading source of these damage awards is the Wall Street Journal, followed by Associated Press, Press Releases and the National Law Journal.

The leading 25 countries receiving US patents (in US$ millions) for the period 2001–2005 are given in Table 4. It is not surprising that the USA is the leading country receiving US patents with a total of 421,393 during the 5-year period. The leading foreign country is Japan, with a total of 169,290 patents, followed distantly by Germany. The following five countries are Taiwan, South Korea, France, the UK and Canada. Of the leading 10 countries, 5 are from Europe, 3 from Asia, and 2 from North America. However, of the leading 25 countries, 13 are from Europe and 6 are from Asia.

Finally, Table 5 presents the leading 10 countries receiving US patents (as a percentage of the total number of patents) for the period 2001–2005. In each year of the 5-year period, the USA has received slightly greater than one half of the total number of US patents, with Japan receiving slightly in excess of 20% each year and Germany between 6% and 7% each year. Italy and Sweden round off the leading 10 countries that receive US patents, with each country having around 1% of the annual total during the period 2001–2005.

Figure 1 shows the US patent applications filed and granted for the fiscal years 1980–2005. Both series have noticeable trending patterns, with the patent applications filed increasing consistently throughout the sample, except for a peak in 1995, but with patent applications granted levelling off in the last 5 years for the sample period. Given the small number of annual observations, it is not sensible to test for unit roots in either series. However, their distinctive patterns throughout the sample period, but particularly during the last decade,

Table 2. Leading 20 Patent Damage Awards, 1980–2005.

Parties	Awards	Date	Source	Court
Polaroid v. Eastman Kodak	$873,158,971	Jan-91	17 USPQ2d 1711	D. Massachusetts
Michelson v. Medtronic Sofamor Danek	$529,000,000	Oct-04	National Law Journal	W.D. Tennessee
Eolas Technologies v. Microsoft	$521,000,000	Aug-03	Wall Street Journal	N.D. Illinois
City of Hope Medical v. Genentech	$500,100,000	Jun-02	New York Times	Sup. Ct. California
Johnson & Johnson v. Guidant	$425,000,000	Sep-03	National Law Journal	Arbitration Panel
Johnson & Johnson v. Medtronic	$270,000,000	Sep-03	National Law Journal	CAFC
InterDigital Communications v. Nokia	$252,000,000	Jul-05	IP Law Bulletin	Arbitration Panel
Advanced Medical Optics v. Alcon	$213,900,000	Dec-05	IP Law Bulletin	D. Delaware
Haworth v. Steelcase	$211,499,731	Dec-96	43 USPQ2d 1223	W.D. Michigan
Hughes Tool v. Smith International	$204,810,349	Mar-86	229 USPQ 81	C.D. California
Procter & Gamble v. Paragon Trade	$178,400,000	Jan-98	Press Release	D. Delaware
Exxon Chemical v. Mobil Oil	$171,000,000	Aug-98	Wall Street Journal	S.D. Texas
Guidant v. Medtronic AVE	$166,681,773	May-02	Judgment	Arbitration Panel
Viskase v. American National Can	$164,900,000	Jul-99	Press Release	N.D. Illinois
Masimo v. Nellcor	$164,000,000	Aug-04	CBS MarketWatch	C.D. California
Hughes Aircraft v. USA	$154,000,000	Jun-94	Wall Street Journal	Federal Claims
Intergraph v. Intel	$150,000,000	Oct-02	Wall Street Journal	E.D. Texas
Freedom Wireless v. Boston Communications	$148,100,000	Oct-05	IP Law Bulletin	D. Massachusetts
3M v. Johnson & Johnson	$129,000,000	Dec-92	Dow Jones Newswire	CAFC
Fonar v. General Electric	$128,705,766	Feb-97	Final Judgment	CAFC

Source: FTI (available at http://www.fticonsulting.com/web/services/Intellectual_Property_Charts_and_Statistics.html).

Table 3. Leading 20 Significant Patent Damage Settlements, 1980–2005.

Parties	Awards	Date	Source
Michelson v. Medtronic	$1,350,000,000	Apr-05	Associated Press
Sun Microsystems v. Microsoft	$1,250,000,000	Feb-04	Press Release
Texas Instruments v. Hyundai	$1,000,000,000	May-99	Wall Street Journal
Texas Instruments v. Samsung	$1,000,000,000	Nov-96	Wall Street Journal
Medinol v. Boston Scientific	$750,000,000	Sep-05	Associated Press
NTP v. Research in Motion	$612,500,000	Mar-06	Wall Street Journal
Northrop Grumman v. Honeywell	$440,000,000	Apr-04	Associated Press
Intertrust Technologies v. Microsoft	$440,000,000	Dec-01	Press Release
Pitney Bowes v. Hewlett-Packard	$400,000,000	Jun-01	Wall Street Journal
Yahoo v. Google	$328,000,000	Aug-04	National Law Journal
EMC v. Hewlett-Packard	$325,000,000	May-05	Associated Press
Intergraph v. Intel	$300,000,000	Apr-02	Wall Street Journal
Medtronic v. Siemens	$300,000,000	Sep-92	Wall Street Journal
MicroUnity v. Intel	$300,000,000	Oct-05	Business Wire
University of Minnesota v. Glaxo	$300,000,000	Oct-99	Press Release
Intermedics v. Cardiac Pacemakers	$250,000,000	Sep-98	National Law Journal
Intergraph v. Intel	$225,000,000	Mar-04	Associated Press
Gemstar v. General Instruments	$200,000,000	Nov-00	National Law Journal
University of California v. Genentech	$200,000,000	Nov-99	Press Release
Gemstar v. EchoStar Communications	$190,000,000	Mar-04	Satellite Week

Source: FTI (available at http://www.fticonsulting.com/web/services/Intellectual_Property_Charts_and_Statistics.html).

would seem to suggest that they are not cointegrated, and hence have not moved together.

Trademark applications filed and granted for the fiscal years 1980–2005 are given in Figure 2. Both series have noticeable trends, but the trademark applications filed have a distinct peak in 2000, after which the series have reverted to a trending pattern, whereas trademark applications granted has a much flatter trend. The gap between the trademark applications filed and granted has widened throughout the sample period. As in the case of patent applications filed and granted, the trademark applications filed and granted would not seem to have moved together during the sample period.

Figure 3 presents the total number of IP cases commenced in US District Courts for the fiscal years 1996–2005, as well as the decomposition for patents, trademarks and copyrights. The sharp increase in the total number of cases commenced in US District Courts in 2004–2005 is due to the significant increase in the number of copyright cases for the same fiscal year. Apart from the last year, the number of trademark cases exceeded those of patent and copyright cases.

The patent cases commenced in US District Courts for the fiscal years 1996–2005 are given in Figure 4. There is a clear trending pattern, except for the last fiscal year.

Table 4. Leading 25 Countries Receiving US Patents (USD millions), 2001–2005.

Country	2001	2002	2003	2004	2005	Total
USA	87,607	86,977	87,901	84,271	74,637	421,393
Japan	33,223	34,859	35,517	35,350	30,341	169,290
Germany	11,260	11,277	11,444	10,779	9,011	53,771
Taiwan	5371	5431	5298	5938	5118	27156
South Korea	3538	3786	3944	4428	4352	20,048
France	4041	4035	3869	3380	2866	18191
UK	3965	3838	3627	3450	3148	18,028
Canada	3606	3431	3426	3374	2894	16,731
Italy	1709	1750	1722	1584	1296	8061
Sweden	1743	1675	1521	1290	1123	7352
Switzerland	1420	1364	1308	1277	995	6364
The Netherlands	1332	1391	1325	1273	993	6314
Israel	970	1040	1193	1028	924	5155
Australia	875	858	900	953	911	4497
Finland	732	809	865	918	720	4044
Belgium	718	722	622	612	519	3193
Austria	589	530	592	540	462	2713
Denmark	479	426	529	414	358	2206
Singapore	296	410	427	449	346	1928
China, P.Rep.	195	289	297	404	402	1587
India	177	249	341	363	384	1514
Spain	269	303	309	264	273	1418
China, Hong Kong	237	233	276	311	283	1340
Norway	265	242	262	243	220	1232
Russian Federation	234	200	202	169	148	953

Source: US Patent and Trademark Office (available at http://www.fticonsulting.com/web/services/ Intellectual_Property_Charts_and_Statistics.html).

Figure 5 shows the number of trademark cases commenced in US District Courts for the fiscal years 1996–2005. There appears to be a cyclical pattern in the data, with a peak in the number of trademark cases commenced 2000.

Finally, Figure 6 gives the number of copyright cases commenced in US District Courts for the fiscal years 1996–2005. The number of copyright cases commenced varied in the range 2000 to 3000 during 1996–2004, but almost doubled in the final fiscal year, which also had a significant effect on the total IP cases commenced at the end of the sample period.

5. Concluding Comments

Intellectual property (IP), such as brand names or trademarks, carries incredible economic power and prestige. Hence, it is not surprising that there has been an increasing recognition by world bodies that IP, whether manifested in patents, trademarks, copyrights or trade secrets, is highly valuable and must be protected

Table 5. Top Countries Receiving US Patents (as % of Total), 2001–2005.

Country	2001	2002	2003	2004	2005	Total
USA	52.80	52.00	52.00	51.30	51.90	52.00
Japan	20.00	20.80	21.00	21.50	21.10	20.90
Germany	6.80	6.70	6.80	6.60	6.30	6.60
Taiwan	3.20	3.20	3.10	3.60	3.60	3.40
South Korea	2.10	2.30	2.30	2.70	3.00	2.50
France	2.40	2.40	2.30	2.10	2.00	2.20
UK	2.40	2.30	2.10	2.10	2.20	2.20
Canada	2.20	2.10	2.00	2.10	2.00	2.10
Italy	1.00	1.00	1.00	1.00	0.90	1.00
Sweden	1.00	1.00	0.90	0.80	0.80	0.90
Total Foreign	47.20	48.00	48.00	48.70	48.10	48.00

Source: US Patent and Trademark Office (available at http://www.fticonsulting.com/web/services/Intellectual_Property_Charts_and_Statistics.html).

through serious enforcement of laws that protect IP. The USA is an interesting natural laboratory for the rest of the world as patent, trademark and copyright litigation battles have been raging domestically for several decades.

The paper discussed the four main forms of IP assets, the legal remedies that are available to enforce the property rights inherent in each type of IP asset, the basic damages theory relating to each form of IP, and how damages may be calculated

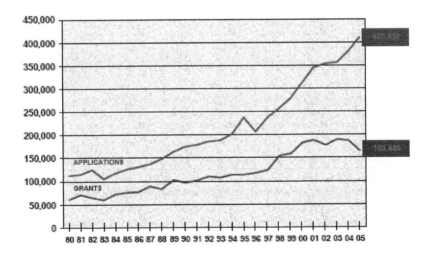

Figure 1. US Patent Applications Filed and Granted, 1980–2005.
Source: US Patent and Trademark Office (available at http://www.fticonsulting.com/web/services/Intellectual_Property_Charts_and_Statistics.html).

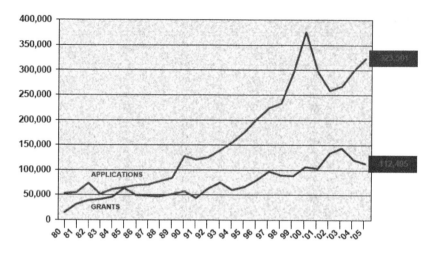

Figure 2. Trademark Applications Filed and Granted, 1980–2005.
Source: US Patent and Trademark Office (available at http://www.fticonsulting.com/
web/services/Intellectual_Property_Charts_and_Statistics.html).

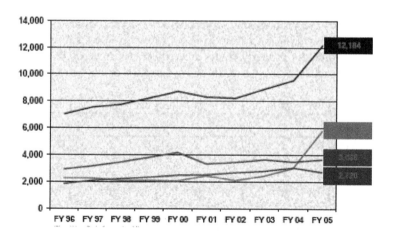

Figure 3. IP Cases Commenced in US District Courts, 1996–2005.
Source: Administrative Office of the US Courts (available at http://www.fticonsulting.
com/web/services/Intellectual_Property_Charts_and_Statistics.html).

when each type of asset is presumed to be infringed. The increased recognition
of the value of IP has led to stronger enforcement of IP protection, an increase in
IP litigation, and growing policy actions that are focused on how that protection
should be manifested. An empirical analysis of how the IP litigation activity in the
USA has changed over time is also presented.

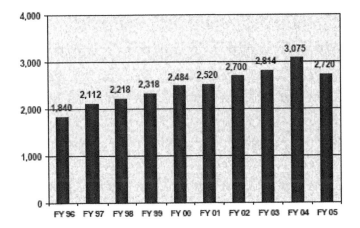

Figure 4. Patent Cases Commenced in US District Courts, 1996–2005.
Source: Administrative Office of the US Courts (available at http://www.fticonsulting.
com/web/services/Intellectual_Property_Charts_and_Statistics.html).

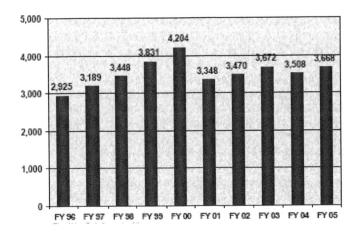

Figure 5. Trademark cases commenced in US District Courts, 1996–2005.
Source: Administrative Office of the US Courts (available at http://www.fticonsulting.
com/web/services/Intellectual_Property_Charts_and_Statistics.html).

Acknowledgement

The first and second authors wish to acknowledge the financial support of the Australian
Research Council.

Notes

1. http://news.bbc.co.uk/1/hi/world/americas/839439.stm.

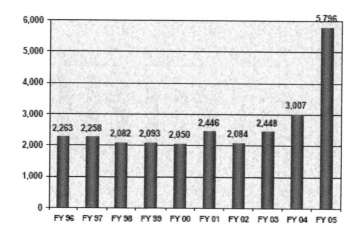

Figure 6. Copyright cases commenced in US District Courts, 1996–2005.
Source: Administrative Office of the US Courts (available at http://www.fticonsulting.
com/web/services/Intellectual_Property_Charts_and_Statistics.html).

2. http://www.commerce.gov/graphics/STOP%20Fakes/STOP%20Fact%20sheet%
   20April%202006.pdf, http://www.nio.gov.uk/media-detail.htm?newsID=11753.
3. 'Counterfeit Medicines,' World Health Organization Media Centre, reported in
   http://www.who.int/mediacentre/factsheets/fs275/en/.
4. http://www.commerce.gov/graphics/STOP%20Fakes/STOP%20Fact%20sheet%
   20April%202006.pdf, http://www.nio.gov.uk/media-detail.htm?newsID=11753.
5. http://www.google.com/search?hl=en&lr=&q=define%3APatent+pool&btnG=
   Search.
6. http://www.uspto.gov/web/offices/com/speeches/01-06.htm.
7. 35 U.S.C. § 284.
8. www.uspto.gov/web/offices/tac/doc/basic/trade_defin.htm.
9. 15 U.S.C. § 1127.
10. Ameritech, Inc. v. American Information Technologies Corporation d/b/a Ameritech,
    811 F.2d 960, 1987 U.S. App. LEXIS 2243; 1 U.S.P.Q.2D (BNA) 1861.
11. 15 U.S.C. § 1117(a).

References

Basmann, R. L. and Slottje, D. (2003) Copyright damages and statistics. *International
    Statistical Review* 71: 557–564.
Besen, S. M. and Raskind, L. J. (1991) An introduction to the law and economics of
    intellectual property. *Journal of Economic Perspectives* 5(1): 3–27.
Chan, F. and McAleer, M. (2006) Trends in U.S. Patent Activity. In D. Slottje (ed.),
    Economic Damages in IP Matters: A Hands-On Guide to Litigation (pp. 15–25). New
    York: Wiley.
Hausman, J. and Leonard, G. (2006) Real options and patent damages: The legal treatment
    of non-infringing alternatives and incentives to innovate. *Journal of Economic Surveys*
    20: 493–512.

Hoti, S. and McAleer, M. (2006) How does country risk affect innovation? An application to foreign patents registered in the USA. *Journal of Economic Surveys* 20: 691–714.

Inglish, B. (2006), Quantification of damages in trademark cases. In D. Slottje (ed.), *Economic Damages in IP Matters: A Hands-On Guide to Litigation*. New York: Wiley.

McAleer, M., Slottje, D. and Wee, P. (2005) *Patent Activity and Technical Change in U.S. Industries*. Contributions to Economic Analysis Number 273, Amsterdam: North-Holland.

Perry, C. and Slottje, D. (2003) Economics, damages analysis and Georgia-Pacific. In *High Technology Litigation Course Book* (Ch. 4). Austin: State Bar of Texas.

Sickles, R. and Ayyar, A. (2006) Evaluation of damages in a trade secrets case. In D. Slottje (ed.), *Economic Damages in IP Matters: A Hands-On Guide to Litigation* (pp. 281–296). New York: Wiley.

Slottje, D. (ed.), (2006) *Economic Damages in IP Matters: A Hands-On Guide to Litigation*. New York: Wiley.

Slottje, D. and Whitaker, E. (2005) Don't send good money after bad. *Executive Counsel* 2: 38–40.

Index

Printed and bound by CPI Group (UK) Ltd, Croydon, CR0 4YY

09/06/2025

14686146-0004